LIBYA ARCHAEOLO[GICAL GUIDES]

TRIPOLITANIA

by
Philip Kenrick

Silphium Press

Libya Archaeological Guides:
TRIPOLITANIA
by Philip Kenrick

Produced by Silphium Books, an imprint of
The Society for Libyan Studies
c/o The Institute of Archaeology
31-34 Gordon Square, London WC1H 0PY
www.britac.ac.uk/institutes/libya

Cover design Primavera Quantrill and Philip Kenrick

ISBN 978-1-900971-08-9

Designed and typeset in Franklin Gothic
by Primavera Quantrill
www.quantrillmedia.com

Printed by Lanes Printers, Broadstairs, Kent

Contents

Sources of illustrations

The maps and drawings in this volume have been prepared by the author, with the assistance of Peter Atkinson. Those which derive substantially from previous publications are dependent on the following sources:

Africa Italiana 2, 1928–9 (fig. 27);

G. Barker et al., *Farming the Desert: The UNESCO Libyan Valleys Archaeological Survey*, London, Paris and Tripoli 1996 (figs. 89, 90, 92, 110);

R. Bartoccini, *Le terme di Lepcis (Leptis Magna)*, Bergamo 1929 (fig. 35);

R. Bianchi Bandinelli et al., *The Buried City: Excavations at Leptis Magna*, London 1966 (figs. 41, 44, 48, 49);

O. Brogan and D. Smith, *Ghirza: a Libyan Settlement in the Roman Period*, London and Tripoli 1984 (figs. 94–96, 98–101);

G. Fehérvári et al., *Excavations at Surt (Medinet al-Sultan) between 1977 and 1981*, London and Tripoli 2002 (figs. 67, 69)

R.G. Goodchild, *Libyan Studies: selected papers of the late R.G. Goodchild*, edited by Joyce Reynolds, London 1976 (figs. 45, 68, 104)

P.M. Kenrick, *Excavations at Sabratha 1948–1951*, London 1986 (figs. 12, 13, 15);

Libya Antiqua 15/16 (fig. 61), n.s. 4 (fig. 72);

Libyan Studies 5 (fig. 58), 14 (fig. 105), 20 (figs. 80, 83);

D.J. Mattingly, *Tripolitania*, London 1995 (fig. 11);

D. Oates, 'The Tripolitanian Gebel: settlement of the Roman period around Gasr ed-Dauun.' *Papers of the British School at Rome* 21, 1953, 81–117 (figs. 75, 77);

Quaderni di Archeologia della Libia 2, 1951 (fig. 46), 3, 1954 (fig. 73), 7, 1975 (fig. 74);

J.B. Ward-Perkins, *The Severan Buildings at Lepcis Magna: an Architectural Survey* (London 1993 (figs. 37, 38, 39, 43);

J.B. Ward-Perkins and R.G. Goodchild, 'The Christian Antiquities of Tripolitania.' *Archaeologia* 95, 1953, 1–83 (figs. 19, 24

D. Welsby, The defences of the Roman forts at Bu Ngem and Gheriat el-Gharbia. In: P. Bidwell, R. Miket & B. Ford (eds.), *Portae cum turribus: studies of Roman fort gates*. BAR British Series 206, Oxford 1988, 63-82 (fig. 107).

The photographs are by the author apart from fig. 97, which was kindly provided by David Mattingly.

Preface

This guidebook is intended to be the first in a series of three, covering the antiquities of Libya in three geographical zones (Tripolitania, Cyrenaica, Fazzan), from prehistoric times until the invasion of the Bani Hilal and the Bani Sulaym in AD 1051. No previous archaeological guidebook or series has attempted to cover this time span, nor indeed has there been anything of the kind apart from *An Archaeological and Historical Guide to the pre-Islamic Antiquities of Tripolitania* by Denys Haynes, first published as *Ancient Tripolitania* in 1945 and last revised in 1965. Libya has much to offer the cultural tourist, ranging from a remarkable array of prehistoric rock-art in Fazzan to impressive monuments of classical antiquity in the coastal region.

The upstanding monuments, both of the great classical cities on the coast and of the more modest ancient settlements of the interior, have been visited and reported by European travellers and explorers from the seventeenth century onwards, and it is therefore over-dramatic for modern books and tour operators to describe them as 'lost cities' or 'lost civilizations.' None the less, Libya has not in recent years been as accessible to tourists as many other countries bordering the Mediterranean and this, more than anything else, has been responsible for the impression of its remoteness. There are also factors in the troubled past of twentieth-century Libya which have discouraged the Libyans themselves from taking proper pride in their own cultural heritage.

The Italians, invaders and colonial masters of the region between 1911 and 1943, explored the ruins of the Roman cities with enthusiasm and used them unhesitatingly as propaganda to demonstrate their prior 'ownership' of the region and to legitimize their presence. It is therefore not surprising to find some ambivalence in Libya today about the monuments, as to whether they represent signs of odious foreign oppression or part of a national heritage to be valued. Likewise, the government itself has sought for a sense of national identity beyond its own borders – at first in the Arab/Islamic world and more recently in the African continent at large.

I hope in some small way in this guidebook to redress the balance, both by reflecting current academic thinking about the identity of those who populated the land in the classical period, when it participated fully in the culture of the Mediterranean world and of Europe, and by showing that there are visible traces of continuity between then and the early medieval period. I have chosen the invasion of 1051 as my cut-off point, because the hiatus between the buildings and settlements which pre-date that event and those which do not come into being until some four hundred years later is much more marked than that between those of the Byzantine period and those of the early Islamic period which succeeds it.

Libya as a single political entity came into existence only in 1929 under Italian administration. Much of its history prior to its recognition as a sovereign state in 1951 has involved either domination by foreign peoples (Greeks, Phoenicians, Romans, Spaniards, Turks, Italians) or a state of impoverishment which has prevented it from making its mark on the consciousness of others. The Arab invasions of the seventh and eleventh centuries AD are, of course, not regarded as emblematic of foreign domination and yet one may legitimately ask in what way they differed from many of the others. In truth, none of these movements of peoples prior to the twentieth century are likely to have involved mass migrations or suppressions of the previous population. There was cultural change, but on the whole it was shared in and absorbed by the underlying indigenous population which has always been there, and which is today most evident in the Berbers of the Jabal Nafusah. The ruling élites of the Roman cities were of Liby-Phoenician descent, as we can see from the names on the inscriptions that they left. On tombs in the countryside we find names that are purely Libyan and the use of a surely Libyan language that we cannot yet read. A visit to the museum at Bani Walid or to the late Roman settlement at Ghirza will rapidly show the presence of a native culture which took what it wanted from 'Roman' civilization without losing its own character or sense of identity.

To demonstrate continuity into the early medieval period from the visible monuments is more difficult: there is little building within the new Arab/Islamic identity that was not swept away in the eleventh century. In the present guidebook this is limited more-or-less to one mosque in Tripoli (with origins in the tenth century, but probably wholly rebuilt in the seventeenth) and to the modest traces of the important medieval city of Sort at Madina Sultan in the Syrtic Gulf. I have, however, deliberately ignored my chosen terminal date with regard to the monuments of the Jabal Nafusah. The justification is twofold: in the first instance, the region does not seem to have experienced the same cultural break in the eleventh century as the coastal areas, with the consequence that existing settlements may well have origins which extend back to the early medieval period, if not further. Secondly, the material culture of the Jabal Nafusah deserves in any case to be much better known.

Finding one's way around

The visitor to Libya who wishes to do more than to see the principal attractions along the main coast road will be faced with substantial obstacles with regard to navigation. The road maps of the country which are publicly available are much more detailed than they were a generation ago, but they still incorporate many inaccuracies, both in terms of new road-building which continues apace and which has not yet found its way onto the maps, and in terms of roads which were once intended to be built but which have never actually existed. There is also a serious dearth of signposts (whether in Arabic or any other script). It was therefore apparent to me that it would be indispensable to provide geographical co-ordinates wherever possible, and to commend to the traveller the use of a GPS (Geographical Positioning System) device. This further circumvents a problem which I have myself experienced, where either the locals express no knowledge of what you are looking for or – and this is typical of an environment where place-names are not codified by maps or signboards – a name is found to have transferred itself from one building or location to another! Formerly, of course, many of the monuments described were accessible only with the aid of local knowledge and of a 4-wheel-drive vehicle. Now, some of them are within easy walking-distance of an asphalted road and may be visited by saloon car. Where this is NOT the case, I hope that I have made it sufficiently clear.

Spelling of names

This is another problem which teases the visitor. Even where names are well established, their transliteration from Arabic has produced very variable results. On the whole, there is a choice of at least three different forms: an Italian phonetic transliteration, which imitates well the local pronunciation of the name; an 'old' English transliteration, which works in the same way, but less reliably, owing to the inherent uncertainties in how unfamiliar names written in English should be pronounced; and a transliteration according to formal, internationally agreed rules, which typically results in something which one simply would not associate with the sound of the spoken name! I have mostly opted, with some reluctance, for the third and least satisfactory solution, on the basis that that is what the traveller will find written on maps. This will inevitably conflict with what one will see in other books or on labels in museums; but in an area where no consistency exists, none can be imposed. I have given alternative spellings, both in the text and in the index, where this seemed likely to be helpful.

Acknowledgements

I am deeply grateful to the Society for Libyan Studies (and particularly to Claudio Vita-Finzi and Paul Bennett, its outgoing President and outgoing Chairman respectively), for the enthusiasm with which it embraced the concept of a new series of guidebooks and made it its own. I am also grateful to Wings Travel and Tours of Tripoli (particularly Alaa al-Shabi, Isam Harrus and Yousef al-Khattali) for their interest and support: they arranged complimentary travel and accommodation for myself and my wife in January 2008 when we made a reconnaissance of many of the sites. My thanks go also to Yasser Mohammed Ali who accompanied us on that tour, indefatigably sought out the obscure places we wished to visit and patiently translated museum labels for me, in addition to being very good and lively company.

   In the course of compiling the text, a number of friends and colleagues have shared their knowledge with me or kindly responded to queries. Amongst these are Lindsay Allason-Jones, Mohammed Arreshy, Antonino Di Vita, Ginette Di Vita-Evrard, Philip England, André Laronde and Michael Mackensen. Of an altogether greater order has been the contribution of David Mattingly, who kindly read and commented on the first draft of the text in addition to providing advice and support in many other ways; his monograph on *Tripolitania* (1995) was always going to be one of the major props of the present work. My wife Sue read heroically through the same draft and chastised me for my occasional obscurities or over-complex sentences. The reader will have cause to be thankful for both of these interventions, which have undoubtedly improved the finished product!

Abingdon, Oxfordshire   December 2008

Historical background

The geography of Tripolitania

This guidebook is concerned with a relatively small part of the area covered by the modern state of Libya (the Socialist People's Libyan Arab Jamahiriya), shown by the pink shading on the map inside the front cover. The vast majority of the country is, however, desert, characterized by sparse and widely separated settlements in the historical and modern periods. The coastal regions are conveniently referred to by the regional names which they acquired in the Classical period: Tripolitania in the west, defined by its three major cities, and Cyrenaica in the east, being the region around the Greek city of Cyrene. The geography of Tripolitania is characterized by a curving escarpment which encloses the flat, arid coastal plain of the Jafarah. There are strings of oases along the coast, with a cultivable coastal strip. The Jabal escarpment captures higher rainfall which also facilitates agriculture and permanent settlement. As the escarpment breaks up into a lower hill-region to the east, the cultivable zone becomes wider, reaching the coast between Tripoli and al-Khums. Behind the Jabal, the rainfall diminishes progressively as one goes south, and the terrain (described by geographers as pre-desert) becomes correspondingly less susceptible to the practice of sedentary agriculture. Further east, as the coastline of the Gulf of Sidra dips southwards, so the desert comes to meet it. The resulting coastline between Tripolitania in the west and the watered upland of Cyrenaica in the east is a real geographical barrier to communication between the two regions: the passage by land is dry and barren, subject to great heat in summer, and watered by few coastal oases. The shelving shoreline is equally inhospitable to sailors, with rocky reefs and few safe anchorages, such that the passage by sea is equally uninviting. A vessel driven towards the shore in a storm is liable to be wrecked and broken up while still as much as a mile out to sea. The Romans referred to the greater and lesser gulfs in the coastline of North Africa (the Libyan one and that bordering the southern part of modern Tunisia) as the *Syrtes* or Dragnets, from the experience of their seafarers that once drawn into this region, it was difficult to escape. There has been, therefore, until comparatively recent times, a significant difference between the cultures and the histories of Tripolitania and Cyrenaica, which justifies their separate treatment in this series of guides.

The Phoenicians

The prehistory of Libya does not really concern us in this volume; while there is important rock-art deep in the desert in Fazzan, and caves with prehistoric deposits in the Jabal Akhdar of Cyrenaica, there are no such visible remains in Tripolitania. This does not mean that early man was absent from this part of the landscape – plenty of scatters of stone tools have been recorded in archaeological surveys – but there is nothing to detain the non-specialist. Instead, we may conveniently begin our account of the history of the region with the Phoenicians. The people of ancient Phoenicia – that part of the Levant identified with the cities of Tyre and Sidon – were early seafarers and explorers of the Mediterranean. They discovered the mineral resources of south-west

Spain (Tarshish – Tartessus – Rio Tinto) perhaps as early as the twelfth century BC and sailed the length of the Mediterranean to exploit them. Naturally, they would have required safe anchorages along the way, and places where they could restock their food supplies. In due course they colonized both western Sicily and the North African coast, thus protecting the passage of the Sicilian Narrows. Carthage (in the suburbs of modern Tunis) was traditionally founded by the Phoenicians in 814 BC, though archaeological evidence does not extend back beyond the eighth century. With the decline of Phoenicia itself under pressure from the Assyrians, Carthage became the dominant Phoenician power in the western Mediterranean. (In this context, it is modern scholarly practice to refer to the civilization of Carthage and its dependants as 'Punic' rather than 'Phoenician'.) The three trading-posts, or *emporia*, which later gave the Tripolitanian region its name (Sabratha, Oea and Lepcis Magna) claimed to have been founded by settlers from Tyre and Sidon. Whatever the truth of this (and it is the kind of ancestry that a city would deliberately invent for itself in later years), they would have been, from the beginning, within the sphere of influence of Carthage. Excavations at Lepcis have revealed buildings of stone going back to the seventh century BC, whereas at Sabratha no occupation is attested before the latter part of the fifth. For Oea, we just do not know. The evidence would lie deep beneath the medina of Tripoli, and as parts of that which have become derelict are redeveloped, an opportunity may at some point arise of finding out.

The other great seafarers in the Mediterranean at this period were the Greeks. They too founded colonies along many parts of the coast, and they and the Phoenicians generally developed mutually exclusive spheres of influence. Conflict did occur between them over a period of centuries in Sicily, eventually resolved to the satisfaction of neither when Rome was invited to take an interest. The Greeks had also attempted in c. 515 BC to found a colony in Tripolitania at the mouth of the Wadi Caam (*Cinyps*). We are told by the Greek historian Herodotus that, three years later, the Carthaginians (*sic* – this may of course mean the inhabitants of Lepcis) drove them out. The legend of the Philaeni (p. 155) concerns the establishment soon after this of a border between the Carthaginians and the Greeks of Cyrene.

The balance of power on the southern shores of the Mediterranean was next disturbed by the expanding ambitions of Rome. This brought her into conflict with the Carthaginians in Sicily, resulting in the annexation of the island as Rome's first overseas possession (First Punic War, 264–241). The next generation of Carthaginians, under the leadership of Hannibal, fought back, taking the war into Italy and almost to the gates of Rome (Second Punic War, 218–202). Carthage was eventually defeated for the second time, and on this occasion much of her territory in Africa was taken from her and entrusted to an ally of Rome, the Numidian (i.e. Algerian) king Masinissa. Over the succeeding half-century, Rome encouraged Masinissa to enlarge his possessions at the expense of Carthage, and in 162 he helped himself to the Tripolitanian *emporia*; despite the protests of Carthage, he was again supported by Rome. Eventually, it seems that the Romans realized the danger of the policy they were pursuing; while weakening Carthage, they were enabling Masinissa to become a threat to them instead. The solution was to intervene directly on a trumped-up excuse (Carthage had taken up arms to defend itself, despite being forbidden to do so), to destroy Carthage and to annexe the territory as a Roman province (Third Punic War, 149–146).

The *emporia* were not directly involved in these military events, but paid their tribute to Carthage and subsequently to Masinissa. The transfer of power did, however, have a liberating effect on their trade, which had been strictly controlled by Carthage; at Sabratha the resulting expansion of the settlement in this period is particularly clear.

Masinissa died during the Third Punic War (in which he did not take part) and was succeeded by Micipsa, who was content with the *status quo*. Trouble next arose after the death of Micipsa (in 118) from his ambitious and unscrupulous nephew Jugurtha. Jugurtha's aggressive activities were unacceptable to Rome, which took the field against him, resulting in his eventual capture and execution in 104. It was during this conflict that Lepcis sought and obtained a treaty of alliance with Rome, and indeed briefly received a garrison of Italian troops for its protection.

The Romans

During the civil war between Julius Caesar and Pompey the Great in the middle of the first century BC, Lepcis (and possibly the other two *emporia* — we cannot always be sure whether references are specifically to the city or more generally to the region) found itself involved with the Pompeian faction, and therefore on the losing side. With the final victory of Caesar, the Numidian kingdom was brought to an end and its territory (including the *emporia*) came under direct Roman rule as the province of *Africa Nova*. Lepcis was demoted from its former allied status (as a *civitas foederata*) to the status of a tributary city (*civitas stipendiaria*) and the tribute exacted was an annual amount of three million pounds (about 1,000 tonnes) of olive oil. Again, we cannot be certain whether Lepcis alone was required to bear this burden, or whether the other *emporia* were included within it.

From now on, the *emporia* were definitely under Roman administration, though inscriptions from the cities show the continued existence of a local ruling elite with (sometimes Latinized) Punic names, holding Punic magistracies and commemorating their benefactions in neo-Punic as well as in Latin. The territory could not, however, be regarded as wholly pacified and a Roman legion, the *Legio III Augusta*, was allocated to it, with its headquarters initially at *Ammaedara* (Haïdra on the Tunisian/Algerian frontier) and later at *Lambaesis* (in eastern Algeria). In 20 BC the commander of the legion, Lucius Cornelius Balbus, led a punitive expedition into the desert, capturing many 'towns', including *Cydamus* (Ghadamis) and *Garama* (Jarma in Fazzan).

In AD 69, when the heart of the Empire was in turmoil following the death of the emperor Nero, a territorial dispute between Oea and Lepcis got seriously out-of-hand when the people of Oea invited the *Garamantes* of the interior to come to their aid. They ravaged the countryside of Lepcis, while its citizens cowered (*trepidabant*) behind their defences until the imperial legate Valerius Festus intervened. Festus drove off the Garamantes and then led another punitive expedition into Fazzan. Before the end of the first century, two further Roman expeditions, this time exploratory, had travelled far across the desert. They may have reached as far as Lake Chad, 800 km to the south of the Tibesti Mountains ('Agysimba, where the rhinoceros congregates').

The second century AD was generally a period of peace and prosperity for Tripolitania. At Sabratha, excavations have shown clearly the expansion of the city in this period, when it more-or-less doubled in size. In all three cities new public buildings in shining imported marble were constructed and older structures were renovated or embellished in this desirable material. The dedicator of the Arch of Marcus Aurelius at Tripoli took pains to point out in the dedicatory inscription that the monument is built of marble throughout! Agriculture was developed further in the marginal zones on the edge of the desert, where surface-finds show that many courtyard-farms were first established in the second century. This was perhaps encouraged by stable treaty relationships now in effect with the tribes of the interior. Along the coast, villas of the very rich sprang up in numbers and quality otherwise matched only around the Bay of Naples. The increasing wealth of the region is reflected in the presence of Africans in the Roman Senate and in the ranks of the Roman army. The formal status of the cities was also enhanced, with the grant of municipal status to Lepcis between 74 and 77, and to Sabratha and Oea around 110. Lepcis became at that time a *colonia*, and this status too was acquired by Sabratha and Oea around the middle of the second century.

It is from this period that we have a vivid vignette of social life, through the public defence, or *Apologia*, of the orator Lucius Apuleius. Apuleius, who is also known to us as the author of a novel, *The Golden Ass*, was born in about 123 at Madauros in Numidia (a little way to the south of Souk-Ahras in eastern Algeria). He studied at Carthage, Athens and Rome, and some years later happened to fall ill at Oea, where he was taken in by Sicinius Pontianus, a former student friend in Athens, who lived there with his rich widowed mother, Emilia Pudentilla. After his recovery, Apuleius gave a public lecture on Asclepius in Oea, which made such an impression on his audience that he was urged to stay there and become a citizen. Pontianus then persuaded him to marry his mother, in order to prevent her for falling into the hands of a less desirable suitor. The marriage was evidently a happy one, though it was not at all to the liking of Pudentilla's relations, thus deprived of her wealth: they conducted a campaign of slander against him, culminating in 158 in a formal charge of having secured his wife's hand by sorcery. Apuleius was made to appear in court before the proconsul Claudius Maximus (also a friend of his), and the hearing took place in the basilica at Sabratha. Apuleius, in a witty defence, exposed the provinciality and ignorance of his opponents and was acquitted. He and Pudentilla, however, then left Oea for good and settled in Carthage.

The upward social mobility of the Tripolitanian elite reached its highest point in the upheaval following the assassination of Commodus in the closing hours of 192. Lucius Septimius Severus, a native of Lepcis Magna, was appointed to the command of three legions in Pannonia (approximately Hungary–Slovenia–Croatia). This in turn gave him the opportunity very shortly to enforce his claim to become the Emperor of Rome.

This is the 'finest hour' in the history of Lepcis, when the emperor lavished on his native city a project of architectural redevelopment which would call on the most sophisticated resources of the Roman Empire for its realization (see p. 91). However, the necessity to defend the prosperous coastal region had not diminished, and military operations had to be conducted against the tribes of the interior during the reign of Severus. In a change of strategy, some of the troops formerly stationed at *Lambaesis* were now moved into permanent forts behind the Tripolitanian coast at Ghadamis (*Cydamus*), Qaryah al-Gharbiyah and Abu Njaym (*Gholaia*). The advance party of engineers arrived at Abu Njaym on 24 January 201. There were also related administrative changes. There had been, since AD 39, a *de facto* distinction between the governorship of the province of Africa by a proconsul (appointed by the Senate) and the exercise of military power by the propraetorian legate of the Third Legion (appointed by the emperor). Now a new province of *Numidia* was created out of the military zone, and within this there appear various public offices (related to the gathering of taxes and the administration of imperial property) associated with the *regio tripolitana*.

We still know relatively little of how the security of the region was maintained. The problems to be tackled were quite different from those in Europe, for there was no settled population to speak of beyond the border, and no purpose to be served in this vast desert region by a linear barrier such as Hadrian's Wall in northern Britain. Rather, the situation called for mobility in both detection of and response to hostile activity, together with measures to control both the seasonal movement of pastoralists on the fringes of the settled zone (transhumance) and the movement of trading caravans across the Sahara. The three legionary forts in the desert constitute the most visible elements of this strategy, but the growing evidence of smaller but elegantly built defensive structures (e.g. at Qaryah ash-Sharqiyah, perhaps Qasr Isawi and the like) suggests a well-established military presence at an earlier date, perhaps even towards the end of the first century AD. The devolution of authority to a regional, and indeed local, level is indicated by epigraphic evidence in the third century for a *praepositus limitis tripolitanae* (officer commanding the Tripolitanian frontier) and of a *regio lim[itis ten]theitani* (at Qasr Duib, relating to a frontier sector based on *Tentheos*, at or near az-Zintan).

The Severan dynasty came to an end with the murder of Alexander Severus in 235, and this was followed by some fifty years of political instability and violence. In the course of this the Third Legion, which had been involved in the overthrow of the African emperors Gordian I and Gordian II, was disbanded in disgrace by Gordian III and its name was erased from many inscriptions in a *damnatio memoriae*. The political and military instability of this period resulted also in inflation and economic collapse. Lepcis, having probably been over-stretched by the demands of the Severan redevelopment project, clearly went into decline; this is less obvious at Sabratha. A new administrative order for the empire was introduced by Diocletian, resulting in the subdivision of previous provinces. It was around 303 that the *provincia tripolitana* came into being, with its capital at Lepcis Magna. The governor was initially *praeses et comes* (President and Count), but in 363 the civil and military powers were separated, with the removal of the latter to the *comes Africae*.

During this period there was clearly rising tension with the semi-nomadic (or transhumant) tribes of the interior. The peace which had existed previously had been based upon two factors: treaty relationships between Rome and the peoples immediately beyond its borders, and the knowledge that any infringement of the relationship would result in swift and massive reprisals. Similar factors affected the troubled relations of the later Roman period. The Roman governors frequently broke the treaties themselves, but no longer had the resources necessary to impose their authority. In 363 there was a major crisis. The flashpoint was the arrest and execution of a local chief, Stachao, for inciting trouble within the province. As a consequence, the *Austuriani*, based in the oases to the south of the Gulf of Sidra (and probably to be identified with the later tribal federation known as the *Laguatan*), invaded the Tripolitanian province. They spent three days pillaging the hinterland of Lepcis (presumably the modern district of Tarhunah wa Masallath) without apparent military opposition; they did not however attack the city as they had no means of assaulting its walls. Some time later, the newly-appointed *comes* Romanus arrived at Lepcis with an army, but refused to proceed against the enemy unless the Lepcitani provided him with supplies, to include 4,000 camels. When these had not appeared after some forty days, he simply left the area. Our informant for these events, Ammianus Marcellinus, was clearly interested in illustrating the infamy of Romanus, but the reality of the situation may well have been that he was genuinely inadequately equipped to undertake a punitive expedition and that, after the depredations of the invaders, the Lepcitani were equally unable to provide him with the necessary means. A further raid by the Austuriani in 365 affected the territory of Oea as well as that of Lepcis, and a number of leading citizens, caught on their country estates, perished. Again, there were no reprisals on the Roman side and the invaders returned again in 366, ravaging the countryside, cutting down olive trees and vines, and actually laying siege to Lepcis for eight days before withdrawing. On two occasions, envoys from the province were despatched to the emperor Valentinian at Trier to complain about Romanus and to ask for help. Romanus, however, was able to frustrate them through friends at court: such was his power and influence that he was even able to ensure the support of the emperor in the face of adverse reports from the civil governor Ruricius, and ultimately to secure the execution or flight of all his opponents. (All of this came to light only in 373 when Valentinian sent an expeditionary force to deal with a revolt in Africa. Romanus was arrested for suspected involvement, and the matter was revealed by his papers.) The upshot of this was that the city probably never again enjoyed the same control over its agricultural hinterland, and was unable to recover its former prosperity. Furthermore, it appears that while the Austuriani were unable to penetrate the city's defences, the buildings within were extensively damaged in precisely the same period by an earthquake. However, archaeological evidence for earthquakes has to be interpreted with care: this is discussed separately below (p. 11).

The experience of Tripolitania in the face of the raids of the Austuriani, both in the 360s and later in the fourth century, shows that the territory was not considered particularly valuable to the Roman state. Those regular military forces which still garrisoned the province were stationed further west, where they could defend the more fertile parts of what is now Tunisia. In the fifth century, the whole region was to be lost to Roman control.

The Vandals

The Vandals were a Germanic warrior tribe living in central Europe, who first became known to the Romans in 406, when they crossed the Rhine under pressure from the Huns to their east. From there, they swept through Gaul and made themselves a new home in southern Spain. Some twenty years later, in 429, their leader Gaiseric took 80,000 of them across the Straits of Gibraltar and advanced eastwards as far as *Hippo Regius* (Annaba in Algeria) at the unwise invitation of the rebellious *comes* Boniface. Having established a new capital there, Gaiseric obtained a treaty with Rome under which the Vandals were formally recognized as *foederati* (allies), charged with the defence of Numidia. Boniface, having made his peace with the empress Placidia (mother of Valentinian III and regent), now found that he could not get rid of his new allies. In 439 Gaiseric again pushed further eastwards and took Carthage without opposition; by 455 he had extended his authority over Tripolitania as well. For the indigenous peoples of North Africa (whom we may reasonably call Berbers), this meant the replacement of one ruling elite by another, but otherwise there will have been little change. Indeed, since the Vandals took little interest in the borders of their empire and preferred to make treaty arrangements with native tribal leaders, daily life may have been less disturbed than previously. They also took little interest in collecting taxes, finding it easier to fulfil their financial needs by piracy. For these reasons, it can be difficult to identify the activities of the Vandals in the archaeological record; their coinage is uncommon, and that previously in use continued in circulation; they were not great builders, innovators or artists. Scholars have therefore readily regarded the period as one of decline in Tripolitania, but this must surely be qualified. Certainly, large areas of Sabratha and Lepcis were abandoned at this time but life in the countryside, now characterized by the defensive farm-buildings known as *qsur* (sing. *qasr*) and by the more extensive settlement at Ghirza, seems to have been vigorous.

The Byzantines

The emperor Justinian, a native of the city of Scupi (now Skopje in the Republic of Macedonia) who came to the throne in Constantinople in 527, initiated a great renaissance of the former Roman Empire, with a determination to recover the lands of the West which had been progressively lost to the Goths (Spain and Italy) and the Vandals (Africa). In 533, he sent his general Belisarius with 500 ships and 16,000 men via Sicily to Carthage. Within three months, the Vandals had been decisively defeated and their territories brought under Byzantine control. (It is important to remember that the term 'Byzantine', used to describe the later Roman Empire based on Constantinople – originally the Greek colony of *Byzantion* – is an entirely modern construct: these people always thought of themselves as Romans, and the last vestige of this still survives in the country known as Romania on the Black Sea coast.)

The Byzantine hold over North Africa was in practice tenuous: everywhere – and this is clearly visible at Sabratha and Lepcis Magna – new defensive walls were thrown up, making use of masonry from the ruins of the ancient cities and enclosing only a fraction of their former areas. (The historian Procopius, who wrote about the building-works of Justinian, reported both that large areas of Lepcis were – and remained – buried in sand and that at some time between 527 and 533 the Laguatan had defeated the Vandals and had emptied Lepcis of its inhabitants.) The Byzantine administration made new treaties with the Berber chieftains, and just as quickly violated them itself. In 543 the Laguatan confederation (arguably identifiable with the Austuriani of the fourth century, and clearly now at least partly sedentary) sent eighty delegates to Lepcis to complain of raids on their crops by Byzantine soldiers. The governor Sergius massacred seventy-nine of them, provoking a revolt which took five full years to put down and to conclude with new treaties. Yet this was a period of genuine revival within the cities, even if on a small scale. Justinian, who was a devout Christian, sponsored a widespread restoration of old churches and also built many new ones. Evidence of this is apparent not only at Sabratha and Lepcis, but also in the countryside (al-Asaba'a, al-Khadra). A century later, however, the ease with which the Arabs swept away the Byzantine administration in Tripolitania suggests that it had enjoyed little support from the local population.

The Arabs
The next wave of invaders to make their impact on the Mediterranean World came not from Europe but from Arabia. United and impelled by the new faith taught them by the prophet Muhammad (570–632), the Arab armies rapidly overran the eastern shores of the Mediterranean, defeating the emperor Heraclius decisively at the Battle of Yarmouk in 636, and pushed their way into Egypt. Alexandria was taken in November 641, and the general Amr ibn al-Aasi decided on his own initiative to move westwards within Africa. In 642 he took the city of Barka, inland in Cyrenaica, while leaving the Byzantine garrison penned up within its defences at Teuchira on the coast. He then sent one of his commanders, Uqba ibn Nafi, on a cavalry raid to Zuwaylah in Fazzan, and made a treaty with the people of the region. Still ignoring the Byzantine coastal cities of Cyrenaica, he pressed on in 643 to Oea, which he took after a month-long siege. (Oea was certainly now the principal conurbation in the region, from which it derived its new name of Tripoli or Tarabulus.) Sabratha he took by surprise through an unguarded gateway; of Lepcis there is no mention in the sources, though excavations have shown evidence of later occupation (or reoccupation – was it once again in terminal decline?). In 644/5 Amr ibn al-Aasi made a second expedition to Cyrenaica, where he expelled the last of the Byzantine garrison, and returned to Egypt laden with booty.

Shortly after this, he was relieved of his command and replaced by Abdallah ibn Sa'ad, who in 647 led another army westwards against the Byzantine forces in *Byzacena* (the southern part of Tunisia), which he defeated at *Sufetula* (Sbeitla). Because of civil war amongst the Arabs and other preoccupations, Carthage itself and the remaining Byzantine possessions in Africa were not finally overrun until 698. In the meantime, a new Arab capital had been founded in 670 at Qayrawan (Kairouan) in central Tunisia. Gradually, a new administrative structure was developed for the African territories, known as *Ifriqiyah*, with a governor (*emir*) ruling from Qayrawan. Non-Muslims were taxed, and the Arabs also developed a penchant for Berber slaves; indeed, it had been stipulated as early as 642 that the inhabitants of Barka could pay part of their tribute by selling their children. This, however, created something of a dilemma for the conquerors. On the one hand, there was a religious imperative to convert the native population to Islam; on the other, the immunity of Muslims from slavery. On the whole, the desire for slaves proved the stronger pull.

Over the ensuing three and a half centuries, what was left of the settled communities in Tripolitania played little part in the political or military history of the Maghreb (the West, an alternative designation for Ifriqiyah). Power in Qayrawan changed hands as governors and their military forces became typically more comfortable and less inclined to go into the field and fight. In 799 a determined officer in command of the military garrison at Tubna (at the eastern end of the Chott el-Hodna in Algeria), Ibrahim ibn al-Aghlab, marched on the city and successfully asserted his authority after a period of turbulence and a succession of ineffective governors. In February 800, he negotiated with the Abbasid Caliph Harun ar-Rashid in Baghdad for the possession by his family of Ifriqiyah in perpetuity, in return for an annual tribute of 40,000 dinars. Thus began the Aghlabid dynasty, which was to rule the region until 909, when it collapsed in a welter of internal strife and bloodshed. In its heyday, however, it provided a period of extended stability, based upon uncompromising military power and the imposition of taxes which enabled vast building programmes within Tunisia, not only at Qayrawan, but also laying out the essentials of Sousse, Sfax and Tunis that are still at the heart of these cities today. Under this regime, the countryside certainly also flourished, but Tripolitania remained something of a backwater, remote and of insufficient potential to be either desirable or dangerous.

The Aghlabids were replaced in Tunisia by the Fatimids, not so much a dynasty as a religious movement, having been an extreme monarchical sect within Shiite Islam (which holds that the leadership of Islam should have followed the bloodline of Ali and Fatima, the only daughter of the Prophet to have produced grandchildren). In 892, a missionary from this sect named Abu Abdallah al-Shii, was sent from Syria to preach to the Berber tribes of the Kabylie mountains in Algeria. He gradually won the allegiance of the Berber tribes, where his personal asceticism and respect for the law contrasted markedly with the behaviour of the Aghlabid emirs. A Berber-Fatimid army progressively took control of the mountainous western territories of the Aghlabids, and eventually drove them out of Tunisia too in 909. Abu Abdallah invited his master, Ubaydallah Said, to join him at the Aghlabid fortress of Raqqada outside Qayrawan, only to find himself supplanted by him as leader. Within a year Ubaydallah had arranged for the murder of Abu Abdallah and his family. The Fatimid regime built up its power on the basis of a wide range of new taxes that were levied with ruthless efficiency. In 914 Ubaydallah felt strong enough to proceed against Egypt, and he briefly held Alexandria, but was then defeated. In the following year he established a new capital for himself on the Tunisian coast at Mahdia.

Political chaos in Egypt in 968 presented a second opportunity for the Fatimid ruler at Mahdia, by now al-Mu'izz, to make an attempt upon it. His army succeeded in gaining control of Egypt within a year, and al-Mu'izz sent instructions for a new capital to be prepared for him at Cairo. In four years, this was ready and the court left Mahdia for good, making a triumphal passage by land to its new Egyptian home. A Berber from the Kabylie (in Algeria), Buluggin ibn Ziri, was left behind as governor.

The Bani Hilal

Under the Zirid emirs, the links with Cairo were progressively weakened and broken, to the extent that when Fatimid authority in Egypt itself was threatened, the caliph al-Mustansir attempted to resolve it by diverting the threat against his one-time subjects in the West. Within Egypt in the eleventh century, there grew up a large body of Arab clans who had migrated casually to Egypt from Arabia, and whose numbers had also been swelled by fugitive peasants. Semi-nomadic, they appeared to be beyond the reach of law and of taxation. They claimed fierce allegiance to Islam, but showed little knowledge of its principles. The problem now was that they had become aware of the power represented by their number, and were becoming more assertive. The caliph (we are told) chose to flatter their chiefs by asking their assistance against the Zirid emir in Mahdia and by promising them control of various provinces. The device worked, and the whole body, known as the Bani Hilal (Children of the Moon) set off westwards in 1051. They came first into Cyrenaica, which had always been governed from Egypt since the seventh century and which was not in revolt. There a part of the horde, henceforth known as the Bani Sulaym, remained, while the rest continued westwards. They defeated a Zirid army at Haydaran near Gabès (in southern Tunisia) in 1052, but did not attack the emir (again an al-Mu'izz) who was protected by his walls at Qayrawan. The swiftness of their progress suggests that, as on other occasions, the inhabitants of Cyrenaica and Tripolitania had not been greatly enamoured of their previous rulers.

The experience of al-Mu'izz in attempting to come to terms with the new invaders typified their character. There was no single chief to negotiate with, and the invaders wanted not the rich cities of the coast, nor taxes, but the steppe of the interior for their flocks. Throughout the region this signalled the end, for several centuries, of any sort of urban life, apart from pockets in the Jabal Nafusah and a few settlements on the coast, which in Tripolitania included only Tripoli itself. Even those coastal settlements lost most of their agricultural hinterland to the nomads, who thus brought about in the eleventh century a cultural change in North Africa which was far more profound than that which had occurred with the first advent of Islam in the seventh. It would not be until the sixteenth-century conflict between the Ottoman Turks and Hapsburg Spain that Tripolitania would again have any strategic interest for the outside world.

Earthquakes and history in Tripolitania
The topic of earthquakes merits a brief discussion on its own account, since several such events have been adduced (primarily by Antonino Di Vita) to explain the collapse of buildings or major changes in the structures of the cities of Sabratha and Lepcis Magna. The evidence for earthquakes in Classical antiquity may be literary (reports of earthquakes in ancient literature) and/or archaeological (physical evidence of catastrophic collapse or major building repairs, occasionally accompanied by inscriptions which indicate the reason for them). Both types of evidence require careful interpretation. Literary reports by later writers may confuse dates, and so conflate into a single event occurrences which actually happened in different places at different times. Likewise, the cause of building collapse or repair is subject to an evaluation of probable reasons, and the date of such collapse may not be determinable within very narrow time limits. Bearing in mind these uncertainties, Di Vita has postulated four earthquakes which affected Sabratha and/or Lepcis Magna during the Classical period.

First half of first century BC. The evidence for this event is limited to Sabratha, and is the weakest of the four. Blocks from the spire and the second storey of Mausoleum B (p. 42) were reused in a building constructed around the base of the mausoleum in the mid-first century BC. Di Vita argues that the monument itself was soundly designed and would not have collapsed through internal failure, and that the surrounding area, previously a cemetery, would not have been built over unless it had been catastrophically damaged. The seismic shock required to tumble the spire of a tall monument might, however, have been relatively slight and without other widespread or serious effects.

AD 65–70. At Sabratha, there was further building activity around Mausoleum B, incorporating blocks from the next section of the superstructure, during the early Flavian period. More significantly, the entire forum area was rebuilt at this time, with the first construction of the basilica and of the *curia* behind façades lined with shops. The Temple of Liber Pater (p. 47), facing the east end of the forum, was rebuilt on massively strengthened foundations, which incorporated decorated blocks from the previous entablature, still in relatively 'new' condition. The Temple of Isis (p. 62) was rebuilt and substantially enlarged in 77/78. In the 'Casa Brogan' (p. 58), walls were strengthened and under-pinned at approximately this time. At Lepcis there were repairs to the market (p. 116), involving reused building-materials (implying hasty repair rather than planned alteration)

306–310. The early Flavian buildings around Mausoleum B at Sabratha collapsed, and the debris shows extensive evidence of fire. There are also a number of coins from this debris, of which the latest were issued in 306; there are none of a massive issue of 310, indicating that the collapse took place no earlier than 306, and probably not more than five years later. A restoration of the Temple of Liber Pater was completed between 340 and 350, from a state of 'ancient ruin': this might have resulted from the same event. At Lepcis there is clear evidence on the site of the Flavian Temple (p. 127) of a violent destruction prior to that of 365, which is not closely dated but could be relevant; the same applies to repairs to the 'schola' (p. 122) and the amphitheatre (p. 131). The Temple of Serapis (p. 113) was also violently overthrown and then restored early in the fourth century. A considerable number of other public buildings at Lepcis are known from inscriptions to have been restored from a state of ruin by the governor Lenatius Romulus, who was *praeses* in 324–6; these include the porticoes and basilica in the Old Forum (p. 109), the porticoes of the market (p. 116) and an undiscovered *basilica ulpia*. Di Vita has suggested that the fourth-century city walls of Lepcis were built as a direct result of this earthquake, making use of masonry from nearby buildings which had collapsed.

21 July 365. The evidence adduced in the previous cases has been entirely archaeological, but now we come to an event of such magnitude that it is reported by several ancient authors. The epicentre determined by geologists was beneath the sea to the south-west of Crete; it wrought huge destruction in Crete (more than a hundred towns destroyed, according to a contemporary writer) and in Cyrenaica ('all and every one of the cities of Libya'). It also generated a tsunami which had devastating effects at Alexandria (still commemorated annually in the sixth century as the Day of Horror), on the west coast of the Peloponnese (where the historian Ammianus Marcellinus saw some years later a ship which had been driven far inland) and on the east coast of Sicily. Names of other cities in different parts of the Mediterranean are adduced by other writers, but we cannot be sure that they are not conflating this 'universal' earthquake with other events around the same time. Potential archaeological evidence for this event (violent destruction of major buildings in a distinctive manner, skeletons beneath fallen masonry, hoards or purses of coins pointing to a date soon after 364) has now been contributed by many excavations: Kisamos and Eleutherna in Crete; Kourion and Paphos in Cyprus; Cyrene, Balagrae and Ptolemais in Cyrenaica; Lepcis Magna and Sabratha in Tripolitania.

The Tripolitanian evidence consists of the following. At Sabratha, an inscription shows that the *curia* (p. 55) was rebuilt between 364 and 367. The basilica on the opposite side of the forum was rebuilt at the same time on a radically new plan (p. 51: period III), making use of columns from the Antonine and South Forum temples which had evidently been damaged and were not rebuilt; decorative marble and marble inscriptions from various parts of the forum area were gathered up and stored in the vaults beneath the Capitolium (p. 54). Likewise, much of the decorative marble from the theatre was found stored in one of the rooms behind the stage, where it seems to have been gathered up after a catastrophic collapse (p. 65). At Lepcis, it has already been mentioned that there is evidence of two successive violent destructions of both the Flavian Temple and the Temple of Serapis. The second (and final) destruction of the Temple of Serapis was accompanied by a deep covering of mud, which Di Vita has attributed to the failure of the dam on the Wadi Libdah behind the city; a similar invasion of mud in the Hadrianic Baths was responsible for both overturning and preserving so many fine statues. (This illustrates well the care with which such inferences must be treated. The mud might alternatively have been brought from the sea on this occasion by a tsunami, but the experience of recent times has shown that – once the dam was ineffective for whatever reason — it could have resulted simply from exceptional weather conditions without the intervention of an earthquake!) The market had also gone out of use by the late fourth century, when it was invaded by poor habitations, and the same is true of the theatre and the amphitheatre. It has been suggested that these habitations grew up in part to rehouse those who had been living in the outer parts of the city which were now abandoned.

The evidence for catastrophic destruction at both Sabratha and Lepcis Magna around 365 is therefore incontrovertible. The question remains whether this could have been caused by the earthquake of 21 July 365 off the coast of Crete. The archaeological (and literary) evidence is of course simply not capable of yielding such precision: a year or two either way, sometimes more, is the best that we can hope for. It is true that seismic movements can occur in close succession along different parts of the same fault-line (between the African and Eurasian plates), but I understand that geological opinion is against the possibility that the Cretan event could have caused the structural damage described above at a distance of some 900 km from the epicentre, other than through the agency of a tsunami (which has not been suggested at all for Sabratha, at any rate). For this reason, I have referred to this event in the guidebook as the earthquake 'of 365', implying that there was such an event affecting the cities of Tripolitania at around that time but that it was not simultaneous with the identified event on 21 July of that year.

Finally, Di Vita adds to his catalogue of evidence the destruction of several of the rich coastal villas of Tripolitania, but here we may be more cautious.

These would certainly have been targeted by the Austuriani in their raids (p. 6), and we do know that there was resulting loss of life on the country estates.

Sectarian conflict
The attentive reader of this brief historical essay will note the virtual absence of any references to Orthodoxy, Donatism, Arianism, the Monophysites and the like, or indeed to Shia and Sunni, Kharijites, Malikites and Ibadites, to name but a few of the different strands of Islam. In the late Roman period and thereafter, matters of religious faith assumed a political importance which they had never previously enjoyed. Conflicts between the various sects within both Christianity and Islam underlay much political and military endeavour. These are complicated to present and to understand fully, and since they have no obvious visual impact on the monuments described in this guide, I have made a deliberate choice not to enter this thorny area.

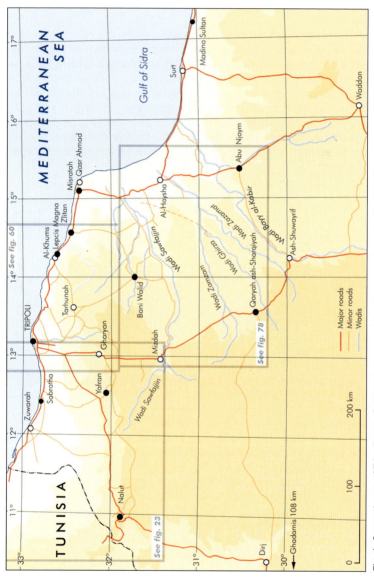

Fig. 1. General map of Tripolitania. Solid dots represent locations mentioned in the gazetteer.

Gazetteer

The gazetteer is arranged in seven sections, two of which are dedicated exclusively to the major sites of Sabratha and Lepcis Magna. The remaining sections represent a sequence of more-or-less coherent regions, within which the sites are mostly listed in geographical order; I have not attempted to compose them into itineraries. I have used the time-honoured device of star-ratings to indicate approximate grades of importance for those who are pressed for time, or who have no desire to examine every detail. All of the locations mentioned are marked on at least one of the four maps in figures 1, 23, 60 and 78. For all of those which are not major modern towns, easily identifiable on maps, I have given geographical coordinates (based on the WGS 84 datum) and navigational instructions.

The principal sites and museums described in this guide are guarded and charge a modest fee for entry; where a museum stands within a site, it is often charged for separately. (At Sabratha, for instance, one requires separate entry tickets for the site, the Roman Museum and the Punic Museum.) Camera tickets may be bought on the same terms, and while they sometimes cause annoyance to tourists who are not forewarned, they provide a refreshing level of freedom for camera use, particularly in museums.

Tripoli and environs

The urban sprawl of Tripoli has grown enormously during the last thirty years and, as in many other parts of the world, outlying districts, villages and oases have become absorbed into a single huge conurbation. The main focus of this very flat and moderately fertile area is the city of Tripoli itself, which has been occupied without interruption since its foundation (as Wy't by its Punic settlers, transliterated as Oea by the Romans) at some time between the seventh and the fifth centuries BC. Its position is determined by the offshore reefs which created a safe natural harbour – though the original coastline has been obscured both by a long historical development and by a massive enlargement and restructuring of the port in the 1970s. Tripoli enjoys the highest rainfall of almost anywhere in Tripolitania (in excess of 350 mm per annum) and it has therefore always been able to sustain itself through its own agriculture. During the Roman period, while generally second in rank to Lepcis Magna, it none the less shared in the prosperity of the region and the coastline on either side of it will have been dotted with the expensive residences of the local elite. We know little of these, but occasional finds such as the tombs at Gurji and Janzur give us glimpses of the funerary customs of these people. In the Byzantine period, Oea had clearly become the leading city of the region, and thus under the Arabs the name of the region itself was adopted for the city and Arabicized as Tarabulus.

TRIPOLI CITY

Medieval and modern Tripoli entirely overlie the ancient *emporium* of Oea, demonstrating a continuity of occupation which is apparent nowhere else in the country (apart, perhaps, from the desert oases). The Arch of Marcus Aurelius, the one visible monument of Classical Oea, has also stood as a cardinal point in the layout of the city from the time of its construction in the second century AD until the present day. For a medieval town, the medina of Tripoli has some remarkably straight streets, and it cannot be doubted that these too are inherited directly from its Classical precursor. The medieval fortifications were largely dismantled by the Italians in the years following the invasion of 1911, on the basis that (a) they no longer possessed any defensive value in the face of twentieth-century artillery and (b) they were a convenient and nearby source of ballast for the construction of new moles and port facilities. Some archaeological observations were made as the walls were being demolished, but these were far from adequate. It seems likely that the medieval walls followed the line of their Byzantine precursors, though this has not been demonstrated. We do know that the ramparts on the seaward side were first built in 796 by Harthama bin Ayan. It is also clear that when Draghut refortified the city after taking it from the Knights of Malta in 1551, he reduced the circuit on the western side. Thus the line projected for the ancient wall on this side in fig. 2 extends beyond that of Draghut's wall.

The level of the modern streets in the immediate vicinity of the Arch of

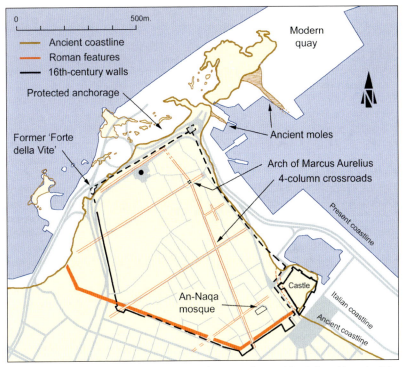

Fig. 2. The medina of Tripoli, showing the ancient coastline and the inferred layout of the city of Oea.

Marcus Aurelius is some 3 m above the Roman paving, and therefore while some of the streets still conserve the general line of the ancient layout, there is some deviation in detail. The tourist will none the less be aware of a wealth of ancient column-drums and capitals built into street-corners. Four of these, at a cross-roads next to the Qaramanli House, appear to stand at an ancient intersection. The ancient port facilities have been entirely smothered by developments both in the Italian colonial period, and more emphatically by a huge enlargement of the port in the 1970s. Fig. 2 shows very approximately the lie of the ancient coastline, whose reefs provided at least two sheltered anchorages, and traces of ancient

moles on the E side of them have been observed.

It was regarded as an early necessity by the Italians to build a railway-line into the port, and in order to do this they demolished the NW bastion of the medieval town (Forte della Vite). In the course of so doing, they discovered an extensive Punic and Roman cemetery, showing that this lay outside the built-up area for at least part of the Classical period. Many of the finds from this cemetery are on display in the National Museum. There have been many other scattered finds, including perhaps a bath-building beneath the castle, but there is nothing else to see in situ.

With regard to the early medieval history of the town, there is little to say:

much of it was destroyed when attacked by the Spanish in 1510. The An-Naqa mosque is clearly very early in origin, and it is included here as a testimony to the intervening period, despite having been destroyed by the Spanish and subsequently rebuilt. Otherwise, the visible buildings of Tripoli belong to the sixteenth century or later and fall outside the scope of this guide.

An-Naqa mosque

This is the oldest mosque in Tripoli, and the only one which traces its origins back to the time before the Hilalian invasion of the eleventh century AD. Its name means 'the camel' and there are at least two legends concerning its foundation and its association with a camel. One places it at the time of the first Arab invasion in the seventh century AD, another at the time of the procession from Qayrawan to Egypt of the Fatimid caliph Al-Mu'izz (969–972). The latter has a greater chance of being chronologically accurate, since the fourteenth-century writer At-Tijani ascribes the building of the mosque to the Fatimids. However, it was effectively destroyed during the Spanish bombardment of 1510, and an inscription records its restoration in 1610 by Safar Dey.

The complex was originally entered from the SW side, where an arcaded courtyard preceded the prayer hall (the windows of which could be opened when there was not enough room for all of the faithful within). At some later time, this access was blocked by the construction of a row of shops, and this is why the current street access, on the NW side, now leads, unusually, directly into the prayer hall. A second doorway to the R of this leads through a corridor into the ablution area, from which one may pass more normally into the courtyard (which is now largely covered with a roof of corrugated sheeting). The prayer hall, approximating to square, presents a forest of columns with intersecting arcades which support the forty-two domes of the roof. The columns and their capitals represent a bewildering variety of spolia from the ancient city of Oea, including the use of reversed column-bases as capitals. The walls and ceiling are otherwise whitewashed and unadorned, forming a rather pleasing contrast. The arcades of the courtyard are similarly supported.

There is on the whole no objection to visitors entering the mosque, provided that one avoids prayer times and that shoes are removed before walking on

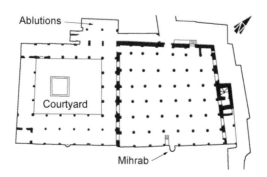

Fig. 3. Tripoli: An-Naqa mosque, plan.

the carpets; at the very least, it is usually possible to enter the ablution area and to look through into the courtyard.

Arch of Marcus Aurelius*

This is the only monument of Classical Oea which is visible in place today. It has stood since antiquity, and appears on maps from the sixteenth century onwards. At the time of the Italian invasion in 1911, a sign on its façade identified it as a cinema, though the colonial powers made it an early priority to clear the monument and the ground around it and to expose it fully for admiration. The sunken garden in which it now stands shows the depth of soil which had to be removed in order to reach the paving of the Roman street.

The arch is a *tetrapylon*, that is to say a four-way arch standing over a street intersection. This was obviously an important focal point, where the *decumanus* leading up from the harbour crossed a major *cardo* at right-angles. Both alignments are still followed by existing streets. The wider, and architecturally more developed,

Fig. 4. Tripoli: the Arch of Marcus Aurelius.

faces of the arch were those towards the harbour and on the opposite side. On each of these sides the opening was flanked by a pair of engaged Corinthian columns standing on projecting pedestals and tied back above by corresponding projections in the entablature. The niches in the piers held imperial statues and there are (damaged and unidentifiable) portraits in medallions above. The spandrels of the arches contain winged victories and the outer corners of the structure are framed by pilasters with elaborately carved vegetal decoration. In height, the over-all effect is weakened by the total loss of the attic. There is no clue as to the form or decoration of this, though it is something of an oddity that the dedication of the arch is carved on the entablature, which must have been an afterthought since this involved cutting back mouldings and decoration which had already been carved.

The shorter faces of the arch, unencumbered by projecting columns, received a more decorative treatment. The SE face (towards the Zumit Hotel) is extremely battered, but the opposite side is the best-preserved of the four. On either side of the opening are trophies of arms on tall poles, with captive barbarian families beneath. Above these, the spandrels contain magnificent portrayals of the patron gods of the city. On the L is Apollo in a chariot drawn by a pair of winged gryphons, and on the R Minerva rides in a chariot drawn by winged sphinxes. Each deity is further identified by their particular attributes, portrayed below: for Apollo his raven, lyre, bow, quiver and laurel-branch; for Minerva her helmet, owl (perching on top of the helmet!), shield, spear and olive-branch. Internally, the arch is covered by a coffered octagonal dome.

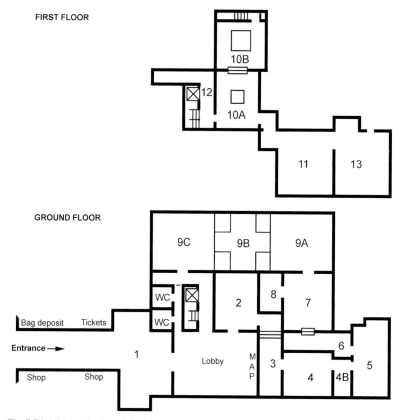

FIRST FLOOR

GROUND FLOOR

Fig. 5.Tripoli: sketch-plan of the National Museum.

The dedicatory inscription tells us that the arch was built in AD 163/4 at the expense of a local citizen and magistrate, Caius Calpurnius Celsus, in honour of the emperors Marcus Aurelius and Lucius Verus. We are also told that it was built on public land and, in case we might not notice it, that it was built entirely of marble. Similarities between the geometry of this arch and that of the contemporary Cruciform Building in the forum of Sabratha (p. 53) suggest that both may have been the work of the same architect.

Temple to the Genius of the Colony

The garden within which the Arch now stands has become a repository for displaced fragments of Classical architecture found in the city and, from the size of some of them, one can be in no doubt that Oea was extremely prosperous in Roman times. Amongst these are some marble blocks from the pediment of a small temple, which were found during the course of clearance works in front of the arch in 1936–37; these have been set up on the high ground between the arch and the al-Athar restaurant on the NW side. The temple from which they had fallen probably lies beneath the funduq to the NE of the arch.

Enough remains of the dedicatory

inscription on the entablature to show that the temple was dedicated to the *genius* (guardian spirit) of the city in AD 183/4 by L(ucius) Aemilius Frontinus. The female figure in the centre of the pediment, with a cylindrical headdress, probably personifies the *tyche* or Good Fortune of Oea. She is accompanied by the patron divinities which recur on the Arch of Marcus Aurelius: Apollo to the L, holding a laurel-branch above his head and leaning on the Delphic tripod (which is entwined by a snake); Minerva to the R, wearing her helmet and holding her spear and shield. These central figures were flanked on either side (and necessarily at a smaller scale) by figures of the Dioscuri, Castor and Pollux, with their horses; only one of them has been found.

National Museum ✱✱✱
During the colonial period, the Italians drove a road-tunnel through the seaward part of the castle in order to link the corniche roads on either side of it. The development of the present port in the 1970s provided made-up ground in front of the castle for a new corniche road, and released the space within for new use. The opportunity was taken of filling it with an entirely new building to house the National (Jamahiriya) Museum, now entered through the grandiose arched portal which used to be the road-tunnel. The result, opened in 1988, has brought together not only antiquities, but also ethnographic and natural history displays which were formerly housed in disparate parts of the castle. The archaeological collection includes many pieces of the highest quality and two or three hours spent here will be well rewarded. There are places to sit (not so much on the ground floor as on the floors above); there are also WCs on the ground floor

close to the stairs, but there are no refreshments. All but the smallest bags are forbidden, though they can be left at the desk just inside the entrance. Camera tickets may be purchased here as anywhere else. There are also a couple of shops inside the entrance which sell postcards and guidebooks.

The lighting, presentation and general labelling of this museum are excellent, with floor plans and many wall-panels in both Arabic and English explaining the themes of the displays. The rooms are identified by numbers, and these are displayed on the walls within the rooms, as well as on the floor-plans. The labelling of individual objects, on the other hand, is generally done only in Arabic. I have attempted in the following pages to supply information on the objects (rather than the themes) where this is not otherwise provided, covering those rooms (essentially 1–16) whose contents fall within the scope of this guidebook.

GROUND FLOOR

Room 1
This houses a few choice masterpieces, by way of introduction. On the left-hand side is a complete monumental tomb of the fourth century AD from the pre-desert settlement at Ghirza (p. 182: this is tomb G from the south necropolis, brought into Tripoli in 1958). Partly within the podium and partly cut into the ground beneath was the funerary chamber, which would have held the ashes of the deceased in a container; above was a form of 'temple,' reduced in this instance to a small central pier surrounded by a colonnade of four columns. In the upper surface of the podium was a small hole communicating with the chamber within so that those visiting

the tomb could pour liquid offerings (libations) to the dead within. Above the columns was an arcade carrying a frieze with primitive but lively figure decoration, and the whole was crowned above by a cornice surmounted by double spirals and stylized palmettes. This is one of a rich variety of monumental tombs found in the pre-desert zone of Tripolitania; Ghirza possesses the greatest single concentration of this type. On the walls in the vicinity are shown a number of other carved elements from similar tombs; those with a more substantial core usually display, on one side, a carved representation of double wooden doors, and two of these are to be seen here: note the portrayal of the locking mechanism. Despite their evident falsity, these doors have often been broken down in later times by would-be tomb-robbers! There are further examples of decoration from these tombs in Room 5.

On the opposite side of the room stands a statue which introduces us to the enormous wealth of sculpture which once adorned the Hadrianic Baths at Lepcis Magna, mostly being high-quality Roman copies of Greek originals. This instance is a naked Venus of the 'Capitoline' type, which was given by Mussolini to Air-Marshal Goering in 1939, returned to Italy from Berlin in 1945 and restored to Libya by the Italian government only in 1999. On the wall behind is another decorative masterpiece, a floor from the villa of Dar Buk-Ammara at Zlitan (p. 150), one of around a hundred opulent country houses which lined the Tripolitanian shore in the second and third centuries AD, giving the coastline a character not unlike that of the Bay of Naples. The central area is composed of panels of shaped tiles of marble (opus sectile) alternating with mosaic representations of fishes. This is surrounded by a narrow band of very fine mosaic (opus vermiculatum) which shows a wide variety of scenes from entertainments in the amphitheatre. The top and bottom bands show musicians, and variously armed gladiators fighting. The left-hand side is largely missing, but down the right-hand side may be seen fights between animals and between men and animals, as well as bound figures (one on a cart) being presented to wild animals for destruction. This damnatio ad bestias was widely practised when suitable victims (criminals or captives) were available: the representation has been associated by some scholars with the expedition of Valerius Festus against the Garamantes in AD 69–70, but it may not reflect any specific occasion. The dating of mosaics on purely stylistic grounds is fraught with uncertainty and current debate suggests that a date as late as the third century is not implausible.

On the left-hand wall, next to the mosaic, is a reproduction of a seventeenth-century map of Tripoli, showing the castle at the water's edge and surrounded by a moat.

As you pass through to the next room, which functions as a kind of central lobby (and off which toilets are to be found), niches on either side of you house two more sculptures from the Hadrianic Baths at Lepcis. On the right is a copy of the Diadoumenos of Polyclitus (an athlete tying a victor's ribbon around his brow), and on the left, a copy of the Apollo of Delphi by Praxiteles, but with the substituted head of Antinous, the Bithynian youth with whom the emperor Hadrian was besotted, and who was drowned in unexplained circumstances in the Nile. The lobby (not part of the numbered sequence) has on the far wall an illuminated map which (if working), shows patterns of occupation and trade in prehistory, the Punic/Greek period, the Roman period and in medieval times.

Room 2, prehistory
A relatively small room, with some impressive fragments of petrified trees in the centre, introduces the prehistoric period. On the right-hand side is a wall-chart illustrating the chronology of North African prehistory. Cases around the walls contain stone implements ranging (clockwise) from the Palaeolithic of the Tadrart Acacus (in the SW of the country, near Ghat) to the Neolithic. The final case (to the right of the stairs) contains examples of Neolithic pottery, together with fragments of ostrich-egg. This material is contemporary with the earliest of the rock-paintings (c. 6,000–1,000 BC: see Room 4).

Room 3, passageway and stairs
Cases on the stairway contain further examples of Neolithic pottery. At the bottom of the stairs, on the right-hand wall, is an illustration of the important prehistoric cave-site of Hawa Ftiah near Apollonia. This was excavated in the 1950s by a Cambridge team and was found to contain a continuous sequence of occupation from c. 80,000–7,000 BC. Excavations on the same site were resumed by another Cambridge team under Prof. Graeme Barker in 2007.

Room 4, prehistoric rock-art
A panel to the R of the door as you enter this room gives a useful résumé of the chronology of North African rock-art. On the left-hand wall are replicas of the typical rock-art that is found in the S and SW (Wadi Matkandush, Tadrart Acacus). The first three are carvings which belong to the Period of

the Large Wild Fauna (from c. 8,000 BC); the fourth is a painting from c. 4,000 BC and the fifth is attributed to the 'Roundhead' Period (from c. 6,000 BC); the curious 'eye' in this composition has been interpreted as having some religious significance. The little skeleton of an infant in the centre of the room is from Wadi Tashwinat in the Tadrart Acacus; it shows signs of deliberate mummification (the earliest known in the world) and has been dated to c. 5,000 BC. In the case at the far end of the room are a couple of saddle-querns, showing early evidence for the grinding of foodstuffs.

Room 4B
A small space separated off from Room 4 (for an audio-visual display) has photographs on the walls of some of the locations from which the replicas in Room 4 derive. There is also a photograph of a cave-painting from the Acacus which shows a 'Garamantian' in a four-horse chariot and what appears to be an imported Roman amphora! This belongs to the Horse Period ('from c. 1,500 BC,' but probably encompassing 1,000–1 BC) in which domesticated horses begin to appear, while the human torso is rendered in an angular hour-glass shape. On the right-hand side of the doorway as you pass through into the next room is a small replica of a painting which illustrates the Camel Period. This period extends from c. AD 500 until modern times.

Room 5, indigenous peoples
The first part of this room (in front of you and to the right) is devoted to the civilization of the *Garamantes*, the native people who dominated the southern region of Fazzan in late prehistoric and in Greco-Roman times. We know a certain amount about the Garamantes

from Classical literature (starting with the Greek historian Herodotus in the fifth century BC), and they are also portrayed in Egyptian sculpture and tomb-paintings. The photographs and cases describe the locations of their material remains, centred on Jarma in Fazzan which still preserves the ancient name of *Garama*, and show some of the artefacts associated with them. The Garamantes were visited several times by Roman military expeditions, but though they traded with the coastal cities to the north, they were never incorporated within the empire. In the centre of the room is a reconstruction of a Garamantian royal tomb, and in a recess at the far end of the room on the left is a *stele* (tomb-marker) in the form of a hand, with a stone offering-table in front of it. This is a very characteristic form of marker placed above the simpler Garamantian burials. Another stone offering-table from Jarma is to the L, and to the R is a small figure described as Isis (provenance not indicated).

In the left-hand half of the room are displays concerned with the extraordinary rock-carvings of Slonta, in the Jabal Akhdar to the S of Cyrene. On the right-hand side are casts of the sculptures, and on the left a photograph of the originals. The carvings are today exposed on the surface of the rock, though what appears to be a column-base suggests that they may originally have been within a cave or rock-shelter. The rock face is carved with a riotous profusion of writhing human and animal figures; it is clear that it constitutes a native religious sanctuary of some kind. On the right-hand side there appears to be some sort of altar with four pigs laid upon it and this is framed by a motif which resembles the bead-and-reel which appears in Classical architecture. Pottery found in the vicinity, where datable, belongs to the fifth and fourth centuries BC.

The third theme of this room is the civilization portrayed on the tombs of Ghirza, in the pre-desert to the S of Misratah (p. 182). We have already encountered one of the Ghirza tombs in Room 1. Here are further reliefs and architectural fragments (mainly from tombs North B and South C) in a style which is technically primitive but full of vivacity; they portray many aspects of life in the pre-desert in the fourth to sixth centuries AD. Typical themes include ploughing (with horses and with camels), reaping, hunting and camel-trains.

Room 6, The Phoenicians
The Phoenician (or Punic) presence in Tripolitania, starting in the seventh century BC, is nowhere near so lavishly represented in the archaeological record as that of the Greeks during the same period in Cyrenaica. Nevertheless, there are here some pleasing pieces of sculpture in travertine. Immediately round to your R is a torso and a pair of feet from the Old Forum at Lepcis Magna; two heads on the R as the passageway narrows are from the area of the harbour at Lepcis, and are thought (because of their headdresses) to represent priests. The charming couchant lion on the R is from Zuwarah (to the W of Sabratha: see fig. 1), the sejant lion (sitting up) on the L is from Tripoli. The case of pottery on the L is intended to display Punic types, though by the time to which these pieces belong (second century BC onwards) there are wide stylistic similarities throughout the Mediterranean World and there is little about them which is specifically 'Punic.'

Further along the passageway are examples of *stelai*, one of which displays the geometrical symbol for Tanit, a goddess identified with the Astarte of the Phoenician homeland and widely worshipped in North Africa. At the far end of the passageway, beyond the stairs which lead up to Room 7, is a travertine torso from Lepcis Magna, and to the left of it part of a draped figure, allegedly from Ghadamis.

Room 7, The Greeks

The first thing that strikes the eye as you climb the short stairway to Room 7 is the text in archaic Greek characters painted around the walls beneath the ceiling. This is part of a text of an inscription of the fourth century BC, purporting to quote from the oath taken by the original Theraean settlers who set out to found the city of Cyrene in the seventh century BC. It reads '[The assembly decided:] since Apollo spontaneously ordered Battos and the Theraeans to colonize Cyrene, the Theraeans resolve to send out Battos to Libya as a leader and a king, with Theraeans to sail as his companions. They are to sail on fair and equal terms, according to households, one son to be chosen [from each family?] of those who are in the prime of life.'

In the centre of the room are the first two of a series of informative reconstruction models that were commissioned for the new National Museum. The first of these shows the Temple of Zeus at Cyrene, one of the great Doric temples of the Greek World, constructed in the sixth century BC and slightly larger in plan than both the Temple of Zeus at Olympia and the Parthenon at Athens. The other model is of the Agora at Cyrene, with its surrounding temples and porticoes, as it appeared in the third century AD.

To your R as you enter the room is a case of ceramics: terracotta figurines,

lamps, unguentaria (perfume bottles), black-slipped and painted pottery mainly of the Hellenistic period (fourth to first centuries BC) but including some earlier Greek imports. To the L of this is a fine head of a goddess, found at Cyrene and attributed to the fourth century BC. Beyond this is another case of pottery and lamps of the Greek and Hellenistic periods. Returning now to the start and going round the room in a clockwise direction, the first case contains some large dishes, unguentaria and a 'Megarian' mould-made bowl with relief decoration. These bowls were made in many parts of the Mediterranean World in the third to first centuries BC, those most widely distributed having come from the neighbourhood of Ephesos in Asia Minor. The objects in this case have nothing to do with Cyrene, but come from tomb-groups at Bin Gashir near Tripoli: they appear to cover a time-span from the second century BC to the first century AD. The next case on this side of the room is also unconnected with Cyrene but contains ceramics from tombs in Tripoli. There are examples of late (Hellenistic) black-slipped wares, of fine red-slipped ware (terra sigillata) from central Italy and from the Carthage region, and some ovoid decorated beakers from northern Italy.

On the far side of the room, framing the doorway, are three sculptures from Lepcis Magna, which seem to have escaped from the room beyond. On the L is a colossal Roman figure of Fortuna from the Colonnaded Street, next to which is a head in archaistic style (i.e. not genuinely early) from the market. On the R is a colossal figure of a drunken Dionysus, accompanied by a panther and supported by a young satyr; this comes from the Old Forum and may be the cult-statue from the Temple of Liber Pater (=Dionysus/Bacchus/Shadrap).

However, before proceeding to the Roman galleries proper, you should cast an eye in the small Room 8, to the L.

Room 8

In the middle of the room is a marble group of the Three Graces, a very popular subject for bath buildings. This is one of two renditions found in the Baths of Trajan by the Sanctuary of Apollo at Cyrene; the other is on display at Cyrene itself. Immediately inside the doorway, on the R, is a small male figure of Dionysus attached to an architectural pier of some sort, perhaps a leg of a table or the like. This comes from Cyrene, as do the two veiled female busts at the other end of the room. These very enigmatic figures are extremely characteristic of Cyrene, where they were used as tomb-markers; they date mainly to the fifth and fourth centuries BC and their faces may be veiled or they may be entirely faceless. Inasmuch as they are clearly associated with the cult of the dead, they have been interpreted as representations of Persephone, the wife of Hades and Queen of the Underworld.

The largest figure in the room is of course an interloper — from Lepcis Magna! (The riches of this site are so great that they find their way into one or more rooms of every museum in Tripolitania, quite apart from filling a sizeable museum at Lepcis Magna itself!) This is a figure of Athena/Minerva from the theatre, typically armed and accompanied by her particular attributes, the owl – isn't its look of devotion irresistible? – and the olive branch.

Room 9A, Lepcis Magna

In the centre of the room is a model of the Severan Forum and Basilica at Lepcis Magna, while the whole is overlooked by a photograph of the market at Lepcis which fills the right-hand wall. The walls otherwise display a fine array of mosaics from wealthy villas along the Tripolitanian coast. Immediately to your right as you enter the room is perhaps the finest mosaic in the collection, in terms of technical quality. This is a large, but fragmentary, piece in the very small tessellated work known as *opus vermiculatum* (with up to 63 tesserae per square centimetre!). The central circular motif is almost completely lost, but it is surrounded by a delicate tracery of plant-life springing from an acanthus, inhabited by a wonderful variety of animals and birds: don't miss the little chameleon towards the right-hand edge! This mosaic comes from the villa of Dar Buk-Ammara at Zlitan and probably belongs to the time of Hadrian (AD 118–137). The largest of the mosaics on the opposite wall comes from the same villa: portraits of the Four Seasons (always looking so bored!) alternate with decorative panels of *opus sectile*, and on either side are panels portraying fishes, animals and 'Nilotic' scenes of men in boats hunting in the marshes of the Nile (often with a hint of satire, showing pygmies struggling with water-birds). The left-hand mosaic on this wall, with four square panels framed by luxuriant borders of fruit and foliage, and with a Medusa head in the centre, is from a suburban villa at Lepcis. In between these two large mosaics are two small panels, one showing *xenia* (gifts of meat and fruit to a guest, from Tripoli, near the Forte della Vite) and the other horses threshing wheat in front of a villa (from Zlitan).

The sculptures which adorn this room were mostly found in the Old Forum at Lepcis, where they were probably associated with the Temple of Rome and Augustus. Starting on your left as you enter the room and proceeding anticlockwise, they are an unidentified female head; Venus; Agrippina the Elder (wife of Germanicus); the emperors Tiberius, Claudius, – ramp – Augustus(?) seated with orb; a colossal head of Livia (wife of Augustus); Livia standing; head of a goddess; head of Drusus Caesar; seated figure of Antonia Minor (niece of Augustus); head of Germanicus; Artemis of Ephesos, from the amphitheatre; Vibia Sabina (wife of Hadrian) as Artemis, from the theatre; Aphrodite, from the Hadrianic Baths; colossal head of Roma; head of a goddess; Aphrodite with Eros and dolphin, from the theatre; colossal statue of Livia as Ceres (from the Temple of Ceres in the theatre); female portrait-head.

Above the ramp leading to Room 9B is a replica of the dedicatory inscription in the theatre at Lepcis, showing the mixture of Punic and Roman culture which prevailed there in the early first century AD: note both the Punic names (Annobal...Tapapius Rufus, son of Himilcho) and title (Sufes, a Punic magistracy) of the sponsor; also the repetition of the content in neo-Punic script. On the left-hand side of the ramp are a colossal head of Tiberius and a head of Vipsania Agrippina (his first wife); in the niche behind is Iddibal Caphada Aemilius, the sponsor of the Chalcidicum (p. 118). On the opposite side is a colossal head of Augustus, and in the niche is Annobal Tapapius Rufus, the sponsor of the theatre and the market.

Room 9B
The focal point of this room is the mosaic in the centre of the floor, which is well seen from Room 10B on the first floor. The design is mainly geometric, with a central circular frame enclosing a head of Amphitrite (a Nereid, the wife of Poseidon), bordered by fishes. It was found in the Villa of the Nereids at Tajurah, to the E of Tripoli, and is attributed to the middle of the second century AD. The cases in the corners of this room are filled mainly with objects from Punic and early Roman tombs discovered in Tripoli in 1912, when the NW bastion of the walled city (Forte della Vite/Borj ad-Dalia) was demolished in order to build a railway-line into the port. The near case on the R contains glass cinerary urns, with some small fragments of sculpture (source not indicated) in the bottom of the case; the further case on the R is filled entirely with glassware from the tombs. (It is only in tombs that one ever finds intact glassware like this.) The further case on the L contains a wide range of imported pottery, mostly (but not all?) from the Forte della Vite cemetery. There is red-slipped *terra sigillata* tableware of the first century AD from Tuscany (typically the items which bear makers' marks stamped in the centre of the floor), from Campania (a conical cup in the centre of the case, more orange in hue) and from La Graufesenque in the south of France (the dish with the yellow/red 'marbled' effect). The rather larger dishes with simple stamped decoration on the floor are from Tunisia and belong to the fourth or fifth centuries AD. Finally, the near case on the L contains small marble sculptures from the villa at Tajurah. On the right-hand side of the room are three statues: a nude male from the Hadrianic Baths at Lepcis; a figure of a woman (of unknown provenance); a nude male from the Old Forum at Lepcis. On the L is a series of second-century imperial portraits, mostly from the theatre at Lepcis:

Fig. 6. Detail of a mosaic from the 'Villa of the Nile' at Lepcis Magna.

Crispina (wife of Commodus), Faustina the Elder (wife of Antoninus Pius), Faustina the Younger (wife of Marcus Aurelius), Marcus Aurelius, Lucius Verus, Hadrian.

The statues which flank the next ramp are almost all from the Hadrianic Baths at Lepcis Magna, and we have now moved definitively from history into mythology. The first figures on either side of the ramp constitute a pair, Apollo (R) and Marsyas (L). Marsyas, a satyr, fancied himself as a flautist and foolishly challenged Apollo (who played the lyre) to a contest: he was flayed alive for his pains. The other figures on the R are the sea goddess Amphitrite, Hermes with (or mostly without) the infant Dionysus, a seated nymph (from the theatre) and Mars in the niche behind. The figure in the corner (not on the raised plinth) is a Roman copy of a resting satyr by Praxiteles. On the L, beyond Marsyas, Isis standing; a fragmentary male figure (perhaps Asclepius); the muse Calliope seated (found near the city wall); a youthful Apollo in the niche. Also on the plinth is a case containing a charming sculpture of a sleeping cupid, which formed part of a fountain; this is from Lepcis, but

the precise provenance is unknown. Next to it, in the corner of the next room, are two female portraits from the Hadrianic Baths.

Room 9C

Above your head as you descend the ramp into this room is a replica of the reused statue-base which stands at the entrance to the *curia* at Sabratha (p. 55). The room is dominated by a photograph of the theatre at Sabratha on the far wall, and in the centre there is a model of the Forum of Sabratha (not very easy to understand because of the attempt to show several, markedly different, chronological phases). Do not be deceived, however: this room is still primarily filled with finds from Lepcis Magna. Around the Sabratha model are three square plinths in Pentelic marble (from Attica) which once adorned the Temple of the *Gens Septimia* in the Severan Forum at Lepcis. These gave added height and prominence to the pink granite columns of the temple portico, and they were all decorated with scenes from the mythical fight between the gods and the giants (who are mainly distinguishable by their fishy tails in place of legs).

The fine mosaics on the right-hand wall are all from Lepcis. The central mosaic was found in the House of Orpheus in the western part of the city (near the Hunting Baths, no longer visible): the long panel across the top shows Orpheus playing his lyre and charming the animals and birds, while the six square panels beneath show objects and activities associated with daily life on a coastal farm estate. The four long panels which flank this piece come from the very opulent Villa of the Nile (p. 130) between the Eastern Baths and the circus. Upper L is a personification of the Nile riding in procession on a hippopotamus; at the right-hand end of the scene is a Nilometer, one of the gauges used to measure the height of the annual flood (which determined the taxes due for each year). Below L is a scene of cupids in a boat race, approaching the porticoed jetties of a seaside villa. Upper R is the magical winged horse Pegasus being dressed by the nymphs; and below R is a scene of fishing, with various nets and with lines. All of these are datable to the late second or early third centuries AD. On the left-hand wall are Nilotic mosaics from a bath building in Wadi Zgaia, near Funduq an-Naqqaza to the W of Al-Khums, with carved Nereid and Medusa-head medallions from the Severan Forum at Lepcis (p. 101) above.

At the farther end of the room are some further pieces of statuary: R to L, a figure of an emperor in Roman armour from the Old Forum; an example of a cipollino column from the Severan buildings; a portrait of Marcus Aurelius (from Tripoli); a torso of a youth from the theatre; a seated figure of a shepherd with his sheep from near the theatre; a statue of a private individual from the *decumanus* to the W of the Severan Arch.

The corridor beyond has an emergency exit only to the R, and leads round L back to the main lobby and to the stairs leading to the floors above. This small space accommodates a number of further mosaics, mostly in the rather coarser technique which characterizes the fourth century AD. Facing you as you leave Room 9C are three mosaics: on the L is a geometric mosaic from the Gurji suburb of Tripoli, and to the R of that is another mosaic from Gurji, with an *emblema* (central panel) in *opus vermiculatum* showing an eel fighting with a squid. Note here how the *emblema* is not correctly aligned with the room as a whole, resulting in awkward wedges of white surrounding it. These very fine panels would have been composed on a tile in a workshop and sold 'off the shelf;' the location in which this example was found may well be secondary (i.e. it has been moved and reused), given the incompetence of its placement in relation to the room and the poor quality of the surround. To the R again is a small hunting scene from the Villa of the Nile at Lepcis. Facing this, on the opposite wall, are two geometric mosaics from Tripoli and Gargarish. To the R of the doorway into Room 9C is another hunting scene from the Villa of the Nile at Lepcis Magna. The two mosaics in this corridor contrast unfavourably, in terms of technical detail, with the four huge panels in Room 9C, and show the loss of quality between the second and the fourth centuries AD. The fourth-century mosaics are not unlike the hunting scenes of similar date in the great villa of Piazza Armerina in Sicily. In the corner of the corridor are two more cases of Roman pottery, once again from the Punic and Roman cemetery of the Forte della Vite in Tripoli.

Passing round to the R, you are faced by a magnificent rendering in Pentelic marble of the head of the Medusa, which formerly adorned the vault of the Arch of Antoninus Pius at Lepcis Magna (later the Oea Gate: p. 123). The emotional intensity of the portrait and the subtle naturalism of the writhing snakes are in marked contrast to the more mechanistic treatment of the Medusa heads from the Severan Forum, carved some sixty years later. Beneath this, on a low plinth, is a remarkable and enigmatic relief from Lepcis Magna (precise findspot unknown) which portrays a dead warrior in barbarian dress (note the trousers) lying on top of four horses (who appear also to be dead) carved in very summary relief. It has been suggested tentatively that this is a representation of the mythical Thracian king Diomedes, who was killed, and whose carnivorous horses were tamed, by Hercules. But, if so, it should have formed part of an entire cycle of sculptures representing the Labours of Hercules, and no other related piece has been recorded. Further along to the R is a mosaic composed of vegetal ornament enclosing four very fragmentary *emblemata*. This is from a seaside villa at Al-Khums, to the W of Lepcis, which is no longer preserved. The last mosaic along this wall is from the bath-building at Funduq an-Naqqaza to the W of Al-Khums. (Compare with that in Room 9C.) At the far end of the corridor, at the foot of the stairs, are a statue of Trajan from the Old Forum at Lepcis, and two bearded herms (busts set on square pillars, with male genitalia indicated below) from the theatre.

FIRST FLOOR

At the top of the stairs to the first floor, there is a statue of a female figure from Lepcis Magna. To your left is a corridor (almost invariably roped off) which is designated *Room 12* and which displays some fragments of Roman frescoes. It also provides a fine view into Room 9C below. In front of you is Room 10.

Room 10A

This room, around an opening which looks down onto the petrified trees in Room 2, houses a number of pieces of smaller sculpture from Lepcis Magna, mainly from the Hadrianic Baths. Amongst the nine pieces along the wall to the R as you enter the room, note the second from the L, a fragmentary but striking winged victory, and the central figure, a portrait of the future emperor Caracalla as a child. On the wall to your L is a case of pottery from the cemetery of the Forte della Vite in Tripoli, followed by a statue of Aphrodite from the Hadrianic Baths. Against the opposite wall is another case of small objects, including some small bronze sculptures, a number of bronze mirrors and a large bronze lantern; some, but not all, of this material is from the Forte della Vite. To the L is another statue from the Hadrianic Baths: this is a priestess of Isis, identifiable by the 'Isiac knot' which fastens her cloak.

Room 11, the Arch of Septimius Severus at Lepcis Magna

The further part of Room 10, up the steps, then leads via another staircase to the floor above. It is therefore more convenient at this stage to proceed through the door opposite to the one by which you entered the room, and to visit Rooms 11 and 13. In the lobby between Rooms 10 and 11 is a case containing three objects from a tomb of the Punic period at Bin Gashir. On the opposite wall we are introduced, by two figures of captives and by a reconstruction drawing, to the Arch of Septimius Severus at Lepcis Magna which constitutes the theme of Room 11. However, first to be noted in the second part of the lobby are a case containing Punic and local Tripolitanian amphorae from various findspots and, almost hiding round to your R, the dedicatory inscription from one of the gates of the legionary fort at Abu Njaym (p. 170). This, along with forts at Ghadamis (p. 84) and Qaryah al-Gharbiyah (p. 196) was constructed at the beginning of the third century AD in order to control trans-Saharan movement. The inscription here names the emperor Septimius Severus (dating the construction to AD 201) and the commander of the Third Legion, Q. Anicius Faustus.

Room 11 displays the original sculptures from the attic frieze of the Severan Arch at Lepcis, for full discussion of which see p. 93. There is a model of the arch in the centre of the room. The principal problem concerning this arch, for architects, is how it was put together. We have only the fallen blocks for the upper part of the superstructure. The steeply-pointed broken pediments are without parallel in Roman architecture, but their position on the monument is unquestionable, however odd they look. What has baffled architectural historians, and has resulted in a number of different attempts on paper at restoration, is how the figured friezes of the attic related to these broken pediments: they are too long to have been placed between them, and yet if they were placed above, the view of the observer would always have been obstructed by the absurd pinnacles (as one sees now in the reconstructed arch on the site).

Along the wall on your L as you enter the room are frieze panels showing the triumphal military procession of Septimius Severus, who rides in a four-horse chariot (quadriga) together with his sons Caracalla and Geta, preceded by barbarian captives and followed by his soldiers. In the background appears a lighthouse, presumably that of the port at Lepcis. The panels on the wall on your R (as you enter) portray a scene of sacrifice, with sacrificial bulls being brought from L and R. Julia Domna, the Syrian wife of Septimius, is burning incense on an altar. On the next wall (continuing anticlockwise) is a scene celebrating familial harmony, with Septimius and his elder son Caracalla joining hands in the presence of his younger son Geta, presided over by Hercules/Milk'ashtart and Tyche/Fortuna: an ironic fantasy, of course, for Caracalla murdered Geta within a year of their father's death. The fourth wall of the room displays the very fragmentary remains of another military procession, possibly similar to the first (and displayed on the opposite side of the arch). The figures of winged victories displayed in the corners of the room did not frame the attic friezes (as displayed) but filled the spandrels of the arches beneath: see the model. For historians of art, these sculptures mark the beginning of the transition from the naturalism of Roman reliefs of the first and second centuries AD (witness the second-century Medusa at the foot of the stairs on the ground floor) to the rigidity and two-dimensionality of Byzantine art. Note, for instance, how Septimius is proceeding to the R in his chariot, while he himself is shown frontally, facing straight towards the viewer; the folds of dress are also shown by rather stylized lines of light and shade, and do not have any real volume or movement;

figures set behind the principal plane of the action are simply raised up, without any diminution of size or change in the depth of relief.

The bust of Septimius in this room is from the theatre at Lepcis. The milestone, recording a distance of 43 miles from Lepcis, was found near Tarhunah, and relates to the road built in the first century AD from Lepcis into its hinterland by the governor Aelius Lamia (p. 93). It is dated to AD 216, in the reign of Caracalla.

Room 13, Christianity
The sculptures on display in this room are mostly decorated architectural elements from early Christian churches. The window-frames, the brackets and some of the column-capitals come from the church at al-Khadra, to the E of Tarhunah (p. 163). They are decorated in a chip-carved technique (as if they are wood). The date of the church and the question whether it was built in a single phase or two successive ones (of which the second would be Byzantine and the first earlier) remains in dispute, but this style of carving may be considered broadly to be characteristic of the fourth to sixth centuries AD. Another church which has contributed to the display is that at al-Asaba'a near Gharyan (p. 74): from this comes the fine tombstone (on the right-hand wall) of *Turrentius*, presbyter of the church, who lived 47 years 'more or less' (*plus [mi]n[us]* – a common formula). The sarcophagus-lid in front of this is from Tripoli, and from the Tripoli area also is a carved block which shows the deep grooves which result from reuse as a well-head; note the chi-rho monogram (signifying *Christos*) on the end, accompanied by the letters alpha and omega. Notable on the far side of the room (as you enter) is a capital in which the acanthus leaves of Classical architecture have been entirely replaced by palm-fronds.

In the centre of the room is a case of clay lamps, made in Tripolitania in the fourth and fifth centuries AD. In the recess on the L (as you enter) are some photographs of mosaic panels from the Byzantine church at Qasr Libya in Cyrenaica (the originals are displayed in a small museum on site) and two cases. These contain cinerary urns, respectively of glass, and of clay or stone. They seem a little surprising in an early Christian context, for inhumation takes the place of cremation in the Roman world with the advent of Christianity. Indeed, the glass urns (like those in Room 9B downstairs) are from the Forte della Vite, and the others are also said to be from Punic tombs in Tripoli!

Retrace your steps now to Room 10 (where there are convenient seats for a brief rest!), and proceed up the steps to the second part of the room. The steps are guarded on either side by busts of Faustina the Younger from the theatre at Lepcis Magna.

Room 10B
First of all, this room gives you excellent views down onto the Amphitrite mosaic below, and to Rooms 9A and 9C on either side. Around the central void are cases of coins and of lamps; the display runs anticlockwise. It begins with a few wheel-made Hellenistic lamps and some fine mould-made Italian imports of the first century AD (known as volute-lamps because of the moulded volutes on either side of the nozzle). Along the right-hand side are mould-made lamps of the second to fourth centuries AD. These were made in many places: they may have

been imported from Tunisia or from Corinth, and there was undoubtedly local production in Tripolitania as well. The final section of the lamp display, on the far side, includes Tunisian and Tripolitanian lamps with Christian symbols (crosses, chi-rho monograms); there is also a lamp with a portrayal of Christ as the Good Shepherd. At the end are four little (plain) lamps of the Islamic period.

As you continue around the central cases, the coin display starts with Punic coins of the Numidian king Masinissa and proceeds in chronological order through the Roman period. The groups can often be identified from the date-ranges shown on the Arabic labels. On the second corner of the coin display is a small hoard of fourth- and fifth-century coins found in Gargarish, together with the flask in which they had been buried. The display ends with a group of coins of Marcus Aurelius found in Tripoli, followed by some square silver coins of the Islamic Hafsid dynasty (1228–1510).

Against the wall on the right-hand side of the room are some further cases, which contain small articles of toiletry, adornment or amusement. There are pins, spoons, knucklebones and dice in worked bone, attributed to the first three centuries AD. Another case contains small bronzes: mirrors, bracelets and finger-rings. Note the finger-ring which incorporates a key. The farther side of the room, against the staircase which leads to the floor above, is lined with some more marble heads from Lepcis. From R to L they are a female head (Old Forum); Aphrodite (market); Augustus (Chalcidicum); Claudius (Old Forum); an old woman (Hadrianic Baths); a male head (found 'near Lepcis'); Septimius Severus (Hadrianic Baths).

SECOND FLOOR

Room 16, Monuments of the early Islamic period

The tour of the next floor begins effectively with this room, which is concerned with monuments datable between the first arrival of the Arabs in the seventh century AD and the invasions on the Bani Hilal and the Bani Sulaym in the middle of the eleventh century. There are few material remains of this period, but virtually none between the mid-eleventh and the fifteenth centuries, which mark a real hiatus in the evolution of the region. Since much of the material here is photographic, the bilingual explanatory panels often give you all the guidance you need. The display in this room starts to the R of the door by which you come in, with a case containing two large glazed bowls (unexplained). Further round to the R, in a recess, is a photographic display concerning the mosque and palace (*qasr*) at Ajdabiyah, dated to the early and late tenth century respectively. The long wall on the R has explanatory panels devoted to Ujlah and other early Islamic settlements in the desert oases, in front of which is a model of the row of tower tombs of the Bani Khattab at Zawilah in Fazzan. These were the tombs of a prosperous Berber family which fled to the desert in 761 to escape the Arabs on the coast.

On the opposite side of the room are photographic displays which describe the mosque excavated at Madina Sultan (p. 153) and the Tripoli mosque of an-Naqa, the origins of which probably go back to the tenth century (p. 18). The model on this side of the room displays an idealized Tripolitanian mosque, showing an early prayer-hall with horseshoe arches, a courtyard with water for ritual washing and accommodation for pilgrims, and a (later) Turkish pencil-minaret. At the far end of the room are three handsome marble tomb-markers of the Islamic period, without explanation. On the wall behind are copies of engravings made by the traveller J.-R. Pacho who explored Cyrenaica and the Syrtic Gulf in 1824–25.

The remainder of the museum contains much of interest, including a fine model of Tripoli Castle in Room 19, ethnographic material, twentieth century history and natural history displays, but an account of these falls beyond the scope of this guidebook.

GURJI, Mithraic tomb

Coordinates: N 32° 51.766', E 13° 6.144'
Directions: The tomb lies 8 km to the W of Tripoli, between two of the main roads leading westwards, at the point indicated. If travelling on the more southerly road, turn R immediately beyond the tomb, into an unmade alley with a plain boundary wall on the right-hand side. The first opening on the R, about 100 m from the corner, is the entrance to the enclosure. The site is guarded, but accessible only by appointment. (Ask at the National Museum.)

This is the site of a painted, rock-cut tomb, first discovered in 1903 and then lost. It was rediscovered in the course of quarrying operations in 1914 and restored, with provision of a cover-building, in 1920. The area is one of soft sandstone that was being quarried already in antiquity, and the builder of the tomb made use of a pre-existing quarry shaft, filled up with earth to the present floor-level of the tomb. The chamber extends beneath the covering rock on the E side, but was mainly open to the sky, requiring a constructed roof in antiquity of which no trace remains. An entrance into the chamber was cut through the rock face on the S side, and is approached by a short flight of steps.

The two principal burials within the tomb are set within rectangular recesses on the N side, and the surfaces are plastered and elaborately painted. The tomb directly in front of you is identified by an inscribed roundel above (fig. 7) as that of Aelia Arisuth, who was about sixty (*vixit annos sexaginta plus minus*); the roundel is supported by two winged *genii*. On the rear face of the recess is a portrait of Arisuth, framed in a wreath supported by two female attendants. On each of the side walls is a reclining *genius* leaning on a reversed torch (symbolizing the life extinguished), whereas on the ceiling is a peacock within an inhabited vine-scroll, symbolizing resurrection. When the tomb was first discovered,

Fig. 7. Gurji: the dedication above the tomb of Aelia Arisuth.

the cover of the chest was intact and was painted with a lioness, inscribed *quae lea jacet* (a lioness lies here). 'Lion' is one of the seven grades of initiation into the mysteries of the Persian good Mithras, whose cult achieved wide popularity in the Roman Empire, and it is therefore assumed that Arisuth was a devotee. (Contrary to the former scholarly opinion that Mithraism allowed only male devotees, it has recently been argued that there is a significant body of evidence for female adherents also.) At the L end of the recess, where the head of the deceased would have been, there are still fragments of a basin moulded in plaster, with a hole in the bottom. This would have allowed relatives visiting the tomb to pour in liquid offerings (libations) to the dead. The recess is flanked on the main wall of the chamber by two acolytes holding candles, and beneath is a lively scene of a chariot-race in the circus. The turning-points (*metae*), each surmounted by three pointed cones, stand at either end of the course, while four teams (red, blue, green and white) compete; blue is winning and white has crashed. Behind the scene is a victor's palm and a man carrying the prize vase.

The recess to the right of the first is similar in character, but its painted decoration is now less well preserved. A tablet above the recess flanked by peacocks (now almost completely lost) identified the resident as Aelios, son of Jurathanus; he was presumably the husband of Aelia Arisuth. On the rear wall of the recess he was portrayed reclining in Paradise: only his feet and the vegetation of the paradise garden now remain. At either end of the recess were again reclining *genii* resting on reversed torches and the ceiling was decorated with flowers, a

vine and a basket of fruit. The lid of the tomb-chest, when found, was painted with a lion and the inscription *qui leo jacet* (a lion lies here). As in the tomb of Arisuth, the plaster basin for libations still survives.

On the opposite side of the chamber is an undecorated recess with twin burial-compartments, which appears never to have been used. The painted tombs have been attributed to the fourth century AD. The portrayal of the face of Arisuth is not unlike that of Egyptian painted mummy-portraits of the same period.

JANZUR, Cemetery and museum*

Coordinates: N 32° 49.709', E 13° 1.656'
Directions: Leave the main road from Tripoli westwards at N 32° 50.290' E 13° 2.460', turning southwards, and then take the next turning to the R. Follow this road (parallel to the main road) for about 1.5 km and turn R at a roundabout. The entrance to the site and museum is about 50 m from the turning, on the L, and is readily identifiable by the name-plate next to the gate.

A small museum, in what is now a suburb of Tripoli, has been constructed in the middle of an ancient cemetery, so as to incorporate some of the tombs within it and to display many of the finds which have been recovered from them. The entrances to further tombs are visible in the garden surrounding the museum. Excavations were carried out here in 1958 and again in 1969–73. The date-range of the cemetery extends from the first to the fourth or fifth centuries AD. The earliest tombs are built in the Punic tradition, and consist of a sunken courtyard excavated in the ground and approached by a flight of steps; one or more rock-cut burial chambers open off this courtyard and in each of these one or more corpses was laid, surrounded by various accoutrements which the dead might require in the afterlife. (Tomb 15, the richest of this series in grave-goods, had been used for a succession of burials over an extended period and yielded a total of 115 objects.) Burials of the second and third centuries AD are characterized by the use of cremation, with the ashes being interred in vessels of pottery, glass, lead or marble. The fact that such cinerary urns are sometimes found in the older tombs suggests a change in rite rather than in population (families presumably continued to make use of the same tombs); other urns were simply buried in the overlying soil. The latest burials reflect a further change of rite with the advent of Christianity: there is a return to inhumation, but in simple cist graves (i.e. cut or constructed like coffins) entirely without accompanying objects. These graves have been attributed to the fourth and fifth centuries AD.

In the centre of the little museum is an array of amphorae which were used as cinerary urns, and beneath these is the most elaborate of the rock-cut tombs, tomb 1, which has been attributed to the second half of the first century AD. It is reached by steps which originally led down to a courtyard, off which the tomb-chamber opens. Within the chamber are cists on either side (found empty) with niches above, but the walls and ceiling are plastered throughout and painted with lively polychrome designs. Opposite the entrance is a figure of a priest burning incense, perhaps intended as a portrait of the incumbent. On either side, the walls are decorated in two registers. The lower register shows scenes of animals pursuing one another amongst trees, whilst the upper one is concerned

Fig. 8: Poppies painted on the ceiling of tomb 1 at Janzur.

with death, and possibly resurrection. Starting on the left-hand side, next to the entrance, the deceased takes leave of his family; we then see him in Charon's boat being rowed across the River Styx into Hades, where he is finally received into the presence of the seated figures of Hades and Persephone. On the right-hand side (continuing clockwise), the imagery is less easy to interpret. We see what looks like a man with a bear on a chain, next to a rock. This is said to be Hercules who is capturing Cerberus, the three-headed dog who guards the entrance to the Underworld. Hercules is often seen as a symbol of the conquest of death, and hence of salvation. The other figures on this side are not readily explained, though immediately to the L of the entrance a figure in flesh colour, carrying a corpse, surely belongs to the Upper World and perhaps has something to do with the circumstances of the death of the incumbent. The ceiling is charmingly decorated with poppies (fig. 8) enclosed within garlands held up by winged *genii*. The finds from this tomb consisted of two urns, a bronze mirror, some other items of bronze and two terracotta lamps. Beyond the entrance to tomb 1 may be seen other, less elaborate, rock-cut tombs.

In the showcases around the walls of the museum are exhibited many of the grave-goods. Cases 1 to 5 (counting anticlockwise from the entrance) display finds from tomb 15: in case 1 are glass cinerary urns and red-slipped pottery which show the extensive character of Roman trade in the first and second centuries AD. The dark red vessels with a maker's mark stamped in the shape of a footprint (S.M.F, for *Sextus Murrius Festus*) are Italian, from the vicinity of Pisa; the dishes of a more orange colour (on the middle shelf) are African, from Carthage. Case 2 contains further examples of African Red Slip ware and related cooking ware from the Carthage region. Case 3 contains cinerary urns and cases 4 and 5 contain other small objects: unguent bottles, mirrors, bone pins, lamps and the like, all attributable to the first two centuries AD. The remaining cases (6–11) contain finds from other tombs, largely repeating what you have already seen. Case 6 contains three large amphorae of Punic style from tomb 7, and case 9 demonstrates the different varieties of cinerary urn which were used in the cemetery. Finally, case 11 shows the range of terracotta lamps that has been recovered, spanning the first to fourth centuries AD, together with bronze coins and mirrors.

Sabratha***

For purposes of modern scholarship, the plan of the town has been divided conventionally into a series of *regiones* (districts) and *insulae* (blocks). These are shown in fig. 9 and provide a convenient means of reference. Numbers in brackets below also refer to this plan.

Excavations have been carried out at Sabratha from 1921 onwards, mainly by the Italians, but with brief interventions by the British (under the direction of John Ward-Perkins and Kathleen Kenyon) between 1948 and 1951. The choice of the site for a settlement was conditioned by the presence of a sheltered anchorage which was capable of being developed into a harbour; it is clear from its later history that it derived its prosperity as a port from the export of both olive oil and exotic goods transported from central Africa by camel-trains. The number of vats exposed in buildings near the shore also suggests a developed commerce in purple dye and fish-products. The earliest evidence for occupation was retrieved from the area between the forum (7) and the water's edge: here were found floors, patches of charcoal and quantities of pottery of the latter part of the fifth century BC. These suggested a seasonal presence of Phoenician traders. Buildings of stone first appear in the second half of the fourth century, and the irregularities apparent in the later layout of the areas to the N (and to a lesser extent the E and S) of the forum reflect its early organic growth.

There is a major phase of both expansion and renovation in the second century BC which probably reflects increasing economic independence from Carthage, which was unable to exert its former domination over the region while preoccupied with its unsuccessful (and eventually terminal) conflict with Rome. The built-up area certainly extended at this time to the S of the later Antonine Temple (5), but not as far as the Punic-Hellenistic mausolea which must have been built outside the town (2). Note the long, narrow *insulae* (city blocks) of this period, which became progressively more orderly as they expanded southwards. The settlement continued to grow and it engulfed the mausolea during the first century BC. The central area, (which had probably always possessed some sort of open space) began to be systematically reorganized around the mid first century AD. At this time the forum acquired the essentials of its subsequent size and shape and the Temple of Liber Pater (8) was built. The Capitolium at the W end (11) and the neighbouring Temple of Serapis (12) may represent precursors of this reorganization and monumentalization of the central public space.

The process of developing a monumental public zone in the centre of the town was then advanced by a natural disaster: the new Temple of Liber Pater, and presumably many other buildings, was felled by an earthquake which has been placed between AD 65 and 70. The temple was rebuilt to a larger plan and on massively strengthened foundations, the layout of the forum was revised and on the S side was added a basilica to serve the judicial and administrative needs of the city.

During the second century AD the forum was again remodelled, with the use of imported marble and granite; space was made for the Antonine and South Forum Temples (4, 5) on its inland side, and at the same time an entire new eastern suburb was established, including the theatre (24), other temples and public baths. The *insulae* of this development are laid out in much shorter, more compact, rectangles than those of the earlier period. At its greatest size, the city extended well beyond what is now visible, covering much, if not all, of the ground between the theatre and the outlying Temple of Isis to the E (23); it also spread southwards beyond the present Punic Museum (31). It was during the second century, also, that Sabratha enjoyed successive advances in municipal status, becoming a *municipium* by the middle of the century and a *colonia* by the 180s at the latest.

Decline came slowly. The city appears to have suffered earthquake damage again c. 306–310, and yet again around the time of the earthquake and tsunami on 21 July 365 which devastated large parts of the eastern Mediterranean. Tripolitania is much too far from the epicentre of that event, off the SW coast of Crete, to have suffered such extensive damage on that occasion; however, the archaeological evidence is strong enough to assert that Sabratha and Lepcis Magna suffered in another earthquake much closer at hand, which was perhaps part of the same sequence of seismic events. (See p. 10.) This is therefore referred to for convenience as the known earthquake 'of 365' but in quotation marks. All of the public buildings were extensively damaged, and the decline of the old religious order is demonstrated with particular clarity by the fact that none of the pagan temples was subsequently restored; rather, their columns and other building materials were now used to build churches and to restore the civil basilica in the forum. There was doubtless considerable loss of life, and outlying areas were abandoned; on the other hand, sufficient vitality remained for extensive restoration work to be carried out in the city centre. It is difficult to attribute specific changes or developments to the Vandal period (AD 455–533) through the lack of inscriptions and of new coinage, but it is reasonable to infer a progressive retrenchment towards the historic centre.

When Byzantine control was reasserted by Justinian's general Belisarius in AD 533, there was a flurry of building activity. A new defensive wall was constructed, which enclosed only a fraction of the previously built-up area; the forum basilica (which had already become a church some time earlier) was again restored and rearranged, and a new and 'very noteworthy' church was constructed close to the shore. The church was decorated with the remarkable mosaics which have been lifted and are on display in the Roman Museum on the site. But this new-found vigour was barely skin-deep. The graves whose outlines can be seen clustered around the forum basilica, occupying the open spaces in the very heart of the town, speak of a community that huddled within its defences. Of the period following the Arab conquest in the seventh century AD, little can be said, in part because its modest vestiges were swept away without interest by the early excavators. However, a plan of late structures overlying the South Forum Temple (p. 43) shows a sprawl of irregular houses; a few Arabic graffiti have been recorded, and the British excavations recovered two Abbasid coins of the eighth century AD. As elsewhere, any sort of settled existence on this site presumably came to an end in 1051, if it had not already done so before.

The principal building-material used at Sabratha is the soft sandstone cut from the quarries immediately to the south of the city (which are most apparent between

Fig. 9. Sabratha: site plan. The coloured zones identified by Roman numerals are the regiones into which scholars have divided the site for easy reference.

1. Regio VI
2. Mausoleum B
3. Byzantine South Gate
4. South Forum Temple
5. Antonine Temple
6. Fountain of Flavius Tullus
7. Forum

8. Temple of Liber Pater
9. Basilica
10. Cruciform Building
11. Capitolium
12. Temple of Serapis
13. Curia
14. Basilica of Justinian

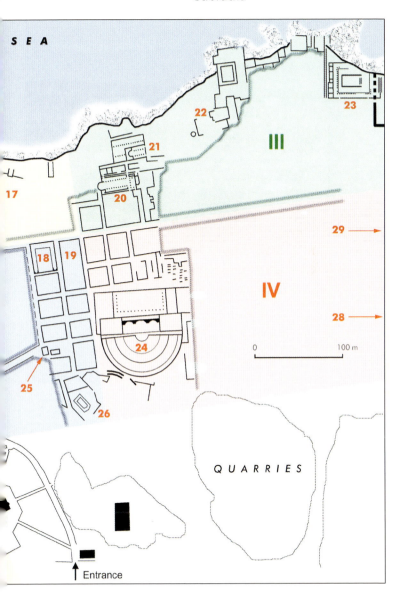

15. Seaward Baths
16. Casa Brogan
17. Byzantine East Gate
18. Temple of Hercules
19. Theatre Baths
20, 21. Churches
22. Oceanus Baths
23. Temple of Isis

24. Theatre
25. Severan Monument
26. Peristyle House
27. Baths of Regio VII
28. Christian catacomb
29. Amphitheatre
30. Roman Museum
31. Punic Museum

Fig. 10. Sabratha: view across the forum towards the theatre.

you and the theatre as you enter the site). This is a very friable stone which was only usable if covered with a protective coating of stucco: in ancient times, the city would have appeared a dazzling white, rather than the soft honey-colour of today. It is one of the insoluble burdens of the conservation of the site that to re-coat every surface would be unsightly to the tourist and prohibitively expensive to carry out; however, without either an intervention of this kind or re-burying the visible structures, many of the buildings will cease to be recognizable in the course of another generation.

Sabratha has been recognized by UNESCO as a World Heritage Site.

Regio VI* (1)

This is the first part of the excavations which you come to as you approach the ancient city-centre from the museums. It shows a well ordered, but by no means uniform, layout and was probably established in the first century BC. The area is dominated by the Byzantine defensive wall beyond it, and in front of that the array of houses is broken by a small, neat piazza flanked by colonnades and with a small shrine in the centre. Also found in this piazza was the painted shrine now in the Punic Museum (p. 71). Towards the western end of the excavated area rises the extraordinary triangular funerary monument known as **Mausoleum B*** (2). This was built in the first half of the second century BC, at which time it was outside the built-up area. It collapsed progressively over succeeding centuries, initially in the first century BC (possibly as the result of an earthquake: see p. 10 f.). Parts of it became buried beneath or incorporated into the houses of the expanding town during the first century BC, and much of its core was used in the sixth century AD to construct a bastion on the angle of the Byzantine defences immediately nearby. The area was excavated by Antonino Di Vita, who meticulously dismantled the later structures and reassembled the original monument. The more important sculptures are on display in the Punic Museum, and those parts are represented on site by replicas.

The whole is triangular in plan, with concave sides. Upon a base of six receding steps stands a first storey framed by attached Ionic columns at the angles, with semi-columns in the centre of each side. On the E side, the central column is interrupted by a false door framed by smaller semi-columns. The second storey was richly decorated with figure-scenes in the middle of each side, framed by *kouroi* (the rather formal male figures of Egyptian portrait sculpture, but softened under Greek influence) standing upon brackets supported by lions at the angles. The scene over the false doorway represents the Egyptian god Bes as lion-tamer; that on the N side shows Hercules killing the Nemean lion (on this occasion with a sword, not with his bare hands); the third panel is too poorly preserved for identification. Finally, above a second cornice, the whole structure tapers to a point. The style shows a mixture of Greek and Egyptian motifs and the whole would have been painted in bright colours: it is almost without parallel but appears to transmit a form of architecture and decoration which must have been current at Alexandria and adapted at Carthage in the Hellenistic period. The obelisk-tombs of the pre-desert zone (e.g. at Msallatin, p. 195; Ghirza, p. 194, Bani Walid Museum, p. 177, and in the Wadi N'fid, p. 203 f.) are later manifestations of the same tradition.

The base alone of a second monument of the same type, Mausoleum A, has been discovered a few metres to the SW.

Byzantine South Gate (3)

The buildings of *Regio* VI had clearly long been abandoned and partially buried by the time that the Byzantine defences were constructed in or shortly after AD 533. The new defensive wall was built entirely of reused blocks, though use was made of the building-line along former street-frontages to provide foundations. The main path into the excavations passes through the South Gate of the defences: the opening corresponding to the parallel street immediately to the W is a modern one. The narrow gateway is flanked by two rectangular towers, of which the easterly one shows traces of a guardroom. The steps leading down on the far side of the gate are modern, and show how far the ground-surface had risen between the early imperial period (represented by the paving beyond the gate) and the time when the Byzantine wall was built. A further rise in level is indicated by the subsequent addition of an outer gate between flanking piers, whose thresholds (with hinge-sockets for the doors) are composed of cipollino columns split in half.

South Forum Temple (4)

As you approach the central area, the next street which you cross was in antiquity the main coast road. In the Byzantine period it had clearly ceased to exist, for it was crossed (and blocked) twice by the Byzantine defensive wall. The blocking towards the E has now been removed in order to recreate this major axis of communication with the eastern quarter of the city. Beyond the crossroads, on the left-hand side, your approach to the centre of the city is now marked by the presence of the South Forum Temple, the construction of which, in the second half of the second century AD, must have involved the

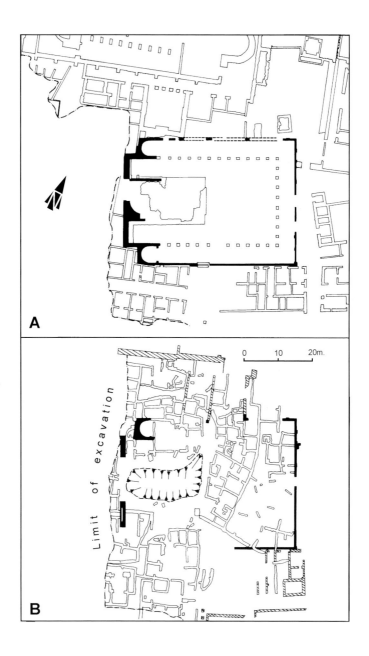

Fig. 11. Sabratha, the South Forum Temple, showing the original structure as excavated (A) and the late structures which were found overlying it (B).

clearance of pre-existing buildings. The temple, whose dedication is unknown to us, faced E and stood on a high podium at the rear of a rectangular precinct; the precinct was surrounded on three sides by slightly raised porticoes, which terminated on either side of the temple in semicircular apses. The precinct is paved throughout with Proconnesian marble, the large slabs being original and the parts composed of small pieces set in a herring-bone pattern representing a fourth-century repair. The walls of the lateral porticoes were also faced with marble veneer. The colonnades were of the Corinthian order, with monolithic green cipollino columns. After the earthquake 'of 365,' many of these columns were used for the restoration of the forum basilica, and at some period the superstructure of the temple was almost entirely quarried away, such that the excavators found a hollow in the centre of the area, which was otherwise overlaid by a disordered mass of small irregular dwellings, constructed in the Byzantine period or possibly even later and showing no cognizance whatever of the structures beneath (see fig. 11).

Antonine Temple* (5)

Passing by the South Forum Temple, one enters a small rectangular piazza, which is dominated on its E side by the steps leading into the precinct of the Antonine Temple. The entrance was more elaborate than the approach to the South Forum Temple, with a central vestibule and halls in each of the two corners, all opening through paired columns into the courtyard beyond. This was lined on three sides with colonnaded porticoes, and the temple stood on a high podium against the rear wall. Some of the columns (similar to those used in the South Forum Temple)

have been re-erected, and a narrow stairway leading up to the temple has been constructed on the foundations of those which originally extended across the full width of the façade. (The top of the podium offers a good viewpoint over the ruins.) The *cella* (the chamber housing the cult statue) also occupied the full width of the podium: the sides were decorated with stuccoed pilasters, and in front was a porch of 4 × 2 Corinthian columns. The interior of the podium contained two vaulted voids or *favissae*: such crypts were often used as repositories or strong-rooms, though one of the voids was, in this case, transformed in a later phase into a water-cistern.

Sufficient fragments of the dedicatory inscription of the temple survive to show that it was dedicated by Manius Acilius Glabrio (to an unknown god or gods) on behalf of the emperors Marcus Aurelius and Lucius Verus: the wording places it between AD 166 and 169. The temple was destroyed in the earthquake 'of 365' and, as in the case of the South Forum Temple, many of its architectural elements were subsequently used in the restoration of the forum basilica. When first excavated, extensive traces were found of graffiti on the stucco covering the inner faces of the *cella* walls. There were examples in Latin, Greek and Arabic, the latest of which certainly post-dated the Arab conquest in the seventh century AD.

Fountain of Flavius Tullus (6)

Before entering the forum itself, there are two features to be noted in the little rectangular piazza. The first of these is an array of disturbances to the paving, all aligned E-W, composed either of files of raised slabs, or simply of elongated cuttings through the paving. They are all graves (with or without cover-slabs) attributable to the latest phase of Byzantine occupation and clustered about the forum basilica which had long since become a church. There are others on the nearer side of the forum, but they will be described in the account of the basilica (p. 52) in due course.

The other feature, which faces you as you make your way towards the forum, consists of a square stone platform with a headless draped statue standing on top of it and a low enclosed basin extending across the front; the statue has been re-erected in this position and may not have come from there originally, though there are bases for statues at all four corners. This was certainly one of twelve fountains with which the city was provided in the second century AD by a certain Flavius Tullus at his own expense. An inscribed marble slab, found in the vaults of the Capitolium, tells us that the fountains were faced with marble and adorned with statues, and that the donor also paid for the provision and maintenance

of the water supply. The associated aqueduct has been partly traced, and must have represented a significant addition to the amenities of the city, previously dependent for water upon wells and cisterns. The slab records the appreciation of the city council (*ordo sabrathensium*) both of his liberality and of that of his son Flavius Pudens who put on a most splendid gladiatorial show which lasted for five days. The council decreed, on the insistence of the people, that a *quadriga* should be set up in his honour at public expense. The slab also tells us that Pudens, 'content with the honour,' paid for the statue himself. We also know from other fragments that there were several copies of this inscription, maybe even one for each fountain: a splendid piece of self-advertisement which cost the citizens nothing more than a little obsequious flattery!

Forum* (7)

The Forum must have been the focal point of public life from the earliest

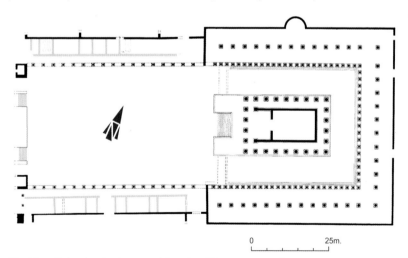

Fig. 12.   Sabratha: the forum and Temple of Liber Pater. The forum colonnades belong to the second century AD, when they replaced earlier lines of shops whose foundations (shown in grey) can still be made out.

days of the settlement. As you see it now, it is lined on the N and S sides with colonnades of grey granite, topped with Corinthian capitals. The E and W ends are defined by the sanctuary of Liber Pater and the massive podium of the Capitolium respectively. But this combines elements of varying date, some of which result from unified development schemes while others came about more casually. Long, narrow trenches, dug across the central area by Kenyon and Ward-Perkins in 1948, were sufficient to show that, while the part in front of the Capitolium may always have been an open space, the eastern part and the precinct of the Temple of Liber Pater hide the foundations of earlier buildings. These have more in common with the irregular layout still visible towards the sea than with the formal rectangularity which was imposed when the temple was built in the mid first century AD. (It is unclear whether the Capitolium, which was substantially enlarged in the second century, was first erected at the same time or earlier.)

There is only very fragmentary evidence for the character of the earliest forum, but we have a much better idea of the transformation which took place following the earthquake of AD 65–70. The outer boundaries of the forum on the N and S were established along their present lines, with a new civil basilica on the S side and the precursor of the later curia on the N. Against these outer walls were built ranges of shops (tabernae), the foundations of which can still be seen quite extensively within the later S colonnade (see fig. 12). The design was radically altered again in the third quarter of the second century AD, when the shops were demolished and the colonnades now visible were

constructed; there are remaining traces of marble paving within the porticoes.

Following the earthquake in the latter part of the fourth century AD, substantial renovation of the area once again took place, with the reconstruction of the curia to the N and of the basilica to the S. The Temple of Liber Pater, on the other hand, does not seem to have been restored; instead its precinct was closed off from the forum by a poorly constructed transverse portico with a coarse mosaic floor and columns of white marble. The forum porticoes must have been repaired, but they had clearly fallen by the time of the Byzantine restoration of the church in the former basilica, whose lines now intrude upon the forum area. By the sixth century the forum must have lost any civic function and by the time of the Arab conquest in the mid seventh it had become a vast graveyard associated with the church. Many cover-slabs of graves are visible in the S forum portico, and many more graves were found in the British trenches across the forum.

Temple of Liber Pater* (8)
The Temple of Liber Pater (= Shadrap, one of the most important Punic gods) occupies a privileged position, framing one end of the forum and facing the Capitolium at the other. His temple is today the most prominent building in the centre of Sabratha, by virtue of its partially re-erected colonnade. Note that in this case the columns and the architectural details are of stuccoed sandstone and not of the marble which was first used extensively in the second century AD. The temple, with its surrounding porticoes, was first erected around the middle of the first century AD, and since the interior of the temple podium has been left exposed by its excavators, much of its history is visible.

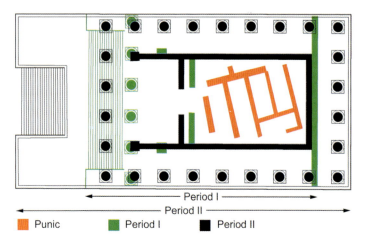

| Punic | Period I | Period II |

Fig. 13. Sabratha: phase-plan of the Temple of Liber Pater.

Within the podium may be seen remains of walls on an oblique alignment (see fig. 13), and these are traces of the housing of the pre-Roman period which were swept away when the temple was built: since the builders knew where the temple platform was going to be, it was unnecessary for them to raze the existing buildings to as low a level as elsewhere. Close examination of the foundations will also show traces of a shorter building which otherwise conforms to the alignment and width of the surviving temple (shown in green in fig. 13). The earlier building was pseudo-peripteral, with a colonnade on three sides and a rear wall extending across the full width of the podium,

Fig. 14. Sabratha: the Temple of Liber Pater.

whereas the later one was peripteral, with colonnades enclosing the *cella* on all four sides. The rear face of the shorter podium can still be seen on the inside of the later building at the SE corner. This change of design occurred only about a generation after the temple had been built, and it is accompanied by two very telling features: the new foundations of the second (enlarged) temple incorporate blocks from the entablature of the earlier building with well-preserved painted stucco decoration, and the voids between the foundations of the *cella* and those of the colonnade were at this stage filled in solidly with concrete rubble. (On the N side, it is this mass of concrete alone which has survived.) These two factors, together with the dating-evidence of pottery from the construction-levels of the second temple, combine forcibly to suggest that the temple was strengthened and rebuilt after collapsing in the earthquake of AD 65–70 (p. 11).

Following this, an inscription allegedly found in the vicinity records the restoration of a Temple to Liber Pater in AD 340–350 from a state of *antiqua ruina*, perhaps implying damage in the earthquake of AD 306–310: it has been inferred that it belongs to this building, though no visible structural change can be identified with it. The temple had surely ceased to function as such following the earthquake of the later fourth century, and the Italian excavation records show that many elements of the superstructure were found stacked in the S portico: this suggests an incomplete move towards restoration following the disaster, such as we shall see also in the Capitolium and in the theatre. A well, dug against the rear of the temple podium, and a screened enclosure in the SE corner

of the precinct are surviving signs of later – and surely secular – activity in the area.

Basilica* (9)

The forum or central market-place of any self-respecting Roman town was always accompanied by a basilica, a lofty aisled building which accommodated civil offices and the administration of justice. The forum basilica at Sabratha was one of the first structures excavated in the 1920s, but it has a long and complex history, which has taken the efforts of many scholars to unravel. The major elements in the sequence are illustrated in fig. 15.

As with other parts of the forum area, there are traces of structures which preceded the construction of the first basilica in the Flavian period, but these are fragmentary and difficult both to date and to interpret. It is clear, however, that when the forum was remodelled after the earthquake of AD 65–70, it was provided, behind the row of shops on the S side, with a civil basilica. The layout of the period I building was of the type known as Vitruvian, since a basilica of this type was constructed by the Augustan architect Vitruvius at Fano in Italy, and was described by him in his manual on architecture. It is composed of a large rectangular hall with an internal colonnade, such that the central area would have been lit by clerestory windows above the colonnade. The distinctive aspect of the 'Vitruvian' design is that the principal axis of the building is the short axis: on entering the building from the forum, in the centre of the long N side, one looked across the main hall towards a large rectangular *exedra* containing the tribunal at which the judges presided over court cases. It was here that Apuleius of Madauros

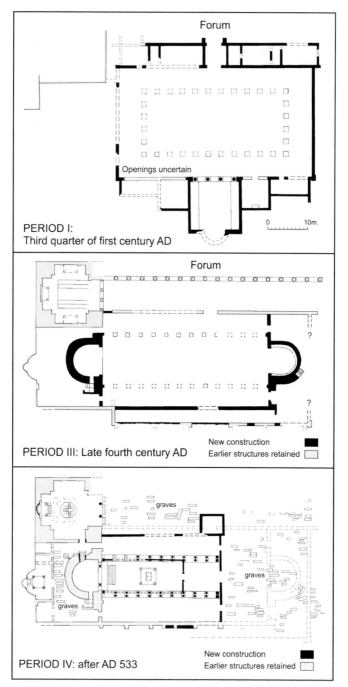

Fig. 15. Sabratha: the evolution of the forum basilica and the Cruciform Building.

stood his trial for witchcraft in AD 158 (see p. 4). The tribunal had initially an apse in its rear wall, and was entered from the main hall through an opening marked by four stuccoed sandstone columns, which were probably identical to those of the main internal colonnade. These have been re-erected (though probably not at the correct spacing). At the time when the South Forum Temple was constructed in the later second century, the apse of the tribunal was suppressed, but the room was remodelled and continued in use. A group of first- and second-century imperial statues was found in this room when it was excavated, suggesting that it had served also as a shrine for the cult of the Roman emperors. The tribunal was flanked, along the S side of the basilica, by two other rooms on each side, which probably served as offices or committee rooms, but their details can no longer be clearly made out. Apart from the tribunal (which lay outside the parts of the building affected by later modifications), the most visible remaining fragment of the Period I basilica is the pilaster at the NW angle, which continued to constitute part of the wall between the basilica and the forum until the Byzantine reconstruction of Period IV. The basilica was paved with large slabs of Proconnesian marble, parts of which survive at the E end (where they are badly broken up by late burials). Elsewhere, their positions can be made out from the surviving mortar bedding, in which also the positions of the bases of the colonnade are partly visible.

Later modifications to the Vitruvian basilica (Period II) consist of the rearrangement of the tribunal on the S side when the South Forum Temple was built, and of some sort of extension to the W. The westward extension must

precede the rebuilding of Period III, but its character is quite unclear. It was enclosed by the boundary walls which are now visible behind the later apse, and it had itself an apsidal feature on its western side. There seems to have been some sort of courtyard, accessed through the W end of the basilica, with rooms opening off it on the N and W sides.

The next major change (Period III) follows the earthquake 'of 365,' which evidently caused substantial damage. The S range, including the tribunal, was abandoned beneath the debris and its doorways were blocked up. Within the space formerly occupied by the Vitruvian basilica and its western extension, and using only its northern wall (which it still shared with the forum porticoes), was built a new and smaller basilica in deliberate imitation of the great Severan basilica at Lepcis Magna (p. 105). The major axis of this building was now E–W, with a hall divided into a nave and aisles by colonnades, and an apse at either end. The eastern apse made use of the original floor, and was lined internally with a stone bench. On the outside of the apse (in the open air), are remains of a staircase which presumably led to galleries above the aisles. The western apse, in contrast, had a floor-level 1.74 m above that of the nave. Traces of coarse tessellated mosaic, both on the raised surface within the apse and at the level of the original floor immediately in front of it and beneath the steps by which it is now approached, show that initially there were no frontal steps and that access to the dais was solely by means of the staircase and door on the S side of the apse. This was presumably the tribunal of the late civil basilica. The colonnades of the new building were certainly supplied from the ruins of the

Antonine and South Forum Temples, for those are the elements which were reused yet again in Period IV (by which time the ruined temples were already buried to a substantial depth, and would not have been obvious sources of building material).

The basilica was substantially rebuilt once again in the Byzantine period, but at some point before then (Period IIIb) it underwent a change of use and became a church. The frontal steps approaching the western apse were added at this time (three of the four churches at Sabratha face W) and an altar (initially of wood) was placed in the centre of the nave beneath a canopy supported on four reused columns, two of red breccia and two of cipollino. The church was also provided with a baptistery by the insertion of a concrete-lined tank in the apse of the earlier western extension. Some part of the area behind the western apse of the basilica was therefore presumably roofed at this time. There are also changes which appear to be designed to strengthen the Period III structure: buttresses added to the new S wall and a wider stylobate for presumably doubled internal colonnades. There is no direct dating-evidence for these alterations, though the radical changes which occurred in the Byzantine period suggest that the Period III building was in serious decay by the time of the re-establishment of Byzantine rule in AD 533.

Following the Justinianic reconquest in that year, the church was once again restored (Period IV). Now the N wall and the E end were wholly abandoned, creating a very much smaller church focussed on the raised apse at the W end. The church was entered through three doorways in its eastern wall, and there was a projecting room at the NE

corner. (Its walls are too slight for it to have been a tower.) The colonnades of the nave were composed of paired columns from the Antonine and South Forum Temples, which had presumably been commandeered already in Period III. Note the curiosity in this final phase of the upturned capitals used as bases at either end. The nave was now repaved at a higher level than before (surely further evidence of the ruin of the earlier building), partly using halved cipollino column-drums, and the altar in the centre of the nave received (either now or perhaps earlier) a new platform created from reversed column-bases and a piece of architrave (with a central recess for holy relics and sockets for colonnettes to support its upper part). Much of the nave surrounding the altar was enclosed by a stone screen.

The apse was further embellished, mostly by reusing marble decorative elements from the adjoining Cruciform Building (see below). Some of these were used to face the frontal steps with marble; the pair of rectangular pilasters which stood at the head of the steps, one of which has been re-erected, were probably moved to this position at this time. The baptismal font behind the apse was now suppressed and replaced by an altar, and a new baptistery was created in the Cruciform Building: a new passageway between the apse and the Cruciform Building provided communication between the two. Every open space surrounding the church, including the forum, the abandoned E end of the former basilica and even the piazza in front of the Antonine Temple, was now pressed into use as a cemetery. The graves are marked sometimes by cover-slabs, sometimes by the upright sides of stone-lined cists and sometimes merely by cuttings through the earlier paving. A number of the cover-slabs bear inscriptions naming those buried below and giving their ages. All belong to the Byzantine period and possibly later, though it is impossible to tell to what extent Christian practices may have persisted after the Arab conquest.

Cruciform Building* (10)

The corner in between the western extension of the basilica and the Capitolium, which occupies the W end of the forum, was occupied by an unusual building of very solid construction, which was externally square and internally cruciform; it was originally roofed with a concrete vault, the fallen masses of which were broken up and removed by the excavators in the 1920s. The building faces, and is aligned upon, the S portico of the forum in the form that it took in the third quarter of the second century AD, and is likely to be contemporary with its construction.

The Cruciform Building was highly ornate on the inside: it was paved with marble, its walls were faced with marble veneer, and each of its three recesses housed a projecting rectangular aedicula, with a raised plinth upon which stood a pair of columns carrying an entablature. The geometry of its construction is very closely related to that of the Arch of Marcus Aurelius at Tripoli (p. 19); it may well have been designed by the same architect. The lavishness of the decoration may be judged from a number of carved elements now lying on the ground: other pieces were found in the vaults of the Capitolium and yet others were extensively used in the Period IV church within the former basilica. These include the columns supporting the altar canopy, some of the marble used to face the steps up to the W apse

and the ornate rectangular pilasters of which one now stands at the head of the steps: these almost certainly stood originally at the entrance to the Cruciform Building, where there are now two cipollino columns. The purpose for which this building was constructed is unclear; it has been suggested that it might have constituted a shrine for the imperial cult following the modification of the tribunal of the early basilica when the South Forum Temple was built.

The second phase in the life of this building was marked by the insertion of shallow, longitudinal sandstone steps on top of the marble floor, converting it into a meeting-chamber (see fig. 15, shown with Period III of the basilica): the effect would have been similar to that in the curia (13) on the N side of the forum, but the chronology of the change and the functional relationship between the two buildings is undetermined.

The third phase is represented by its conversion into a baptistery for the Byzantine church (Period IV in fig. 15). The decision to use it for this purpose was probably made after the rebuilding of the church, for which so many of the elements of the Cruciform Building were robbed. In any case, the N and S aediculae were wholly removed down to floor level, that on the W was rearranged with frontal steps so as to contain an episcopal throne, and an elaborate cruciform font within an octagonal casing was set in the centre of the room. The floor was raised to a uniform level throughout (necessitating steps leading down into the former forum area) and an opening was cut in the S wall in order to communicate directly with the apse of the church.

The last (undated) vestiges of the use of this building are marked by the removal of the remainder of the S wall and the cutting of a surface gully crossing this area, together with an early Arabic graffito scratched on the concrete surface of the font.

Capitolium (11)

The Capitolium which fills the W end of the forum shows evidence of two periods of construction. There is no direct dating evidence for the earlier building, of stuccoed sandstone, though it was probably built in the first century AD and may have determined the subsequent alignment of the entire forum area. The building was of typical Etrusco-Roman type, with three *cellae* for the Capitoline Triad (Jupiter, Juno and Minerva), standing on a high, wide podium and fronted by a double row of four columns. The temple was approached from the forum by two staircases flanking a platform for orators, behind which rose a single broad flight of steps leading up to the temple itself. At some time in the second century AD, most probably in conjunction with the renovation of the forum and its embellishment with colonnaded porticoes, the Capitolium also was upgraded and given a more imposing appearance. The façade was extended to occupy the full width of the podium by the provision of flanking side-chapels (of which the details are unclear), the columns were replaced and everything (including the frontal steps) was faced in marble. The apex-block of the temple pediment now lies on the front of the podium.

Following the earthquake 'of 365', the Capitolium seems to have shared the fate of the other pagan temples: it was not rebuilt and the finer building materials were removed for reuse elsewhere. The very solid podium clearly remained intact and, when excavated, the *favissae* within were found to contain large quantities of inscriptions,

statues and decorative marble friezes from surrounding buildings: these had clearly been systematically gathered up and stored there for future reuse. (They used to be displayed there, but in recent years the entrances to the vaults have been walled up.) In the Byzantine period, as in the case of the South Forum Temple and elsewhere, the ruins of the Capitolium were overlaid by an accretion of late structures which were removed by the Italian excavators.

Temple of Serapis (12)

Immediately to the N of the Capitolium, and separated from it by the once winding street that led inland from the harbour, is the precinct of the Temple of Serapis. Its identification rests on the discovery within it of a small marble statue of that Alexandrian god. Two Punic coin-types struck at Sabratha some time before 7 BC (possibly as far back as the second century) show an image of a temple, with a head of Serapis or Melqart respectively on the reverse: Serapis was therefore of some importance in the local cults before the Roman period. The precinct is at a slight angle to the alignment of the forum and Capitolium, and this must be one of the oldest temples at Sabratha; however, pottery found here in a small excavation by the British team in 1948 indicates that it is no earlier than Augustan (i.e. late first century BC or early first century AD). Like the Temple of Liber Pater (8), this temple was set, in the Hellenistic fashion, in the centre of a colonnaded courtyard rather than against the rear wall (as were the later Antonine and South Forum Temples). The colonnades were originally of stuccoed sandstone (preserved behind the temple as a result of being incorporated into the building at a later date), subsequently replaced by columns of grey breccia with capitals and bases of white marble.

The temple was raised on a podium but, unusually, had no colonnade or porch of its own. The *cella* had three doors in its façade (the sandstone sills can still be made out), and, probably at the time when it was lengthened at the rear, its sides were embellished with shallow pilasters. As with the other early temples at Sabratha, so this one also was altered and embellished with marble at some time in the second century AD. The surrounding colonnades have already been mentioned; the frontal steps were extended forward by overlaying slabs of marble or grey limestone; and it is very likely that fragments of a marble frieze decorated with winged solar discs (an Egyptian motif), found in the vaults of the Capitolium, also formed part of the ornament of this temple in its later phase.

In late antiquity, presumably after the earthquakes of the fourth century, the structure was stripped to pavement-level and other buildings were erected on the site. By the Byzantine period, when the apartment-block to the N was built, partly encroaching into the precinct, it is clear that a considerable depth of soil must have been covering the earlier ruins.

Curia* (13)

Behind the N portico of the forum lies the *curia* or municipal council-house. The visible remains post-date the earthquake 'of 365' (having been completed no later than August 367), but they clearly replace an earlier building of similar size and function, which had probably occupied the same position since the forum was laid out in the first century AD. Access to the *curia* from the forum was through two (possibly three) doorways which led

Fig. 16. Sabratha: the forecourt of the curia.

into a small rectangular colonnaded forecourt, with a rectangular apsed *exedra* in the centre of the far wall. The coarse mosaic of white marble with which the colonnades are paved is similar to that found in the transverse portico across the front of the Temple of Liber Pater (p. 47) and to that at the W end of the Period III basilica on the S side of the forum (p. 51). The columns were evidently reused from elsewhere, for some are of cipollino marble and others of grey granite; they were surmounted by arcades, of which one has been schematically reconstructed. The *curia* proper was entered through a doorway behind this reconstructed arch, but before proceeding, note the inscribed statue base which also stands in front of the entrance. Like everything else here, it is reused and a previous inscription or dedication has been chiselled off in order to make space for the new lettering. The honorand is named as L(ucius) Aemilius Quintus and he is a *fl(amen) p(erpetuus)*, a priest of the Temple of Rome and Augustus. He is honoured here by the Council and People of Sabratha (line 8: *ordo et populus splendidae col(oniae) Sabrat(hensium)*) because he brought to the ears of the emperor their communal distress (line 5: *miserias communes*): here is a vivid testimony to the period following the earthquake, when we know that Sabratha was trying to recover from a great natural disaster and was at the same time being harassed by raiders coming out of the hinterland. It is of interest that at a time when Christianity was in ascendancy over the pagan cults, the tenure of an ancient priesthood should still be a matter of honour.

The council-chamber itself is lined on either side with low, broad steps, which would have supported the seats of the *decuriones*. Across the far end, on a similar raised step, would have been the seats of the magistrates. A shelf behind the magistrates probably supported statues, framed by niches on the wall, which continued along the sides of the room. The floor and steps were faced with marble, most of which has disappeared. Traces in the cement bedding show that some of these paving-slabs were made from reused inscriptions, placed face-down.

Basilica of Justinian* (14)

Between the *curia* and the Temple of Serapis, a narrow street leads N to a small, irregularly paved piazza which is now almost on the foreshore. On the western side of this is a Byzantine residential block and on the right, once fronted by a portico held up by four sawn-off columns, is a church, also constructed after the Byzantine recovery of Tripolitania in AD 533 and known as the Basilica of Justinian. As it now appears, this is a poor building, constructed from a wide variety of reused, non-matching materials: note how columns of different heights have been pressed into service together by raising them up on square plinths. The distinctive yellow-brown limestone which has been extensively used in the walls has been brought over here from a monument in honour of Septimius Severus, the lowest courses of which still stand at an intersection close to the theatre (25). The sense of decadence and ruin is exacerbated by the loss through quarrying or erosion of the eastern end of the building, where there was probably a projecting apse. The chancel began at the sixth bay from the W, where it was enclosed by a low screen with a central opening. Beyond this, the altar stood beneath a marble *ciborium* supported by four slender

Fig. 17. Sabratha: the basilica of Justinian, seen from the piazza in front.

columns. The base of the altar may be recognized by its central reliquary recess and by the sockets for the four colonnettes which supported its upper part. In the nave stands an *ambo*, the base of which is cut from a cornice-block belonging to the Capitolium.

And yet, this is undoubtedly the 'church worthy of great renown' listed by Procopius in his work on the buildings of the emperor Justinian. Its particular glory lay in the mosaic decoration which covered the entire floor area. The mosaics were lifted by the excavators and form the focal point of the Roman museum. They are described in detail on p. 69 f.; suffice it to say here that they are undoubtedly the work of craftsmen from the Eastern Mediterranean, who must have been brought to Sabratha specifically for this purpose.

To the E of the Basilica of Justinian stands a quarter of densely packed houses fronting onto an irregular pattern of streets. The structures now visible belong to the Roman imperial period, but they reflect a layout which grew up organically with the early settlement. (British excavations in this area found evidence of occupation going back to the fifth century BC.) The traces of earlier buildings found within the podium of the Temple of Liber Pater (fig. 13) and in trenches across the forum area show that a much more extended sprawl of houses was swept away when the forum area was 'regularized' in the first century AD. This is certainly a residential area, and some of the houses at least had upper storeys (usually built in mud-brick above the masonry of the ground floor); yet as one walks through it one sees unmistakable signs of commercial activity. There is the base of a large circular mill and vats lined with pink waterproof cement, which would have been associated with the production either of fish-products (*garum*, a sauce not unlike anchovy paste) or of purple dye from the murex mollusc. Some of the spaces look more like storerooms or warehouses than residences, and one can readily visualize this as a typical harbour quarter. However, there were residents of some pretension as well: the House of Leda, which has

Fig. 18. Sabratha: the latrines of the Seaward Baths.

supplied some fine painted wall-plaster now in the museum, is just across the road from the Basilica of Justinian.

Seaward Baths* (15)

Behind the NE corner of the precinct of the Temple of Liber Pater is an irregular piazza, from which one enters the Seaward Baths, a complex probably built in the late first century AD, and then embellished with marble in the time of Hadrian. These now stand perilously above the sea and they have already been eroded to the point that it is difficult to understand their layout. The entrance from the piazza leads into a rectangular hall terminating in an apse fronted by two cipollino columns. To the left of this hall, a vestibule leads into the most recognizable feature of the complex, the hexagonal latrine. Latrines are frequently associated with bath buildings, since both require running water; the seats around three sides of the room are placed over a drain, and in front of the seats is a channel which provided clean water for one to wash oneself (with a sponge).

All is faced in marble. To the right of the entrance hall, a mosaic-paved corridor leads eastward to other parts of the complex, including a lobby with a fine polychrome geometric mosaic.

A statue-base found in the forum honours the provincial governor in 378 for restoring 'the ruined baths', presumably after the earthquake 'of 365', and there are certainly signs of late repairs to the floors (note the coarse mosaic in the long corridor) which would be consistent with this.

Casa Brogan (16)

Running southwards from the Seaward Baths is a very long, semi-regular *insula* which stretches behind the Temple of Liber Pater and the Antonine Temple. It is immediately evident that the visible structures stand at quite a high level relative to their surroundings, and for this reason the Kenyon/Ward-Perkins expedition decided to explore part of it in depth. This part became known (after the supervisor of the excavation) as the 'Casa Brogan.' The excavation was highly successful, revealing a depth of 3.5 m of stratified deposits which extended in time from the fourth century BC to the fourth century AD. It appeared that the *insula* acquired its basic form in the second century BC, after which the various parts of it underwent continuous adaptation and renovation. There was evidence here for the rebuilding and strengthening of walls following the earthquake of AD 65–70, and there was a further major reorganization (and amalgamation?) of properties following the earthquake 'of 365.' A number of mosaic floors post-date this event, showing the continuing vitality of Sabratha despite the disaster. An *emblema* from one of the rooms, enclosing an (almost unintelligible) inscription, is on display in the first room in the E wing of the Roman museum. As you walk down the E side of the *insula*, you should note further evidence of commercial activity in the form of sunken cement-lined tanks, probably for the preparation of salted fish-products.

Byzantine East Gate (17)

At the far end of the street, turn left towards the eastern quarter of the city, following what used to be the main coastal highway. On your left-hand side rises the Byzantine defensive wall, which formerly cut across the street at two points, showing that it had ceased to function long before the sixth century. At a slight angle in the road are the denuded foundations of a *tetrapylon*, but nothing is known of its original character. Just beyond this, the Byzantine Wall turns away seawards, and half-way along this stretch may be made out the East Gate. As in the case of the South Gate (3), there must have been inner and outer doors, but here the structure projects beyond the wall instead of being set behind it.

Temple of Hercules (18)

Continuing along the road, one passes through an area which has not been excavated, but which was certainly entirely built up in antiquity. The abandonment of the road by the fifth century AD is demonstrated in this stretch by the presence in its course of Christian burials, like those in the forum area. (It was probably easier to dig graves in the street than amongst the rubble of abandoned buildings.) The next excavated building, on your right-hand side, is the Temple of Hercules. (Hercules, here the Punic Melqart in Roman guise, is celebrated on coins of Sabratha, as is Serapis: above p. 54.) The layout is similar to that of the South Forum Temple: a porticoed precinct with inset apses at the ends of the lateral porticoes, and the temple set on a podium against the rear wall. The temple itself has been reduced to its foundations, but the lateral porticoes may be made out, at a slightly higher level. They shows traces of a paving in grey breccia and there was formerly painted stucco on the walls. In front of the temple was a statue of Hercules seated, a copy of a Greek original by Lysippus: a very battered fragment of this survives.

The inscription which ran around the portico of the temple records modifications completed at some time between AD 186 and 193; we do not know, however, precisely when the temple was built. This is of some importance, for it is clearly integral to the planning of the eastern suburb, which should perhaps, therefore, be placed around the middle of the second century.

Theatre Baths* (19)

Immediately to the E of the Temple of Hercules are the Theatre Baths, a

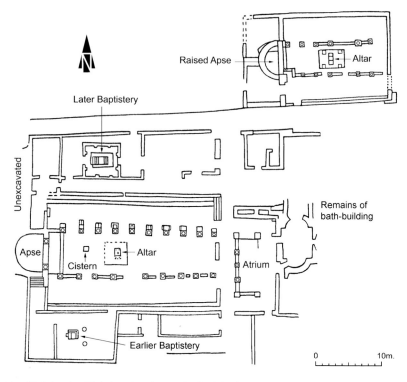

Fig. 19. Sabratha: Christian churches to the N of the theatre.

compact public bathing establishment. A corridor entered from the street leads to three rooms which were probably *apodyteria*; at the far end, a doorway on the left leads into the *frigidarium*. This was a rectangular barrel-vaulted room with two cold plunge-baths on the S side, flanking a niche which served also as a light well. (In this niche was displayed the remarkable marble candelabrum of Orpheus charming the animals, now in the Roman Museum: p. 69.) Fallen masses from the vaults still show moulded stucco surfaces and several layers of painted plaster. The hot rooms (now quite difficult to figure out) were entered from the N side of the *frigidarium*. There are numerous mosaic floors throughout the complex, with pleasing geometric designs in black and white. Two square *emblemata* in the *frigidarium* have been lifted and are on display in the Roman museum.

Churches in the East Quarter* (20, 21)
Beyond the Theatre Baths, follow the path which leads seawards directly opposite the centre of the theatre. This brings you shortly to two Christian churches, both of which seem to have been constructed initially in the late fourth century (after the earthquake 'of 365'?) and to have been modified, indeed substantially rebuilt, later. It was suggested in the first extended account of these churches that such

substantial restoration was unlikely to have taken place during the Vandal period and must therefore have taken place in the aftermath of the Byzantine reconquest in 533. However, a more recent generation of scholars has felt that we have been too ready to regard that interlude as one solely of decline. An opinion that the rebuilding (which admittedly shows no specifically 'Byzantine' characteristics) took place in the 480s, when the Christian Church was recovering from a period of persecution by the Vandals, deserves serious consideration.

The pathway leads you into the atrium or forecourt of the larger church (20), open to the air in the centre and with a portico around all four sides. Behind this (to the R) are remains of an earlier bath-building, which in its time must have been the principal public bath in this quarter of the city. Three doorways led from the atrium into the nave and aisles of the church, which is also inserted within an earlier building. (Hence the double walls along either side.) The colonnades were of grey granite, and the total absence of architraves suggests that they were surmounted by arcades. Eight of the ten bays of the nave were enclosed by a screen (the slots for which are visible in the column-bases), and within this space was placed the altar, of which the marble base and part of the surround survive. The apse at the W end was always raised above the nave, though in the second phase it was raised still higher. Originally accessed only by steps on the S side, in this later phase it was provided with frontal steps, of which only the outermost foundation-course remains. The traces of mosaic in the apse, and in the nearest part of the nave, belong to the earlier phase and have been cut through by the later alterations.

This church has two baptisteries, the earlier of the two being on the S side and identified as contemporary with the original construction by its paving with a similar style of mosaic. The roof of the room was supported by two central columns, and in the floor was a simple rectangular font approached from the W side by steps. The later baptistery occupies a similar position on the opposite side of the church, and is substantially more elaborate: the font has steps at both ends and is enclosed within a rectangular structure lined on the inside with pilasters.

The second church (21) is smaller, and has been inserted within a large, three-aisled building, perhaps a warehouse, of which only the footings remain. Its form is very similar to that of the larger church, with (probably) arcades on top of the colonnades of reused cipollino columns. The surviving altar platform in the centre of the nave dates to the later restoration, when the floor level was raised by some 35 cm. The apse at the W end had a slightly raised floor, which again was raised further in the restoration. The slightly divergent lines of the earlier structure, visible on the N side of the apse, show that the building must have been more or less ruinous before it was restored. To the later phase belong the two sacristies behind the apse, accessed from the aisles and separated from one another by a low partition-wall topped by a slab of green marble.

There are extensive burials around these churches, some of which are almost contemporary with their construction. This fact, together with the positioning of the churches, which does not respect the former street-layout, indicates that the area must have been in ruins when the churches were built. Close to the NE corner of the theatre (and just outside the fenced perimeter) is another dense late burial-ground amid the ruins of earlier buildings, presumably associated with a church outside the hitherto excavated area. The removal of the contemporary ground-level around them, in order to expose the earlier structures beneath, has left them looking rather more prominent than they would originally have been.

Oceanus Baths* (22)

Proceeding further to the E, one passes the remains of a circular structure in stuccoed sandstone with a basal moulding. It is much too large for a fountain (and there is in any case no trace of waterproof cement or other works for the supply or drainage of water); it seems more likely to have been the base of a funerary monument, erected here at a time when it was well outside the built-up area.

Immediately beyond this are the Baths of Oceanus, which take their name from a fine portrait head of Oceanus in mosaic, which is now in the Roman Museum. This small bath-suite is indeed characterized by the richness of its mosaic decoration, both on the floors and on the rims of its plunge-baths. The large rectangular room which had the head of Oceanus in a hexagonal frame at the centre, surrounded by complex geometrical patterns, was probably the *tepidarium*. It had an apse at the S end and two lateral cold plunge-baths. The hot rooms, also with mosaic floors, opened off this: note in the doorway the representation of the necessary accoutrements of Roman bathing: a flask of oil to rub yourself with; strigils (curved scrapers) to scrape off the oil, dirt and sweat; and sandals, because the floors of the hot rooms were too hot to stand on with bare feet.

This was not a public facility, but was associated with the large structures immediately to seaward. It is not clear whether these represent a private residence or warehouses of some sort – in which case the baths would have belonged to a guild or club. The first phase of the baths is dated by brickstamps to AD 123, though the Oceanus mosaic is later (third quarter of second century?), succeeding an earlier mosaic with a head of Diana/Luna (also in the Roman Museum).

Temple of Isis* (23)

Beyond the Oceanus Baths, and beyond an area which foundations on the foreshore show to have been substantially built up, stands the Sanctuary of Isis. The re-erected columns of the temple itself, seen against the blue of the sea, are a striking marker of the easterly boundary of the built-up area. The temple stood, in Hellenistic style (like the temples of Liber Pater and of Serapis), on a podium in the centre of an enclosure whose porticoes ran around all four sides of it. The association with the cult of Isis is assured by the discovery of a statue and a statuette of the goddess (both in Room 3 of the E wing of the Roman Museum), together with part of a dedicatory inscription in her honour.

The temple which can be made out now is a replacement for a smaller shrine which was destroyed by the earthquake which devastated the forum area and the Temple of Liber Pater; the new building was completed in AD 77/78. The entire sanctuary faces E, the general choice for temples in the Greek world where there are no constraining factors; it means, however, that in this case it faces away from the city. It was approached from the E by a broad flight of steps and a

Fig. 20. Sabratha: the reconstructed stage-building of the theatre.

monumental portico; these have been partly lost to the sea, but they are also now separated from the precinct by a defensive wall built along the rear wall of the portico in (presumably) the fourth century AD. (This is the only place where this wall has been identified, so the project may never have been completed.) The internal porticoes were raised above the paving of the precinct by a continuous row of four steps; the colonnades of both the porticoes and the temple itself were of stuccoed sandstone and the capitals were Corinthian, as in the case of the contemporary buildings in the city centre (basilica, Temple of Liber Pater). The temple stood on a high podium with complicated substructures, including both a large cistern and vaults accessed both from the rear of the podium and from the interior of the temple above. (This possibly had something to do with the rites of the Isiac mysteries.) Of the superstructure of the temple, apart from six re-erected columns, nothing

remains. The excavators noted that the fallen material (where not removed for reuse in antiquity) had collapsed uniformly in a westerly direction and was accompanied by extensive traces of burning, presumably in the earthquake 'of 365'.

The western portico, behind the temple, has a number of small rooms opening off it. A number of statue-bases and altars were found here, some at least associated with the gods of the Underworld. It appears that Isis was in business, and rented out rooms to associated deities!

Theatre** (24)

The theatre is undoubtedly the most striking monument at Sabratha, and deservedly so. When first uncovered, in 1926, none of the columns were standing, and the rear wall of the stage-building rose only to about two-thirds of the first storey. However, enough of the architectural elements were present for a full reconstruction to be possible on paper and the Italian colonial authorities (under the governorship of Italo Balbo) decided to make the investment in a substantial reconstruction in stone. The restored building was inaugurated in 1937 when Mussolini attended a production of *Oedipus Rex*.

The theatre, as it stands now, is one of the largest in Roman Africa (with a diameter of 92.6 m) and is a fine example of the type which characterizes the western Roman Empire: the stage-building itself is articulated by three niches in the rear wall, each with a doorway through it and a projecting rectangular 'porch' in front of it, so that the combined effect of the three tiers of colonnades, variously coloured or fluted, and the receding surfaces behind provides a ceaseless interplay of light and shade. All that the reconstruction lacks is the coffered wooden ceiling which projected forward above the stage, providing not only (limited) protection from the weather but a soundboard to improve the acoustics. The *cavea* (auditorium) of the theatre is semicircular, and originally rose considerably higher than it does now. (On the outer ring, parts of only two of the original three storeys of the façade have been re-erected.) The seating capacity has been estimated at approximately 5,000. The arched openings in the façade led to a sequence of ramps and stairways connected to different areas of seating, which were divided by walkways into three principal tiers. All of these were separated from the semicircular central space, the *orchestra,* by a marble parapet. Within are four shallow steps upon which the more privileged members of the audience could place their cushioned chairs.

The stage would have been fitted with wooden boards as it is now; the front of it, faced in marble, is broken up by a sequence of rectangular and curved recesses, all elaborately decorated with carvings in relief. Counting from the L, the scenes which fill them are the following.

(1) Two philosophers disputing; to the right a sundial, a bundle of scrolls and a writing-tablet, all on pedestals.

(2) The Nine Muses.

(3) A scene from a mime (a slave caught stealing), flanked by pieces of furniture.

(4) The central, and most important scene: personifications of Roma and Sabratha joining hands in the presence of soldiers, flanked by figures at an altar to the L and a sacrificial bull to the R.

(5) A scene from a tragedy, flanked by comic and tragic masks.

(6) A satyr (badly damaged); the Three Graces; the Judgment of Paris, with the three goddesses in the centre (Aphrodite, Athene and Hera) and Paris (trousered, in Phrygian dress) to the right, being introduced to the contestants by Hermes (with caduceus).

(7) A scene from a pantomime (?).

Roman theatres often had curtains in front of the stage, but since there was no possibility of suspending them from above, they were raised on a bar from a slot immediately behind the front of the stage. The Sabratha theatre has such a slot, but it is not now visible.

At either side of the stage, passageways (*vomitoria*) led directly into the *orchestra* from the outside; there were also lateral doorways on the stage itself which led into halls (green rooms) on either side. That on the W side was paved and veneered with multi-coloured marbles, the effect of which has been schematically recreated on the wall towards the stage. Behind the stage was a covered portico (*porticus post scaenam*) enclosing a garden.

The date of construction of the theatre is controversial. Giacomo Caputo and John Ward-Perkins, the two foremost authorities, had irreconcilable views on the subject. Ward-Perkins insisted that the style of the architectural decoration is very close to that of the Antonine buildings in the centre of Sabratha and that there are no obvious links to the style of carving on the Severan buildings at Lepcis Magna. He proposed a date in the last quarter of the second century AD. Caputo, on the other hand, argued for a Severan date precisely because he did see resemblances to the Severan work at Lepcis; moreover, he argued that Septimius, together with Caracalla and perhaps the Praetorian Prefect Plautianus, may be the sacrificants at the altar in the central relief in front of the stage, suggesting a date around or after 204. The demise of the theatre is more easily defined. The building suffered catastrophic collapse and fire during the fourth century, after which much of the architectural marble was gathered up into the green rooms on either side of the stage. This reflects what we know of the forum and Capitolium in the earthquake 'of 365' and its aftermath, and the theatre must clearly have suffered a similar fate. Subsequently, small huts were constructed in its ruins, which were otherwise occasionally pillaged for building-material: a capital from the stage-building was found in the church overlying the forum basilica (9), and two brackets from the top of the *cavea* are in the precinct of the Antonine Temple (5).

Severan Monument (25)

The street which leads away directly from the western *vomitorium* of the theatre enters a small irregular piazza just one block away, and then bends southwards onto the alignment of the older street-grid to the W. In this piazza are two large, low rectangular platforms which must have supported monuments of some kind. One of them, of the local sandstone, is reduced entirely to its foundations and nothing further can be said of it. The other, however, whilst also much reduced by the reuse of its blocks elsewhere, may be identified as a monument to the emperor Septimius Severus. It is distinctive inasmuch as it is built of the fossiliferous yellow limestone which is widely used at Lepcis Magna and which comes from quarries at Ras al-Hammam nearby. This stone, which must have been shipped to Sabratha deliberately, occurs in only one other building on the site, the Basilica of Justinian (14). Close examination of that building shows it to have been constructed precisely by the demolition of the Severan Monument, for it incorporates blocks with the same cornice-moulding and indeed even parts of the inscription from the monument. Careful study of all the evidence shows that the original podium stood four courses high above the basal plinth, and that it bore a dedication to Septimius which is probably to be dated to the year 202. There is no surviving evidence for what stood on top of the podium, but its size suggests a large sculptural group, perhaps a *quadriga*. (Being of bronze, this would readily have been melted down at a later date for other purposes.) Sabratha's most obvious tribute to the African emperor therefore took the form of a monument at a prominent street-intersection, dominating the approach to the theatre from the W.

Peristyle House* (26)

To the SW of the theatre, and prominently visible from it, is a substantial peristyle house. Both its character and its alignment show that it predates the eastward expansion of the city, and that it was probably constructed in the first century AD as a wealthy suburban villa. Its rooms are arranged around a central peristyle, which was rectangular but slightly bowed at one end. The effect of the garden that one might walk into from the surrounding portico is rather diminished for the visitor, both by the excavation of the central area to below the stylobate of the colonnade, and by the absence of the floor of the portico. The latter is due to the fact that there was a lower corridor or *cryptoporticus* running beneath the portico, which therefore had a suspended wooden floor: the slots for the ends of the beams are readily visible. The *cryptoporticus* was accessed from a staircase on the W side, and led to a series of underground rooms, corresponding to those at ground-level above. The columns of the peristyle are of stuccoed sandstone, fluted and with Corinthian capitals. Some of the rooms on the W side, which are built on solid ground, are embellished with either black-and-white or polychrome mosaics: note the circular maze, which was a popular motif.

Outlying monuments

There are some other monuments at Sabratha which do not readily form part of a circular tour, but which are still of interest if you have the time for them. The closest of these are the **Baths of Regio VII*** (or 'Office Baths': 27), which lie behind the offices of the Department of Antiquities and to the SW of the Punic Museum. Like the Oceanus Baths (22), this is a bath-suite extensively

decorated with mosaics, attached to a villa (which is largely beyond the area exposed) on the edge of town.

The present entrance is on the W side, through a portico of stuccoed sandstone columns which led into a large rectangular vestibule. From this, the villa was entered to the R and the baths to the L; also on the L was a door leading to a latrine with a black-and-white geometric mosaic. On entering the baths, one came first to two antechambers which may have served as *apodyteria* (the further one may have been a vestibule for an original entrance from the N), and then (to the R) to the *frigidarium*, with two opposed cold plunge-baths, one hexagonal and the other rectangular with an apse. At the E end of the *frigidarium*, two round-ended lobbies with heated floors constituted *tepidaria*. These gave access to a circuit of three hot rooms: the southernmost was heated only beneath the floor, but the other two have flue-tiles within the walls as well, so that they benefited directly from the heat of the furnace. The central room was probably a *laconicum* or sweat-room, while that to the N was a *caldarium* with two hot plunge-baths.

The baths (and presumably the villa) were built in the second half of the second century AD, and were destroyed in the earthquake 'of 365.'

About 500 m. to the E of the theatre, the cutting in 1942 of a trench for a sewer towards the sea accidentally revealed the presence of a **Christian catacomb (28)**, which appears to have been in use between the early fourth century and the end of the fifth century AD. This is now protected by iron grilles, but access may be obtained by enquiry at the Antiquities Office. There are several, broad but low, branching

Fig. 21. Sabratha: the arena of the amphitheatre.

galleries cut in the natural sandstone, with *loculi* for inhumations. The smaller *loculi* in the walls of the galleries were often sealed up and plastered over, with painted or incised Christian symbols and inscriptions naming the dead. A tomb-cover in mosaic, naming its incumbent as Auguria, is on display in the central hall of the Roman Museum, above the door (p. 70). A curiosity here is that tombs are excavated even in the floors of the galleries (and covered with slabs). Broken tombs still reveal bones within.

The amphitheatre* of Sabratha (29) lies about a kilometre from the entrance to the site (at N 31° 48.236', E 12° 29.640'), and is most easily reached by road, taking the northern Sabratha ring-road eastwards and then turning N past the sports arena on an asphalt road. The amphitheatre is then a couple of minutes' walk across the open ground (largely rubbish dump) to

your L and beyond a derelict boundary-wall. The structure is mostly below the surrounding ground-level and, like the amphitheatre at Lepcis, must have made use of a pre-existing quarry for the hollow of the arena; in this instance, however, the outermost ring of seating was supported on arcades. The seats are well-preserved, though unlike Lepcis, there has been no attempt at restoration. They appear now, at least on the S side, to end precipitously and without protection above a considerable drop; this is because the vaulted passageway around the perimeter of the arena, which supported the lower rows of seats, has collapsed at this point. This passageway, which could be sealed off from the spectators, provided the means of introducing gladiators or animals to the ring. A similar purpose was served by the cruciform passage beneath the floor of the arena: this had originally a timber ceiling (the slots for the beams are clear), and passed completely underneath the seating on the S side in order to communicate with the exterior.

The capacity of the amphitheatre has been estimated as about 10,000 people. It is thought likely to have been built in the late second century.

Roman Museum** (30)

This museum was built in 1934, and its focal point has always been the mosaics from the Justinianic church to the N of the forum, which occupy the central hall. The lateral wings house on the right (W), pottery and other small finds and on the left (E) sculpture, further mosaics and fragments of wall-painting. The W wing has been closed for a number of years now, and there has apparently also been an intention for some time to build an entirely new museum. This would be a pity, inasmuch as the existing position is good and the design is an elegant piece of colonial work which is sympathetic to its contents; the 'usual' problem of maintaining the integrity of the roof may not, however, be susceptible to unending repairs. Many of the site plans of Sabratha still show what is now a rather enigmatic feature in the formal gardens immediately to the W of the Roman Museum: this is all that remains of a one-time railway terminus! (The platform may still be made out.)

In the central court of the museum are a number of statues, but since a succession of recent guidebooks clearly indicates that they are some-what mobile, it is perhaps unwise to list them here: hopefully they still include two fine (but headless) Roman emperors in ceremonial armour. On entering the left (E) wing by the first door inside the frontal portico, one reaches a display that is rather more static, though some

of the finer pieces have been replaced (at the time of writing) by labels which indicate that they are on tour with the Gaddafi Foundation.

Room 1: mosaics
On the opposite wall as you enter this room is a large mosaic, composed of three *tondi* surrounded by lavish geometrical patterns. The *tondi* contain portrait heads of a lion and a panther, and a very simplified and rather stylized rendering of the Triumph of Liber Pater, with Dionysus/Liber Pater together with Ariadne in a chariot drawn by two panthers, accompanied by a dancing Maenad (behind) and by Pan (in front). This is from a house in *Regio* IV, near the theatre. The mosaic on the wall to the L, with an inscription within a laurel wreath (in bad, late Latin, dated after AD 365), is from the Casa Brogan in *Regio* II (16). On the right-hand side of the wall bearing the Liber Pater mosaic are (or should be) two small panels from the Theatre Baths (19), inscribed BENE LABA ('Wash well') and SALVOM LAVISSE ('Washing is good for you'). They show sandals (for walking on the hot floor), strigils (for scraping oil and sweat off the body) and oil-flasks, all essential accompaniments to a visit to the baths. There are various other fragments of mosaic here from the excavations. The large tessera-size and rather simple designs reflect a late date, somewhat after the 'best' period of North African mosaic art: these examples show that Sabratha was still prosperous in the later fourth century AD, when Lepcis and its dependent luxury villas were in steep decline.

Room 2 : painted wall-plaster
Most of the painted wall-plaster on display here is from the so-called House of the Tragic Actor (in *Regio* V, *Insula* 3,

close to the theatre). Also on the walls here (to the L of the doorway leading to the Room 3) are two graffiti, one with architectural sketches, in the base-coat of plaster from a corridor in the theatre. On the floor is a mosaic from the House of the Tragic Actor which encloses four *emblemata* in the fine tesserae known as *opus vermiculatum*: one panel is a still-life of a *xenion* (gift for strangers) composed of meat, vegetables, a pig's trotter and fruit; the others show Tritons and Nereids consorting with one another.

Room 3: sculpture
This room is filled entirely with sculpture. The pieces are (clockwise from the door by which you enter) head of Caligula (Basilica, 9); two Aphrodites (Seaward Baths, 15: one nude, one clothed, both headless); Jupiter as Serapis (Office Baths, 27); Bacchus (Seaward Baths); colossal bust of Jupiter on an inscribed base (Capitolium, 11: dedicated to Jupiter by Africanus); Isis (Temple of Isis, 23); Tanit as Caelestis (Capitolium); Mercury(?); torso of youth (S Forum Temple, 4); bust of Concordia (Capitolium, also dedicated by Africanus: shame about the lettering!); a pierced candelabrum representing Orpheus charming the animals (Theatre Baths, 19, attributed to the third century AD); fragmentary cupid on dolphin with an inscription in neo-Punic (near the forum basilica); another cupid (Office Baths); Isis (Temple of Isis, third century AD); prisoner? (*Regio* IV); Juno (Capitolium); a pilaster with a figure of Dionysus accompanied by a panther (*Regio* IV); two representation of Diana; satyr (Forum).

Room 4: portrait heads and mosaics
This contains a display of heads, but apart from a fragmentary female head

in marble from the Antonine Temple (5) and part of a marble ram from *Regio* IV, the remainder are all casts. Above the door is a mosaic of a lion from *Regio* V and there is also here a fragment of a mosaic of Oceanus/Neptune. Three other mosaics which were on the walls are away on tour at the time of writing: these are the Head of Oceanus (in a hexagonal frame) and a mosaic of Diana/Luna from the Oceanus Baths (second and first phases of the building, respectively: p. 62), and a portrayal of the Three Graces from *Regio* II.

Room 5: painted wall-plaster
The display here is again dedicated to painted wall-plaster: several of the pieces on the L are from the House of Ariadne in *Regio* IV (near the theatre) and the arched pieces on the R are from the House of Leda in *Regio* II, *Insula* 6 (close to the basilica of Justinian: 13). The latter show scenes from the legends of Dionysus and Ariadne, and Leda and the Swan. On the floor is a mosaic panel representing Autumn, and another with birds and a vessel. Above the door on the way out is a fragment of an octagonal mosaic with a figure of a Nereid combing the tail of the winged horse, Pegasus (from the Seaward Baths: the same theme is treated in one of the large mosaics in Room 9C of the National Museum in Tripoli.)

Central hall
Returning thus to the courtyard, one now enters the central hall, which was designed specifically to display the magnificent mosaics from the basilica of Justinian (14). Casts of the column-bases and other church fittings have been placed to give an idea of the arrangement within the building; the mosaics with geometric patterns

Fig. 22. Sabratha: the floor-mosaic from the basilica of Justinian.

geometric designs now displayed on the walls of the room find their closest parallels at Antioch in ancient Syria, and there can be little doubt that the craftsmen who created it came from the eastern Mediterranean.

Also from the same church are the two columns which supported the altar-canopy, with crosses surmounting orbs carved on their shafts, two panels from the chancel screen and two altar-tops (one rectangular and dedicated by a certain Stephanus, the other rounded at one end).

Above the door into this hall is a mosaic tomb-cover from the catacomb (28). It displays a chi-rho monogram in the centre (with alpha and omega, but the wrong way round!), and records Auguria, who lived (*bixit* for *vixit*: this is typical of late Latin) more-or-less 65 years. On either side of the door are cases of late Roman lamps (of both Tunisian and Tripolitanian origin): many of them bear crosses or Christian monograms. In the left-hand case there are also stamped plaster stoppers which were used as bungs for amphorae.

now on the side-walls were originally on the floors of the aisles: note the cut-outs which correspond to the column-bases.

The principal mosaic in the nave of the church is composed of a magnificent inhabited vine-scroll, rising from an acanthus calyx. The bunches of grapes are being pecked at by all sorts of birds and it has been claimed that the motifs in the central loops of the intersecting vine-stems are an allegory of life: the phoenix in the first loop symbolizing resurrection, the caged quail in the second the imprisoned soul and the peacock displaying in the fourth loop the soul in Paradise. Repairs were made to the mosaic both in antiquity (coarse mosaic and marble chips) and in modern times (terrazzo paving). The style and character both of this mosaic and of those with

Punic Museum (31)

The first room in this building is devoted largely to the conservation and display of the original carved elements of the triangular Punic-Hellenistic Mausoleum B (2). In the centre of the room are displayed elements of the second storey, with lions (formerly surmounted by *kouroi*) at the corners and figured reliefs in between. On the left-hand side is the relief of Bes as lion-tamer, and on the right-hand side is Hercules killing the Nemean Lion (with a sword: note the socket in his clenched fist). These fragments still show extensive signs of their original paint. Against the L wall of the room are further fragments from higher up on the same storey, and from the crowning obelisk. On the rear wall of the room is a reconstruction drawing, showing how the various elements must have fitted together. On the right-hand side of the room are three pieces of sculpture from Sabratha which belong to the Punic period, and towards the rear on this side is a charming little stuccoed and painted shrine which was found in the piazza in *Regio* VI (1).

In the corridor which leads off to the R are some further fragments of Punic sandstone sculpture, including a small figure of Bes and a flat *stele* with a curious cartoon-figure scratched upon it. Behind glass on the R is a reconstruction of a burial found at Mellita, on the coast about 20 km W of Sabratha. It takes the form of an extended skeleton in the remains of a wooden coffin, surrounded by various grave goods: an amphora, pottery with a slightly metallic black slip (imported from the Bay of Naples) and other items of the second century BC.

In the room beyond, the cases of pottery, glass and other objects derive from burials found at various sites in the vicinity of Sabratha: they belong generally to the last two centuries BC and the first century AD. On the end wall, in a recess, should be a marble basin with an inscribed dedication to Baal-Ammon (away on tour at the time of writing). To the R of this is a fragment of mosaic with the sign of Tanit, a fragment of marble veneer with neo-Punic writing on it, and an explanatory table showing the evolution of various alphabets. The corner and the entire opposite wall of this room are occupied by a display of Punic *stelai*, mostly recovered in difficult conditions during the course of construction work to the west of the ancient city, just beyond the old tuna fishery. Here it seems that there was a sacred area or *tophet* dedicated to the goddess Tanit. The *stelai* have variously serrated upper margins and are decorated with crudely incised or red-painted motifs, including the Tanit symbol (stick-figure with a triangular body), trident, palm, pomegranate etc. A few bear traces of writing, and where these can be deciphered, they appear to be proper names. Beneath the *stelai* (where preserved *in situ*) were found small jars (of which a number are displayed in the last two cases on the left-hand wall) containing burned skeletal remains. Where identifiable, these were of young (sometimes neonatal) sheep, goats and cows which had been offered in sacrifice. The *tophet* seems to have been in use approximately between the mid third century BC and the late first century AD.

The Jabal Nafusah and Ghadamis

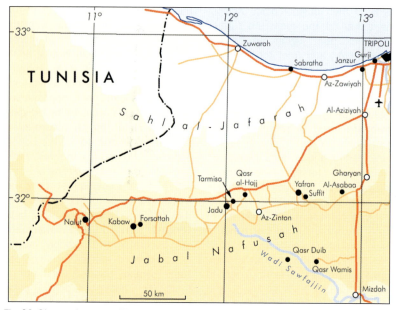

Fig. 23. Sites to the west of Tripoli.

The region to the S and W of Tripoli is dominated by the escarpment of the Jabal Nafusah, which rises in a long curve to the S of the coastal Jafarah plain. The approach to the high ground is through broken hills towards the E, but the scarp becomes an increasingly dramatic and solid barrier towards the W. The Jafarah at its foot, away from the coast, is waterless and barely cultivable, whereas the higher ground attracts a greater rainfall which permits the cultivation of olives, dates and cereals. Proceeding further southwards, the land falls gently to the S and the E, draining eventually towards the Greater Syrtis (or Gulf of Sidra) through the wadi systems of the Sawfajjin, Zamzam and Bayy al-Kabir. Away from the edge of the scarp, the rainfall diminishes rapidly into a zone of marginal agriculture (the pre-desert) and thence into the Hamada al-Hamra, the stony desert plateau to the S.

Historically, the Jabal Nafusah, whose terrain lends itself to hidden and readily defensible settlement, has been a refuge for those resisting or avoiding the cultural fluxes of the coastal region. There is plenty of evidence of Roman settlement in the area (though little has been identified of earlier date); after the Arab conquest of the coast, the population of the Jabal retained a distinctively Berber character, which is still apparent today in both the people and the language. The practice of Christianity (exemplified by the church at al-Asaba'a) seems to have persisted for several centuries and when the Berbers did adopt Islam, they adhered to the puritanical Ibadite sect (widely regarded as heretical), in contrast to the Malikite tradition followed by the majority. It seems that from the time of the Arab conquest until the advent of the Italians in the twentieth century, the partially sedentary Berbers of the Jabal were constantly dominated and menaced by the nomadic Arabs of the Jafarah, who raided their flocks and exacted tribute from them. This antagonism and repression seems to have been even greater after the arrival of the Bani Hilal in the eleventh century.

There are more visible traces of medieval settlement in the Jabal Nafusah than anywhere else in Tripolitania, though because of the primitive forms of the architecture and the mode of construction (rough stones bonded with mud and rendered on the surface), the necessity of constant renewal makes it difficult to date buildings other than by their most recent repairs (recorded by inscriptions in the plasterwork). Particularly striking in this region are the communal granaries, with notable examples at Qasr al-Hajj, Kabaw and Nalut; that at Nalut proclaims an origin in the seventh century BC, which may be treated with scepticism, but they probably do go back at least to the early medieval period. The granaries are built up of individual cells (*ghorfas*) which held the provisions of a single family within a communal structure accessed by a single guarded entrance. The life of the Berbers could involve absences from their villages of several months at a time with their flocks, and it was therefore important to them to have a safe repository for their food stocks, which represented their wealth far more than houses or other possessions. It is interesting to note that the writer Diodorus Siculus, of the first century BC, reports that part of the 'Libyans' live without cities, but that their chiefs have towers near water sources in which they store the reserves of their booty. The antecedents of these granaries may well therefore extend as far back as the Classical period. Primarily designed for storage, many of them have also a defensive aspect, as a refuge against oppressors. It is also notable that many of them were reported to have been destroyed by the Turks in the face of a rebellion in the mid-nineteenth century: this would have been an effective way of reducing opposition and terrorising the population. The remaining granaries went progressively out of use during the course of the twentieth century.

Another feature of the Jabal Nafusah, of which I have tried to give some idea in this guide, is the frequent presence, in the countryside as well as in the towns, of very small mosques. Some of these could have accommodated barely a dozen people at one time and yet they represent a very long-standing tradition, in a few cases demonstrably going back to the tenth century or earlier. Many are carefully maintained, but even some of those which are derelict are clearly still revered and visited on special occasions. Some of them, named *taghlis*, preserve through their name a presumed identity with an earlier church (*ekklesia*), though no certain cases have been identified where this is suggested by their layout. I have listed a few of the more accessible, but there are many others, some of which are in (now) quite isolated positions in the landscape. Many of the Berbers of the region have changed from Ibadite to Malikite in their religious practice, and there is also now a substantial population of Arabs; it is impossible, however, to distinguish from the mosques themselves by which sect they were erected or used.

Ghadamis is a remarkably well preserved example of a true oasis town. It is included here because it has roots which go back to Classical antiquity, and because it is most likely to be visited by tourists today in conjunction with an exploration of the Jabal Nafusah. The difficulty of attributing dates to the buildings which make up the old town of Ghadamis is similar to that encountered in the Jabal: the forms may be of considerable antiquity, but as part of a living town they have been endlessly renewed. Since there are good descriptions of the standing architecture in recent popular guidebooks, I have confined my account here to the fragmentary evidence for occupation in Classical times; very little systematic study of this material has hitherto been published, and it is possible that the evidence concerning the legionary fort and its associated settlement is more extensive than we appreciate.

The entries in this section of the gazetteer are arranged more or less geographically, proceeding westwards from the vicinity of Gharyan to Ghadamis.

AL-ASABA'A

Coordinates: N 32° 2.726', E 12° 52.886'
Directions: For both of the monuments described here, turn R off the main Gharyan–Yafran road at a distance of approximately 21 km from the centre of Gharyan, next to a memorial commemorating a Libyan act of resistance to the Italian invasion. (This is the point to which the map coordinates refer.)

Church

The location of this church (at N 32° 3.300' E 12° 51.169') was described in the 1960s as 'situated on a windy ridge overlooking the Djebel escarpment, on the edge of the Asaba'a plain, about 3 km NW of the Mudiriya of el-Asaba'a.' The area is now extensively built-up, with a maze of minor roads between new buildings: the Mudiriya is no longer identifiable and the miserable remains of the church are strewn with rubbish and hemmed in between water tanks and houses on the crest of the ridge (which is still windy). The church is at a distance of about 3 km from the

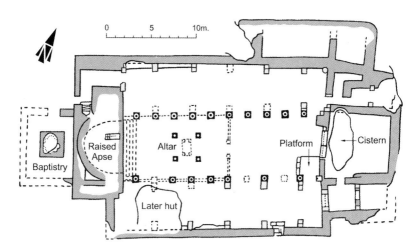

Fig. 24. Plan of the church at al-Asaba'a.

Fig. 25. The lonely communal granary near al-Asaba'a.

turning off the main road, slightly N of W; it is 2 km SW of the *qasr* (below).

The church was found incorporated in an Arab *zawiya*, and was excavated in 1926–27. It was a rectangular structure of normal basilical plan, with a nave and two aisles, and a single raised apse at the W end. There were various additional rooms on the N side and at the E end. The nave colonnades probably carried arcades; bases, shafts, and capitals were of limestone, the capitals being partly Ionic from an earlier building, partly Corinthian, and, in one instance at least, of uncanonical, local form. The six westernmost bays of the nave were enclosed by screens held in slots in the column-bases, and the altar stood in the middle of this enclosure under a *ciborium* supported on four slender, spirally-fluted columns. Little of this is now visible, apart from some column-bases and the remains of the baptistery behind the apse, with a cruciform font of Byzantine pattern. A hoard of coins, found on the site of the altar, suggests that the main structure dates from before the Byzantine reconquest. Other finds made in the church include carved

limestone brackets similar to those found at al-Khadra (p. 163) and, in the apse, the handsome tombstone of the presbyter Turrentius, which is now on display in Room 13 of the National Museum in Tripoli (p. 32).

Communal granary

I was directed to this communal granary or *qasr* by chance, when trying to find the church. The map coordinates are N 32° 4.089' E 12° 52.092', but it is difficult to describe how to find it through the sprawl of irregular building development in the area. Leave the main road at the point indicated previously: the *qasr* is about 3 km to the NW, beyond the ridge and below the crest of the escarpment of the Jabal. It stands at the end of an asphalt road, in a desolate stony landscape. Despite the presence of the road, which can only have been built in order to reach it, it has an air of total abandonment and isolation and, surprisingly, there are no obvious signs of any associated settlement.

The building is of the open-courtyard type, like the granaries at Qasr al-Hajj and Kabaw (pp. 78, 81), and is the most easterly example known to me. There is a single tunnel-entrance and the courtyard is an irregular, elongated oval, with most of the surrounding cells still standing three or four tiers high. It clearly belongs within the same series as the other Berber granaries of the Jabal Nafusah, and as such may have origins which go back to the early medieval period.

YAFRAN

Coordinates: N 32° 3.630', E 12° 31.379'
Directions: Yafran may be reached from the Tripoli–Nalut road in the Jafarah by turning off towards the Jabal at Bir Ayyad (N 32° 7.763' E 12° 27.469'). On the road along the top of the Jabal, going W from Gharyan, turn R at N 31° 59.736' E 12° 38.299'; if approaching on this road from the W, turn L at N 31° 58.844' E 12° 32.677'.

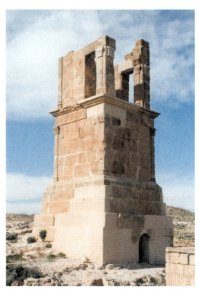

Fig. 26. The Roman mausoleum at Suffit.

Yafran is an important administrative centre, and is now an extended built-up area which encompasses a number of Berber villages strung along the edge of the Jabal escarpment. It has a notable old mosque, Tiwitrawin, which stands in a prominent and isolated position about 3.5 km to the NE of the town centre, immediately above the road at N 32° 4.644' E 12° 32.971'. This is quite a complex building compared with the other early mosques of the region, not least because it has a tall square minaret, from the open upper floor of which the call to prayer could be issued most effectively. Access to this floor follows a tradition found in late Roman fortified farms: there is a staircase leading from within the mosque onto the roof, but after that it is a matter of climbing up by means of projecting foothold-stones. The interior of the mosque is divided into three rooms, and there is a separate, semi-subterranean, chamber at the NE

end which is accessed from outside and which contains the tomb of a holy man. There is also on the SE side of the mosque a roughly enclosed courtyard with its own *mihrab*, for additional worshippers (as at Forsatta, p. 82).

Suffit Mausoleum*

This is to be found about 16 km by road to the SE of Yafran (on the road towards Gharyan), and may readily be seen from a distance as a tall rectangular building on high ground next to a concrete water-tower. Turn E off the road by a filling station at N 32° 0.831' E 12° 35.354'. Follow the road uphill: it passes immediately below the mausoleum, which is at N 32° 1.648' E 12° 35.595'.

This imposing Roman tomb stands just below the crest of a hill, from which there is a commanding view in every direction. There are traces of a rectangular building – perhaps a watch-tower – on the summit, and this is surrounded by a rock-cut ditch. The

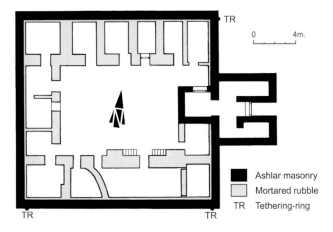

Fig. 27. Plan of the Roman farm building at Hinshir Suffit.

recently restored mausoleum stands three storeys high and has lost its crowning element, which was probably a squat pyramidal roof. Like other mausolea of similar scale, it is built of large ashlar blocks throughout. An arched doorway in the plain rectangular sub-base gives access to the burial chamber, which is lined with six small niches. (They are a little shallow to have accommodated cinerary urns, but may have served for lamps.) The slot in the doorway, where the original blocking-slab would have dropped down once the remains had been placed inside, is clearly visible. The next tier of the monument rises above the sub-base on a stepped, moulded podium; its faces are plain but it is framed by Corinthian pilasters at the angles, supporting a frieze composed of a simple vegetal-scroll and a projecting cornice. The tier above this is aedicular (i.e. open on one side, like a miniature temple); the *aedicula* is framed by rectangular pillars at the front corners, formerly joined to one another across the front by an arch, and to the enclosing wall behind by flat lintels. The pillars are decorated on each face with Corinthian pilasters.

No inscription belonging to this monument has been found, though there is an uninscribed *tabula ansata* on the front of the lower storey. The quality of the masonry suggests that it belongs to the second or third century AD.

Hinshir Suffit

On the next hill, 250 m to the NE of the mausoleum, are the remains of a fortified farm with which it was almost certainly associated. The farm, known as Hinshir Suffit, was excavated in 1926 by Renato Bartoccini, who identified two distinct modes of construction as shown in fig. 27; he attributed these to successive phases. The main rectangular enclosure is built of large, well-finished ashlar blocks with a single entrance on the E side. At various points around the exterior there are projecting tethering-rings for animals, variously treated, in the form of animal heads and the like. Three of these are still detectable, as marked, though the pierced hole is broken away in each case. A secondary element of the design is a square, projecting entrance with the door-sill set deep within the flanking walls. While the butt-joints between this and the original structure suggest that it was not original to the design, the masonry is entirely similar, and it may represent only a revision while the work was in progress, in order to make the entrance more readily defensible.

Bartoccini's second phase is represented by the use of small rubble masonry, both for a sloping external revetment on the N and W sides (not shown) and for almost all of the internal walls. These have almost entirely dissolved now, and little can be made out. However, since the inner facing of the ashlar outer walls must also have been in the same rubble masonry, these two distinct modes of construction may not have been separated in time, but only in purpose. Bartoccini made out a series of rooms around all four sides of a central courtyard; narrow stairways on the S side showed that there was access to the roof above (though not necessarily an upper storey). The room which was entered between these stairways was reported to contain stone mangers and was presumably a stable. One such manger or trough now lies displaced on the surface. A room on the opposite side of the courtyard was lined with pink waterproof cement (still just detectable) and must have been a cistern for rainwater channelled off the roof. The defensive character of the entrance was augmented by the addition of an inner room, entered not axially but from one side; there are numerous other examples of this device in the pre-desert region.

Bartoccini recovered various fragments of colonnettes and some late Roman lamps. He attributed the two principal phases of construction to the third and the sixth centuries AD respectively; in the light of more recent discoveries this confidence is probably no longer justified. The building may originally have been constructed as early as the late first or second century (see Qasr Isawi, p. 201, with which it shares many similarities), and may well have been occupied continuously until the late Roman (Byzantine) period.

QASR AL-HAJJ

Coordinates: N 32° 2.703', E 12° 9.903'
Directions: The village is just off the road along the bottom of the Jabal Nafusah from Aziziyah to Nalut, between Bir Ayyad and Shakshuk. Turn S off the main road at N 32° 4.180' E 12° 9.784', then turn R in the village after 2.6 km; this will take you directly to a car park in front of the granary. The facilities here include a public toilet (in the garden that has been laid out in front of the granary, next to the payphone!).

Granary**

This is one of the better-preserved communal granaries of the Jabal Nafusah. In this case it takes the form of a hollow ellipse, ringed by cells in which local families stored their foodstuffs, both liquid (oil) and solid (cereals, dates, olives). The mode of construction is also typical of the region, being built of unshaped stone rubble bonded with large quantities of mud and gypsum. When kept in good repair by constant refacing, it may last a very long time, but once the rain begins to get into the structure, collapse is catastrophic. The *qasr* at Kabaw lost a substantial segment in this way just a few years ago, and the ruins of the old village around Qasr al-Hajj also show how this type of architecture disintegrates into shapeless heaps of rubble, once abandoned.

The building has a single entrance, and only tiny windows (for ventilation) on the outside, and it would have had a single guard/doorkeeper. The cells within all open towards the centre, the higher ones being accessed either (here) by ladders or (at Kabaw and Nalut) from small projecting wooden balconies or loading-platforms, generally so arranged that it was possible to make one's way up by jumping from one to another. Each cell was closed by a door made from split palm-trunks and fastened with a lock (originally wooden, more recently a cheap padlock). The insides of the cells are usually divided into compartments or bins, with large built-in storage-jars for liquids. Local guides may tell you that the number of cells (114) corresponds to the number of *suras* in the Qur'an, but a glance at the style of construction will show that this is entirely coincidental! Nonetheless, the regularity of the design here suggests a building constructed to some kind of plan in one or at most a few phases, in contrast to some of the other granaries which seem to have grown organically by the random accretion of additional cells (e.g. at Kabaw or Nalut).

JADU

Coordinates: N 31° 57.416', E 12° 1.727'
Directions: Travelling W from Gharyan along the main Jabal-top road, fork R at N 31° 55.467' E 12° 6.318'. Travelling E from Nalut, fork L at N 31° 53.942' E 11° 59.089'; Either of these roads will lead you to the centre of Jadu. The fork for Tarmisa is on the eastern approach.

Jadu is listed here not so much for its own historic centre, which is hardly in evidence, as for the sake of the little rural mosques which abound in the countryside round about. As elsewhere

(Forsatta, Nalut), they are very difficult to date but they may go back to perhaps the eighth or ninth centuries AD. The spread of Islam to the Jabal Nafusah was slow, because of its remoteness and the resistance of the Berbers to the invading Arabs; Christianity therefore long retained a foothold here and local tradition maintained that a number of these mosques had previously been churches. However, though some of them make use of reused Roman building material, there is barely any direct evidence for prior use as a church. The mosques described here are just two specimen examples, amongst a dozen or more in the close vicinity.

Ibukar mosque

Coming from the Nalut direction on the main road, fork left for Jadu as described above. After 1.2 km there is a turning to the L just before an electricity sub-station. Take this and fork L again after 2.4 km (still on asphalt). After 250 m, fork L onto an unmade track, which is viable in a saloon car in dry weather. Follow this, as far as possible in a straight line, for 1.4 km. The mosque becomes visible on high ground to your R: a small squat building of mostly undressed stone, with a recent square building next to it at N 31° 54.905' E 11° 58.374'. The mosque has two barrel-vaulted aisles and, curiously, no *mihrab*. This is because the present doorway is the former *mihrab*, the original doorway (just to the R, when looking out from the inside) having been blocked. From the outside, it is clear that this building makes use of some substantial dressed stones from a Roman building; immediately to the L of the present door, on the outside, is a sculpted stone (from a tomb?) showing a camel ploughing, but at the time of

Fig. 28. Roman architectural fragments in the Umm at-Tabul mosque near Jadu, including an upright from an olive-press.

writing (2008) this is hidden by fallen debris.

Beneath the mosque, and accessed by a ramp from the outside, is an underground room, probably a natural limestone cave. It is notable that a number of these mosques are associated with such features, which were perhaps used as tombs – for a holy man, or the founder of the mosque.

Umm at-Tabul mosque
This mosque stands about 2 km to the N of the Ibukar mosque. To reach it, take the same turning next to the electricity sub-station, but continue for 3.7 km, at which point the mosque, very ruinous but again with a modern cream-painted building next to it, will be visible to the L, some 600 m from the road. There is no obvious access route for vehicles; the mosque stands at N 31° 55.987' E 11° 58.296'.

This mosque is in a very perilous state, not helped by the fact that someone has recently dug deep holes in the floor. (Allegedly, this is done by Moroccans who are looking for buried treasure: it is a not infrequent hazard!) An ancient instability in the *qibla* wall has been remedied by three very solid buttresses against the outside of the building and three inserted arches within. The piers of the arcades are very irregular, and many of the arches have had additional props inserted beneath their crowns, but the interest here lies in the incorporation of the uprights of a Roman olive-press, and of a number of column-shafts and Corinthian capitals. There was presumably a Roman olive farm in the immediate vicinity. The plasterwork of this mosque is also quite elaborate, particularly in the *qibla* aisle, with a wide variety of decorative motifs. There is also some stucco decoration in high relief around the *mihrab*.

TARMISA*
Coordinates: N 31° 59.654', E 12° 2.820'
Directions: Leave the Yafran–Jadu road at N 31° 57.204' E 12° 2.725', heading N, and follow this road through the modern village until it comes to an end at the coordinates given. The path leading into the old village is directly in front of you, and crosses a rock-cut ditch (where there was probably once a wooden bridge).

This small Berber village, approximately 5 km from Jadu and now abandoned, occupies one of the most dramatic cliff-top spurs overlooking the arid Jafarah plain beneath. The narrow pathway into the old village passes beneath a look-out tower and then leads into such a warren that it is difficult to tell what is the street and what is part of a house. On the bare

Fig. 29. Interior of the communal granary at Kabaw.

of the museum at Lepcis Magna (p. 140), is decorated with a Christian chi-rho monogram within a wreath and flanked by a pair of stylized palm trees: this must belong to the late Roman period, and may have come from a church. Inside the mosque, the *mihrab* is to your L, but the plan is otherwise totally irregular.

KABAW (CABAO)

Coordinates: N 31° 50.704', E 11° 19.637'

Directions: From the Tripoli–Nalut road along the Jafarah, turn S at Tiji (N 32° 0.847' E 11° 20.017') and climb the Jabal escarpment; from the road along the top of the Jabal, between Jadu and Nalut, turn N at N 31° 46.584' E 11° 19.505'. In either case, branch W in the centre of the modern village at N 31° 46.584' E 11° 19.505' and follow this road for 1.2 km to the car park below the *qasr*.

rock surface, small cup-sized hollows are frequent. These have been created over long years through their use for crushing date-stones: these are fed to camels, and are also made locally into a kind of paste, rather like *halva* (sesame paste). The spur eventually tapers to a point with vertiginous, unguarded cliffs. Just before this, on the left and up a few steps, is the door to a small mosque (now conveniently labelled 'Mosque'): note the arched stone door-frame with its carved roundels: this is unusually regular for Berber architecture and may have been brought from a Roman building nearby. An inscribed block, found at Tarmisa in 1914 and now in Room 20

Granary*

Kabaw is a typical Berber village built on the edge of the Jabal Nafusah escarpment, which has now expanded in a modern sprawl above and around its historic centre. The focal point of the old village is the communal fortified granary or *qasr*, which now dominates a sea of collapsing houses, in at least one of which can be found an olive mill and press, occasionally still operated (for the benefit of tourists) by a camel. The *qasr* is similar to that below the Jabal at Qasr al-Hajj (p. 78), in that it is circular in shape, with the cells disposed in tiers around a central open space. The cells here are not arranged in such an orderly fashion, however, and they seem to rise in random columns from the ground. Another difference from Qasr al-Hajj is that the open ground in the centre is also honeycombed with cells beneath, and it is possible to get from one side to the other entirely underground! The upper cells are reached by leaping precariously from one of the projecting loading-platforms to the next.

The original date of the *qasr* is no more readily determined that that of others in the region: it is presumably medieval and passed out of regular use only during the last century. The local community attempts to maintain it to some degree, but a large segment of the circumference collapsed during winter rains a few years ago.

FORSATTA *

Coordinates: N 31° 51.616', E 11° 22.933'
Directions: Heading N from the centre of Kabaw, turn E at N 31° 51.393' E 11° 20.245'. Drive through the modern village of Forsatta until the asphalt road comes to an end (the coordinates are for this point).

This village is chosen for description, not because it is in any way exceptional, but because it presents, within relatively easy reach of an asphalt road, much of the character of the pre-modern settlement of the Jabal Nafusah. As is the case at Qasr al-Hajj, Kabaw and Nalut, little of what you can see can be ascribed to a precise date, but the ruins are testimony to a civilization which flourished with little change in these remote parts from early medieval times until the first half of the twentieth century.

From the end of the asphalt road, a rough path over the rock leads on in the same direction, down the hillside towards the clearly visible ruins of the old village. Houses cluster on the steep slopes of the escarpment beneath the *qasr* which crowns a narrow spur,

while lower down can be made out the mosque of Sidi Abu Yahya Zakariya, which is still maintained and venerated. The walk down to the mosque takes about twenty minutes.

The mosque, with four aisles, is large compared to most in the region, and is well looked after. Like a number of others, it is preceded by an irregular courtyard which has its own *mihrab*: this would have accommodated extra worshippers at festival-times, with the *mihrab* provided so that they too should know in which direction to face for Mecca. The teacher after whom the mosque is named lived in the late ninth and early tenth centuries AD.

There are still several oil-presses in the ruined houses of the old village.

Back up on top of the escarpment, two more, much smaller and more typical, mosques may be visited without difficulty. The first, Taghlis, is now within the modern village at N 31° 52.102' E 11° 22.340'. (Retrace your route from the end of the road for about 1.6 km, then turn off to the R, about 400 m). It is on top of a hill with a fine view, which it shares with a water-tower. The mosque is a rectangular building, of two aisles internally, divided into a number of rooms. A plaster inscription (now fallen) recorded that it was made by Shaikh Sulayman 'Amr al-Azzabi, and another that it was repaired in 965 AH (AD 1557/8). The plan seems most unlike that of a mosque, and the *mihrab* is directed very nearly S (rather than SE); this suggests that it was originally built for some other purpose. Despite its name ('Taghlis' is thought to be possibly a corruption of *ekklesia*) and the fact that the building is basically oriented E–W, there is nothing else to suggest that it was previously a church.

About 1 km further to the N, at N 31° 52.595' E 11° 22.197' and this time

82

Fig. 30. The qasr of Nalut amid the ruins of the old town.

in an isolated position in the fields, is the Hawariyin ('Apostles') Mosque. It is possible to get to within 150 m by saloon car, but only by means of an unmade track. This mosque is very characteristic of many in the Jabal Nafusah, both by virtue of its very small size and because of its seemingly total isolation from other buildings. (It is, however, notable that since the writer last visited these mosques over thirty years ago, a number of them – and even some very ruinous ones – have acquired simple ancillary buildings of concrete, which show that they are still visited sufficiently often to warrant the provision of some sort of shelter.) This tiny mosque is divided into three aisles inside, one of which is walled off as a separate room. Its arcades make use of some limestone column-drums which have been brought from elsewhere, presumably a Roman building, and the curved stone lintel over the entrance, which is alien to the rest of the construction, may have come from the same source.

NALUT

Coordinates: N 31° 52.060', E 10° 59.100'
Directions: Approaching from Tripoli across

the Jafarah plain, one climbs the escarpment of the Jabal Nafusah immediately beneath the town: the ruins of the old town, clustered about the communal granary (the *qasr*) are above you to the R, while the modern town is in front of you and to the left. In order to reach the old town (to which the coordinates given above apply), turn back sharply to the R just as you approach the intersection at the top of the climb (beneath a fibreglass dinosaur!), park in the open space and walk round to the R.

Granary**

Nalut is an important administrative centre for the western Jabal, and like other conurbations, it has sprawled vastly in recent years. In so doing, it has left behind the historic town, whose remains cluster on a separate spur, projecting steeply above the edge of the Jabal escarpment. The ruins of the old town are tended with some care by the community, and they are signposted and labelled in English. A notice on the outer wall of the *qasr* informs you that its origins go back to the seventh century BC, for which I know no other authority, but it is certainly likely to go back several centuries. Nalut is recorded in documents of the eighth and ninth centuries, but there are traces of an earlier *qasr* and mosque on the slopes beneath the modern town (i.e. on the left as you climb up from the plain). The settlement must therefore have moved to the more defensive location of the present *qasr* at an undefined date, perhaps in the eleventh century. The *qasr* at Nalut takes a rather different form from others in the region (e.g. Qasr al-Hajj, Kabaw): while it is entered in the same way by means of a single portal, it has no internal court-yard but rather a circuit of four narrow streets with cells rising on either side. The loading-platforms upon which one stood in order to hoist up the baskets of goods are still much in evidence here; there were at one time over 500 cells in the building. An inscription in the plaster of the entrance-tunnel records repairs after it was assaulted by the Turks in 1240 AH (AD 1824). Note the fact that the single entrance faces towards the narrow tip of the spur on which the *qasr* is built, so as to prevent any massed frontal attack.

Around the *qasr*, apart from those buildings which are falling progressively into ruin, there are several which are being maintained for their tourist interest. You may see here an example of a traditional oil press, with a palm-trunk as the press-lever: the design is virtually identical to that of the Roman presses whose remains may be seen in the Tarhunah area (e.g. at Hinshir Sidi Hamdan, p. 165 and fig. 77). There are also several mosques of considerable antiquity. On the E side of the *qasr* is the so-called 'Grand Mosque', which is on two levels. The upper hall is whitewashed and mostly kept locked: within, one enters a wide and lofty central aisle parallel to the *qibla* wall; there is another aisle to the R and two to the L, beyond which is the recess of

the *mihrab*. The piers of the arcades are square in section, and all surfaces of this stuccoed architecture seem to merge seamlessly into one another. Above the roof of this building is a typical minaret: a little open spire on four legs, built of the same materials as everything else. It is not as high as a man, and presumably served mainly as a marker: the *imam* might stand next to it and clutch it when issuing the call to prayer.

Immediately below the Grand Mosque is another prayer hall, now increasingly ruinous, but composed of several arcaded aisles; the *mihrab* is visible and there is simple stucco decoration on the arches. A third mosque, readily identifiable by the same form of open minaret, stands beyond the entrance to the *qasr*. In the gaping E side of this building, one can see directly into a room with little cupboards set into the walls: this was the Quranic school associated with the mosque. The prayer hall itself is well-preserved, with four aisles and various inscriptions in the plasterwork.

GHADAMIS

Coordinates: N 30° 8.033', E 9° 29.833'
Ghadamis is a desert oasis town of remarkable character. Its position in history is assured by its location on one of the major routes across the Sahara, leading from Tripoli, between the stony plateau of the Hamada al-Hamra to its E and the sand sea of the Grand Erg Oriental to its W, south-westwards to the Niger around Tombouctou. For centuries an important trade-route between central Africa and the Mediterranean, its decline began with the development of alternative sea-routes in the nineteenth century and with the suppression of the slave trade. The visitor of today goes there to

admire its adaptive architecture, which has developed covered thoroughfares and cool airy houses, well suited to protecting its citizens from the heat of the desert sun; the old town has been designated by UNESCO as a World Heritage Site.

The locality has yielded tools of the Palaeolithic and Neolithic periods, but is first recorded in history in connection with the Saharan expedition of Cornelius Balbus in 20 BC as *Cydamus*, one of the cities of the *Phazanii* – therefore a tribal centre – conquered by him. Latin inscriptions found at Ghadamis make it clear that there was a Roman garrison here in the early third century, composed of a detachment of the *Legio III Augusta*. This may have been withdrawn by the time of the construction of Qasr Duib (p. 200) in AD 244–6. However, permanent contact with the Roman world is attested already before then by extensive quantities of second-century pottery found both throughout the oasis of Ghadamis and in the smaller oases along the route from the coast, at Sinawin, Shawan, Tfalfalt and Mataras. We are also told by Procopius that in the sixth century the *Cidamenses* were converted to Christianity, that they had a bishop, and that they entered into a treaty with the emperor Justinian. Ghadamis was conquered by the Arabs under Uqba ibn-Nafi in 667; it is related that the Berbers who refused to be converted to Islam withdrew

to the fortified hilltop of Ras al-Ghul, some 10 km to the NW of the oasis (at N 30° 11.439' E 9° 29.211'). There are clear signs of fortification around the hilltop, but I know of no archaeological investigations at the site or evidence of date.

At Ghadamis itself, the standing evidence of occupation in the Roman period is limited to the so-called 'idols' (*asnam*) on the high ground to the W of the oasis. These rather shapeless pillars of rubble masonry, of which two still stand to some height, show on close inspection that they are just the cores of monumental tombs. They were once faced with dressed stone and probably surrounded by colonnades like those at Ghirza (p. 190); they are therefore likely to be of approximately similar date (fourth/fifth centuries AD). It is also evident that they are the last visible remnants of an extensive necropolis. In the museum in the old Turkish/Italian fort may be seen a Latin inscription from such a tomb, some arcuate lintels and other carved frieze-blocks, which have probably also come from tombs. As for the columns and capitals which adorned these structures, they are probably those which may now be seen in the Yunis Mosque off the main square of the old town. No trace has been found of the Roman military post here, from which it may be inferred that it was not as substantial as the forts at Qaryah al-Gharbiyah (p. 196) or Abu Njaym (p. 170).

Lepcis Magna***

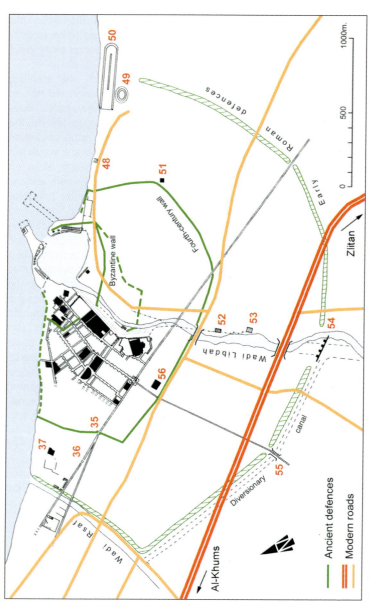

Fig. 31. Lepcis Magna: plan of modern roads and outlying areas.

Lepcis Magna now lies virtually within an eastern suburb of al-Khums, which has grown vastly around its little port in the late twentieth century. Most of the ancient site lies within a protected archaeological zone, but its suburbs, outer defences and cemeteries are still constantly being eroded by modern building activity. The site has long been known to European travellers, and the inclination of some travel writers (and tour operators) to describe it as a 'lost city' seems somewhat misplaced. The earliest person to have paid any systematic attention to it in modern times was the French consul Claude Lemaire, who between 1686 and 1708 was excavating marble columns as a business, shipping them back to France and selling them as building-material. In 1816 Yusuf Karamanli, Pasha of Tripoli, was persuaded by the British consul Hanmer Warrington to allow the British to excavate at the site and to take what they wished 'as a gift for the Prince Regent.' Warrington was hoping for 'works of art' and was disappointed in this, but in the following year Commander (later Rear-Admiral) W. H. Smyth shipped out a considerable number of architectural fragments, which were subsequently used to compose a classical fantasy at Virginia Water, at the southern end of Windsor Great Park.

Archaeological investigations, as opposed to these quarrying activities, began seriously only in 1920 under the Italian colonial administration, and were pursued with vigour until the outset of the Second World War. Since the war, many different countries have been permitted to send archaeological missions, including the British, the Americans (in 1960–61), the French and the Italians. The excavations of the major public buildings have been accompanied by large-scale programmes of consolidation and restoration, with the result that Lepcis Magna is today not only recognized by UNESCO as a World Heritage Site, but is also arguably one

---

Key to numbered entries in the text and on the site-plans in figures 31, 32 and 44

1. Entrance to main site
2. Arch of Septimius Severus
3. Hadrianic Baths
4. Great Nymphaeum
5. Colonnaded Street
6. Church
7. Severan Forum
8. Temple 'of the Gens Septimia'
9. Severan Basilica
10. Byzantine Gate
11–22. Old Forum
23. Temple of Serapis
24. Oriental Sanctuary
25. Unfinished Baths
26. Market
27. Arch of Tiberius
28. Arch of Trajan
29. Chalcidicum
30. Theatre
31. Porticus post scaenam
32. Monument to Macer
33. 'Schola'
34. Temple on the Decumanus
35. Oea Gate
36. Arch of Marcus Aurelius
37. Hunting Baths
38. Harbour
39. Flavian Temple
40. Neronian portico
41. First-century harbour entrance
42. Lighthouse
43. Signal-tower
44. Doric Temple
45. Foundations of mole
46. Eastern Baths
47. Temple of Jupiter Dolichenus
48. Villa of the Nile
49. Amphitheatre
50. Circus
51. Qasr Shaddad mausoleum
52, 53. Cisterns
54. Dam
55. Bridge over canal
56. Museum

LEPCIS MAGNA

MEDITERRANEAN

24

11–22

25

23

39

35–37 ←

10

31

9

26

7

30

27

8

29

28

6

Wadi

32

5

34

4

33

3

2

1

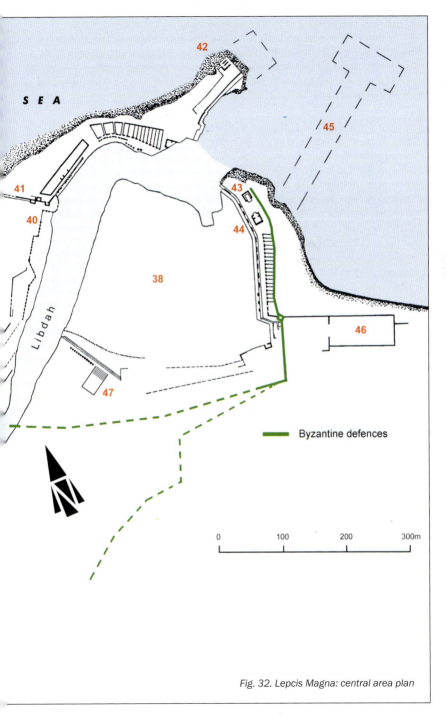

Fig. 32. Lepcis Magna: central area plan

of the best-preserved and most evocative cities of the ancient Roman Empire. While many of its best portable finds are displayed in the National Museum in Tripoli, there is such a wealth of them that not only does Lepcis itself have an excellently displayed and interpreted museum, but there are displays of sculpture from Lepcis, and of pottery from tombs in the vicinity, also in the museums of Zlitan and Bani Walid.

The initial settlement of the site is attributed by literary sources to Phoenicians from Tyre, and this is entirely consistent with the archaeological evidence. The earliest occupation levels, identified in both American and Italian excavations beneath what is known as the Old Forum (11), have yielded both Corinthian and Phoenician pottery of the seventh century BC. Substantial stone structures were associated with these levels, but these have been insufficiently explored hitherto to understand their character. The limits of the Punic settlement must, in the inland direction, have fallen short of the later position of the Roman theatre (30), for beneath the stage-building have been found Punic rock-cut tombs, extending in time between the late sixth and the end of the third centuries BC. (See the display in Room 2 of the museum.)

The visible remains are generally no older than the first century BC, and the subsequent expansion of the city may be readily traced through public buildings dated by inscriptions and through changes in alignment of the street-grid. The city was sufficiently prosperous in the mid-first century BC for the imposition of an annual tribute of three million pounds of olive oil by Julius Caesar to be not unrealistic (Lepcis had taken the side of Pompey during the Civil War), and towards the end of that century it had citizens of sufficient wealth to sponsor major public buildings such as the market (26: 9/8 BC), the theatre (30: AD 1/2) and the *Chalcidicum* (29: AD 11/12). It must therefore have already grown to considerable size, and probably up to the edge of these buildings. Between them, they served to disguise a change in the street-grid which allowed further expansion inland to meet the main coastal road more or less at right-angles. This expansion had presumably reached the coast road by AD 29/30, when a gate named the *porta augusta salutaris* (no longer visible) was constructed just to the N of the later position of the Arch of Septimius Severus (2).

The lack of excavations to the SW of this road prevents us from charting in any detail the further expansion of the city in this direction, but it is thought that an outer defence in the form of an earth bank and ditch, later used on the N and W sides of the city as a diversionary canal for the Wadi Libdah (p. 134 and fig. 31), must have been constructed in the first or second century AD. This enclosed a total area of some 425 ha, though not all of it will have been built upon, and at its eastern end the bank terminated close to the amphitheatre (49) which was built in AD 56. It would have taken considerable manpower to defend such a line, and we cannot tell whether this was the 'wall' behind which the citizens cowered in AD 69 when the city of Oea invoked the support of the Garamantes in a territorial dispute with Lepcis (p. 3).

The continuing wealth of the city in the second century AD is demonstrated by the completion in AD 137 of the Hadrianic Baths (3), by the introduction of imported marble to renovate and embellish a number of existing buildings (e.g. the theatre and market) and by the erection of further honorific arches to Trajan (28), Antoninus Pius (35) and Marcus Aurelius (36). The circus (50) next to the amphitheatre was finally completed in AD 162. The physical expansion of the city was also accompanied by a progressive advance in administrative status: it was elevated to the rank of *municipium* in the seventies of the first century, and to that of *colonia* in 109. (Exceptionally, this did not involve the settlement of military veterans, which otherwise justified this rank.) However, the apogee of the city, and the reason why it makes such an unforgettable tourist destination today, is represented by the developments carried out in the reign of the emperor Lucius Septimius Severus and his son Caracalla in the early third century.

Septimius Severus (fig. 59) came from an aristocratic family of Lepcis which had already sent members to sit in the senate at Rome. He himself was a senator, and as governor of Pannonia (approximately Slovenia/Croatia/Hungary) at the time of the assassination of Pertinax in 193, was in a good position to use the three legions under his command to secure recognition as the new emperor. It took him a further three years to eliminate two other rivals, but he then enjoyed a reign of a further fifteen years before dying at York in 211, while on campaign in Britain. Many earlier emperors had displayed their power to the people of Rome by constructing magnificent public spaces, fora and temples, in the centre of the Eternal City, but by the time of Severus there were so many of these that there was little further scope for such projects. He commemorated himself there by an arch which still dominates the Roman Forum, and by the erection of a monumental decorative façade known as the *Septizodium,* where the Via Appia passes beneath the Palatine Hill on its way into the city. (Part of this survived until 1588, when it was dismantled by Pope Sixtus V as a source of building material!) Septimius decided, however, to lavish on his natal city the splendours which he might otherwise have bestowed on the capital. He sponsored the creation of a new civic centre, with a forum (7), a basilica (9) and a temple (8); he carried out a wholesale redevelopment of the harbour (38) and he linked these features together with a broad street (6) lined on either side with shady colonnades such as he had seen when serving with the army in Syria. The cross-roads where the main coastal road intersected the principal street of the city was embellished by an extraordinary *quadrifrons* or four-way arch (2). The scheme shows many signs of really high-quality architectural and urban design, with a subtlety that made clever use of irregular spaces and made them appear, to the casual observer, entirely regular. Not only did it make use of the best decorative marbles that the emperor's quarries could provide, but it is clear that craftsmen skilled in the working of those stones came with them from Asia Minor and elsewhere. Nowhere else in the Roman World can we examine and appreciate in such detail a project conceived on such a scale.

This building program took a good twenty years to complete, and indeed never was fully completed. When work stopped after a formal dedication by Caracalla in 216 (five years after the death of Septimius), much of the architectural detail had still been only roughed out, and it has been argued that the project should have included a second forum, as large as the first and placed symmetrically on the opposite side of the basilica (as in Trajan's Forum in Rome). The necessary space was certainly cleared, but nothing was built. The paucity of modifications and of new building at Lepcis attributable to the following period rather suggests that the city was largely bankrupted by the undertaking, and the fall of the Severan dynasty in 235 will doubtless have resulted in that portion of the city's wealth which was now bound up in imperial estates being diverted elsewhere.

At some time in the first half of the fourth century, probably following earthquake damage in 306–10 (p. 11), a new circuit of defensive walls was built: this is most readily visible today in its north-western part, particularly where it makes use of the Arch of Antoninus Pius as its West or Oea Gate (35). This represents a reduction of the previously defended area from 425 ha to 130 ha. Other constructions dated by inscriptions to this period demonstrate continued vitality, as might be expected, given the stimulus of Lepcis becoming (in c. 303) the capital of the new province of *Tripolitana*. But the city was soon in a decline, hastened both by natural disasters (earthquakes) and by raids on its agricultural hinterland carried out by the tribes of the interior (p. 6). The Vandals took no obvious interest in the area during the fifth century, and when the Byzantines drove them out and re-established 'Roman' rule in 533, it is recorded that much of Lepcis was already deserted and enveloped by the sand. Indeed, the writer Procopius goes so far as to say that during the reign of Justinian but prior to the reconquest (i.e. between 527 and 533) the *Laguatan* of the interior had driven the Vandals out of Lepcis and had emptied it of its inhabitants. The area enclosed by the latest walls amounted to only 44 ha: it enclosed the harbour, the Severan civic buildings (whose massive perimeter walls were well-suited to defensive use) and a small area around the Old Forum. The state of dereliction, even in this area, is indicated by the level at which the postern gate was built behind the temple of Rome and Augustus in the Old Forum (21), and the raised floor-level of the baptistery which installed in the NW corner-chapel of the Severan basilica.

Like the other cities of classical Libya, what was left of Lepcis was not immediately abandoned following the Arab conquest in the seventh century. Excavations in the area of the Flavian temple (39) have yielded evidence for occupation, including pottery-making, down to the tenth century AD. It is likely, however, that the last vestiges of settled occupation came to an end with the arrival of the Bani Hilal in 1051, if not before.

The order in which the monuments are described below corresponds to a circuit of the central area, followed by an excursion to the W along the Oea road and then to the harbour and the outlying monuments to the E. The amphitheatre and circus to the E are most readily reached by road; the harbour is also most conveniently reached from this road, provided that the gates on this side are not padlocked. Otherwise, it has to be approached by a fifteen-minute walk from the main entrance. The size of the site and the richness of the monuments are such that two days can easily be spent here with profit; in one day, the principal monuments of the central area can be visited; if you have only half a day, try to include items 1–9 and 26–31.

A note on the name
In modern literature, the forms Lepcis and Leptis can both be found; Italian speakers particularly favour the latter form as being more euphonious to them and easier on the tongue. This confusion certainly existed in antiquity also.

The original Libyphoenician name took the form **Lpqy**, whence Lepcis, the form that is found exclusively in the local inscriptions; the alternative spelling occurs, however, in many literary sources, and may be influenced by the name of the Roman town of Lepti (Minus) on the Tunisian coast. This last may also have been responsible for Lepcis acquiring the contrasting epithet 'Magna', from the mid-first century AD.

Features at the entrance (1)

On entering the site, one's eye is inescapably drawn to the impressive Arch of Septimius Severus, but before descending the steps to admire this feat of reconstruction, give a moment's attention to a curiosity to your L. Here are some enormous pieces of 'raw' Pentelic marble which were dredged up at Qasr Ahmad, the port of Misrata (about 100 km to the E of Lepcis), during development work some years ago. Quite clearly, the marble must have been on its way from Piraeus in Greece for use in the Severan building project at Lepcis, when either the ship carrying it sank on approaching the harbour, or the blocks fell into the water when being landed.

If you now descend the modern steps (which show the depth of soil now overlying this part of the site) to the paving of the Roman period, you will see on the left-hand side of the road, immediately before the arch, a handsome milestone (fig. 33) which records that in AD 15/16 the proconsul L(ucius) Aelius Lamia built a road into the interior (*in mediterraneum*) for a distance of 44 miles. This is the road which ran via Qusbat onto the Tarhunah plateau, ending in the vicinity of Ain Sharshara (p. 161). It has been plausibly argued that this represents the extent in this direction of the *territorium* of Lepcis, encompassing the most fertile land of the region.

Fig. 33. Lepcis Magna: the milestone of Aelius Lamia

Arch of Septimius Severus** (2)

The four-way Arch of Septimius Severus, dedicated to the emperor by his native city, may now be admired again in something like its original form. There are considerable difficulties however, with regard to its reconstruction, for it appears to break so many accepted rules of architecture. The arch was clearly already partly collapsed in the Byzantine period, for at that time two of the capitals of the corner-pilasters were taken imaginatively to create an ambo (pulpit) in the Severan basilica (9) when that was converted into a

Fig. 34. Lepcis Magna: Arch of Septimius Severus.

church. What you now see in the basilica (with a sense of *déjà vu*) are replicas, the originals having been returned to the arch. At the beginning of the twentieth century a single span of one of the four openings remained in place, and that fell down a few years later. What stands before you is therefore the painstaking work of Italian archaeologists (Sandro Stucchi, Antonino Di Vita and others) over some twenty years. The architecture is bizarre and there is not universal agreement as to how the various elements were originally arranged, but the reconstruction as you see it is certainly a reasonable interpretation of the evidence.

The arch stands at a critical nodal point, where the street leading inland from the heart of the city (conventionally, the *cardo maximus*) intersects the main east–west coastal road. Its importance (though not its utility) is enhanced by setting it on a plinth of three raised steps, thus making its interior impassable to wheeled traffic! The structure was of limestone faced with marble; each face was framed between Corinthian corner-pilasters decorated with vegetal scrolls, and there were winged victories in the spandrels of the arches. In addition, a pair of engaged Corinthian columns projected from each face, carrying extraordinary pointed broken pediments, so positioned as to interfere with the observer's view of the reliefs on the attic above. (This is one of the puzzles of the design.) The reliefs on the attic (now displayed to best effect in the National Museum in Tripoli, p. 31) include two triumphal processions (which were presumably set on opposite faces); a scene of sacrifice involving the imperial family; and a symbolic scene of familial harmony, with Septimius and his elder son Caracalla clasping hands in front of the younger son Geta and in the presence of Hercules and Tyche. Other reliefs consisted of tall, narrow versions of the conventional scene of captives standing beneath military trophies on poles (compare the Arch of Marcus Aurelius in Tripoli, p. 19), and eight figured panels which faced one another in pairs inside the openings of the arch. (Four of the originals of these are on display in Room 4 of the Lepcis Museum.) Some of these show conventional groups of gods (including Septimius as Jupiter-Serapis and Julia Domna as Juno), but one shows the siege of an oriental city, perhaps illustrating the Parthian campaigns of Septimius. The vaults of the four arches were coffered, as was the interior of the dome. The pendentives which mark the transition from the square structure below to the dome above are decorated with imperial eagles standing on globes, with their wings outstretched.

The style of the different parts of the arch is very mixed: some of the decoration suggests sculptors from Aphrodisias in Asia Minor; other pieces – particularly the historical reliefs – show similarities with the carving on the Arch of Severus in the Roman Forum or with contemporary sculpture in Syria. The date of the arch is not precisely fixed: it must have been constructed after 198, but before 209. It is perhaps most likely that it was thrown up in haste to coincide with the visit of the emperor

to his birthplace in AD 203. The issue is further complicated by the fact that the core of the arch was constructed of limestone from Ras al-Hammam (which was no longer being quarried by the end of the second century) and was designed in Punic cubits, whereas the design of the marble veneer was worked out in Roman feet! Di Vita has therefore suggested that a pre-existing arch was adapted to a new purpose.

From the Severan Arch, proceed to the R (south-eastwards) and follow this street until the next excavated junction, at which you can turn L. As you go, note the pattern of the street paving and the evident presence of a drain running beneath the centre. At the street corner, just before the turning and slightly above head-height, note the carved apotropaic panel. It takes the form of a *tabula ansata* in which is portrayed a variety of objects intended to ward off evil. These are the Evil Eye itself (at the R), something which looks like a leek (!), and a creature which has the hind-parts, legs and tail of a horse, but which is otherwise a winged phallus; this is a very potent object, the power of which is increased by the fact that it has further genitalia of its own! Representations of this kind are common at Lepcis, and indeed generally in the Roman world. They are imbued with magical power and are placed particularly at street corners, which one must concede to be obvious focal points of evil! At their simplest, just the male genitalia may be represented: these do NOT ever represent an advertisement for a brothel, whatever the guides (or guidebooks) may suggest to the contrary. One of the most complex representations at Lepcis may be seen in the street on the NW side of the portico behind the theatre (31).

Hadrianic Baths** (3)

After turning the corner, the road which you are following leads you into a huge rectangular space terminated by apses at either end. This is the *palaestra* attached to the Hadrianic Baths, which open off the right-hand side. Huge public bathing establishments of this kind may be imagined as a Roman counterpart to the leisure centres of the modern day: not only did they include facilities for bathing in a congenial social environment, but the *palaestra* provided space for athletics, there was a swimming pool, capacious public toilets and a number of peripheral rooms which could have served other purposes. Sometimes they included a library, though there is no direct evidence for this here. The *palaestra* was surrounded by a portico of Corinthian columns with shafts of cipollino marble; on the N (left-hand) side there were also two colonnaded *exedrae* or recesses which would have provided congenial shaded spaces for sitting out and conversing.

The baths were dedicated in the reign of the emperor Hadrian, in 137. (The dating of the proconsulate of the dedicator, P. Valerius Priscus, has been revised downwards from 126/7, which will be found in earlier publications.) This was the first monumental complex at Lepcis to make extensive use of coloured marbles imported from other parts of the Mediterranean world; not only for columns, but also as a decorative, multi-coloured facing for walls and floors. The complex was laid out according to the principles established in Rome by the Baths of Trajan, with a grandiose symmetrical suite of cold and heated rooms (see fig. 35). The central entrance from the palaestra led into the *natatio* (N), a swimming pool surrounded on three sides by a portico of Corinthian columns in pink breccia. The further side of this space is largely occupied by a row of massive piers, which are not original but probably date to renovations under Commodus (180–192), when the *frigidarium* and adjoining areas were substantially rebuilt (due to subsidence?) by a local magistrate, Rusonianus. Four doorways led from the area of the *natatio* into a corridor which surrounded the massive central hall of the *frigidarium* (F). This great hall, 30 × 15 m in plan, was roofed after the Commodan restoration with three concrete cross-vaults springing from eight massive Corinthian columns of cipollino. The floor and walls were covered with marble, and the vaults were decorated with glass mosaic. On the south wall have been reassembled fragments of the inscription recording the restorations carried out by Rusonianus, who obtained permission from the emperor to divert funds allocated to gladiatorial displays for the purpose. The name of the emperor Commodus was erased after his downfall, and that of Septimius Severus was substituted. In one of the small rooms nearby (marked x on fig. 35), a fallen segment of the ceiling mosaic is displayed. At the E and W ends of the hall, arches opened into cold plunge-baths, again lined with marble and surrounded by Corinthian columns of grey granite (fig. 36).

From the *frigidarium*, the bather would progress, through the central opening in the S wall, to the warm room or *tepidarium* (T). In its original form, this had a single central plunge-bath, but after the Commodan modifications it was supplied with three, the two lateral ones being formed by closing off that part of the corridor which had originally surrounded all four

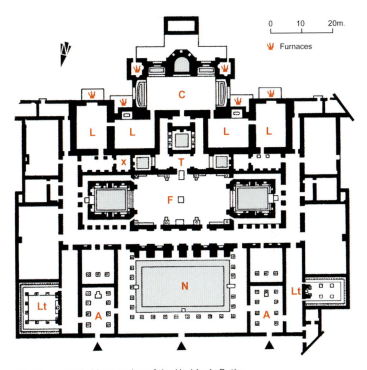

Fig. 35. *Lepcis Magna: plan of the Hadrianic Baths.*
A. Apodyterium
C. Caldarium
F. Frigidarium
L. Laconicum
Lt. *Latrine*
N. Natatio
T. Tepidarium

sides of the *frigidarium*. The central bath was surrounded by an elaborate columned enclosure, behind which a small vestibule led to the hot steam room or *caldarium* (C). This was another vast covered space, measuring 22 × 11 m and roofed with a barrel vault. The five hot plunge-baths here date from the Commodan restoration, and the previous arrangement of the room is unclear. The room is placed on the S side of the complex in order to take advantage of the heat of the sun, but the huge windows must still have been glazed in order to keep the heat in. Not only were the floor and the basins in this room heated, but the walls also:

traces may be seen of the hollow flue-tiles with which they were lined. By this means the heat from the external furnaces was drawn across the floor and up each of the walls behind the surface veneer. The gases were then typically gathered in a manifold which ran around the room just beneath the vault, and this would have had vents to the exterior at each corner. On either side of the *caldarium* were pairs of *laconica* (L, L), hot dry rooms in which further details of the heating system are clearly visible. Behind the baths, close to the Wadi Libdah, is a row of stone-built water-cisterns; near these was discovered an inscription recording

Fig. 36. Lepcis Magna: marble opulence in the Hadrianic Baths.

was completely covered, with its roof supported on four columns of cipollino standing on plinths. The columnar halls on either side of the *natatio* (A, A) are likely to have been *apodyteria*, undressing-rooms.

The effect of the coloured marble everywhere would have been extremely lavish, and this was further heightened by large quantities of marble statuary. The spaces between the columns around the various pools were filled with figures of gods, mythological figures and emperors, while the *exedrae* on the far side of the *palaestra* provided a suitable setting for statues of local worthies and their spouses. An enormous wealth of these was found by the excavators, and they now grace the museums of Tripoli, Lepcis and Zlitan. The remarkable state of preservation of many of these statues is due to the fact that they were found overturned in a thick layer of mud. It has been suggested that this resulted from the rupture of the dam upstream on the Wadi Libdah (54) in the earthquake 'of 365', though if an earthquake was the cause, a tsunami seems a more likely explanation for the mud. The baths must have been severely damaged and were not subsequently restored.

Great Nymphaeum** (4)
At the E end of the *palaestra* of the Hadrianic Baths, there is an irregular open space which constituted a cardinal point in the great civic development scheme of Septimius Severus. Directly opposite is the entrance to the grand

the provision of a water-supply in 119/20 by a certain Q(uintus) Servilius Candidus. This is likely to have been the aqueduct which brought water to Lepcis from the Wadi Caam, some 20 km to the E (see p. 147).

The other peripheral rooms of the complex are now of uncertain purpose, apart from the two suites of latrines (Lt, Lt) on either side near the entrance. Here may be seen the remains of the marble seats, placed above a flushing drain, and with a water channel running in front of the feet of the sitter, by means of which (with a sponge), one might clean oneself. The large suite, on the E side, was open to the sky in the centre, but protected by a Corinthian portico above the seats. The opposing suite (necessarily smaller in order to fit the bold design into an awkward site)

Fig. 37. Lepcis Magna: reconstruction of the Severan Nymphaeum.

colonnaded boulevard which led from this point, past the new forum and basilica on its left-hand side, to the remodelled harbour. The main carriageway was over 20 m wide, and it was flanked on either side by covered porticoes which were themselves 10 m wide. Arches led from the piazza into these porticoes. But this was part only of the scheme. Originally, an exactly similar colonnaded street led from the piazza inland, behind the Hadrianic Baths and along the edge of the wadi. Unfortunately, over the course of the centuries, the wadi has reasserted its ownership of this space and there is almost no trace left of the Roman street; we do not know how or where it met the coastal road. The angle between the two streets was filled by a monumental *nymphaeum* (4) or fountain, part of which still stands almost to its original height. This took the form of a two-storey semicircular

recess (see fig. 37), built essentially as a solid mass of concrete, with a stone facing towards the piazza which was in turn veneered with marble. The recess and the flanking walls were articulated with superimposed colonnades framing niches, which would presumably have housed statues. Water flowed from spouts beneath the niches into the semicircular basin beneath, and overflowed thence through seven further lead spouts into the long trapezoidal basin in front. This basin has been altered during the course of its existence, with the construction of a lattice screen across the front of it, but something of the sort must always have been part of the design. The solidity of Roman concrete is well demonstrated here, both by the half of the hemicycle that still stands, and by the other half which, undermined by the return of the wadi, has fallen onto its back more or less as a single mass.

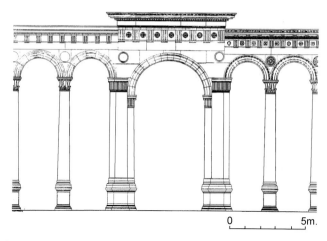

Fig. 38. Lepcis Magna: reconstruction of the façade of the Colonnaded Street at one of the minor junctions.

The stylistic parallels to this form of decorative architecture are to be found in theatre stage-buildings (such as that at Sabratha) and other monumental *nymphaea*. This kind of façade is also used to good effect in the early second-century library of Celsus at Ephesus.

The side of the piazza opposite the Great Nymphaeum has been much altered in the Byzantine period, but now shows the columns of a partly-reconstructed curved portico. This is apparently later in date than the *nymphaeum*, and perhaps represents an attempt to finish off the piazza at a time when both money and architectural flair were running out.

Colonnaded Street* (5)

The former grandeur of the Colonnaded Street can readily be appreciated from the fallen elements which are still liberally scattered on the ground at the landward end; further down towards the harbour, its remains are still being progressively washed away by occasional floods of the Wadi Libdah. In appearance, it must have resembled the

colonnaded streets that Severus would have come across when commanding the army in Syria: such streets may still be seen, for instance, at Apamea and Palmyra, or at Jerash in modern Jordan. The carriageway was lined with porticoes of cipollino columns (over 350 in number), the height of which was accentuated both by raising them upon square plinths and by the fact that, instead of flat architraves, they carried arcades above. The internal height of the porticoes, which had flat roofs, was therefore over 11 m (which may be compared with the current maximum permitted vehicle height in the EU of 5 m!). For most of its length, the capitals and bases of the columns were of grey-white Proconnesian marble and the capitals were Corinthian. The stretch fronting the forum and basilica, however, was given added emphasis by exchanging the Proconnesian marble for the honey-colour of Pentelic marble from Attica; the Corinthian capitals were also exchanged for the 'Pergamene' lotus-and-acanthus type which is used inside the forum. The junctions with side-streets were handled by creating wider openings between the columns, spanned by arches. The elements of that next to the S corner of the forum, including two huge monolithic piers of white limestone, are scattered close to where they stood, and have enabled the reconstruction drawing in fig. 38.

The interior of the porticoes was probably never finished in accordance with the original design: no trace of paving has been discovered, nor indeed do the walls show any sign of stucco or of marble veneer. Beyond the forum and basilica, on the same side of the street, there is a fine grey limestone arch, typical of first or second-century construction and presumably surviving from some earlier structure on this line. Further on, there is a second semicircular *nymphaeum*, much smaller than the Great Nymphaeum at the head of the street, and which simply opened off the rear of the portico. It was, however, originally decorated in a similar fashion with two tiers of niches in the rear wall. In the Byzantine period it was crudely adapted into a small church.

Church (6)

As you enter the Colonnaded Street from the landward end, you see first two great portals in the enclosing wall on the left-hand side. The structure to which these originally gave access is unknown to us; almost all trace of it was removed in the sixth century, when a church was inserted into this space. One can make out the remains of the nave and the aisles, terminating in an apse at the SE end, against the outer wall of the Colonnaded Street. The apse was flanked by two sacristies, and there was a baptistery with a typical Byzantine cruciform font in the E corner. Beside the church was an extensive cemetery: some of the graves have flat cover slabs; others were upstanding chests, faced and covered with stucco. Many of the graves had painted or (in one case) incised inscriptions.

Severan Forum** (7)

Proceeding further along the Colonnaded Street, the visitor sees on the left a long row of *tabernae* (shops) which open off the portico. In the centre of these and at either end were entrances which led into the *forum novum severianum*, the New Severan Forum. This is now one of the greatest monuments of Roman antiquity which has come down to us, both because of the grandeur of its original conception and because of the resources which were devoted by the Italian colonial authorities in the 1920s and 1930s to its excavation and partial restoration. In order to appreciate the difficulties of this task, it is worth recalling the words written in 1927 by Renato Bartoccini, when reporting on the opening campaign.

> I shall remember always the impression which I formed when I first explored the area. Interrupted here and there by masses of masonry, the heavy mantle of sand spread itself across the broad expanse of buildings which had lost their roofs, piling itself up against obstacles and then dropping down into deep hollows between one wall and the next. Towards the west, sand was followed by more sand, but at a much lower level and sometimes anchored by dense patches of evergreen scrub; on the east, the deep trench of the wadi marked an intractable barrier to the march of the dunes, guarded more effectively by the strong offshore wind which funnels down its course than by the pathetic and intermittent trickle of water in its bed.

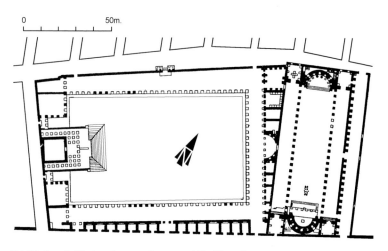

Fig. 39. Lepcis Magna: Severan Forum and Basilica, plan.

All this is fine weather – but when the wind gets up, what a sight! The humps of the dunes become corrugated, from their summits rise tall plumes of dust and gradually and mightily the whole mass begins to move. Walls, columns – a pilaster – previously unseen, reawaken from decades of slumber, while elsewhere others are swallowed up, perhaps so to remain until we reach them with our teams of workmen. All is confusion on this shifting terrain: one has to close one's mind to the fear that it inspires, for otherwise one would never dare to face up to so formidable an opponent. Indeed, it is true that here the excavation has to be undertaken in the spirit of moving to the assault of a well-defended fortress: the application of the normal criteria for the conduct of such work to the clearance of the Imperial Forum at Lepcis would lead only to ignominious failure.

It will be evident from the plan (fig. 39) that the architect responsible for the project was highly skilled in imposing an apparent regularity on a very irregular site, conditioned by the prior development of the city.

At various points, subtle wedge-shaped spaces disguised necessary changes of orientation. Thus the interior of the NW forum portico tapered from one end to the other, a wedge-shaped array of *tabernae* between the forum and the Colonnaded Street masked another change of alignment there, and the triangular space between forum and the basilica was similarly masked by a row of rooms of differing size. The outcome was the creation of a truly rectangular space, about 100 × 60 m, paved with Proconnesian marble (almost completely gone, though the concrete bedding shows clearly how the slabs were laid) and surrounded on three sides by lofty colonnaded porticoes. The space was dominated at the SW end by a temple on a lofty podium (fig. 41); here the porticoes were articulated into two open columnar halls on either side of the temple, with two further halls in the corners. The colonnades were composed of cipollino columns, with bases and lotus-and-acanthus capitals both of Pentelic marble; above these ran an arcade of greyish-white

Fig. 40. Lepcis Magna: the Severan Forum.

limestone, incorporating a series of circular medallions in Proconnesian marble, one above each column. The medallions, representing either Medusa-heads (with snakes in their hair) or Nereids (sea creatures of some sort, which appear to be surrounded by dolphins or even crocodiles), are carved with great vigour and individuality. The arcades were surmounted by a carved vegetal frieze and a cornice. Standing on the cornice above each column was, at the very least, a square pedestal of Proconnesian marble. There are many of these lying about in the forum, and it has recently been argued that they carried an upper colonnade (the model in the National Museum in Tripoli follows this interpretation), but of the corresponding columns (which must have been nearly a hundred in number) there is very little trace. A considerable stretch of the arcading itself has been re-erected, which gives some idea of its appearance, though one has, of course, to imagine it raised up on top of the columns. It may readily be seen here how much of the intended decorative detail (e.g. the mouldings around the

arches) was only roughed out with a drill or not even begun.

The internal faces of the walls surrounding the forum were decorated with multi-coloured marble veneer: the many square holes in the masonry result from the bronze clamps which originally held it in place, and at ground-level there remain occasional pilaster-bases and fragments of slabs in position. In the Byzantine period, when the forum became a military barracks, the doors into the *tabernae* along the Colonnaded Street were blocked up, and new openings were made through the SE wall of the forum. The high level of the sills of these openings reflects the accumulation of soil in the area in the late period. On the NE side, the interior of the portico was elaborated with a row of engaged columns running along its length and framing entrances into a series of rooms which masked the difference in alignment between the forum and the basilica. The basilica was reached either through a central opening, set at the back of a semicircular *exedra*, or through openings at either end of the range:

that at the right-hand end was a simple doorway, while at the other end the greater interval between the buildings was filled by a fine colonnaded hall.

On the NW side, the rear wall of the forum portico presents a fine plain elevation towards the street on that side, with handsome ashlar masonry rising above a foundation course of orthostats (upright blocks). The central entrance into the forum on this side is framed by a projecting porch. The entire length of this wall has, in fact, been re-erected, having been found uniformly fallen inwards into the forum. The excavator, Bartoccini, was very puzzled by the ample evidence that this had been brought about deliberately, and with the use of gunpowder! The effect of the mining is not very apparent on the NW wall, where the damage to the stonework has been made good with cement (though the line of damage, approximately at shoulder-height, may easily be made out). In the street behind the temple, however, where the wall did not fall (because it had the mass of the temple podium behind it), the voids created by the explosions, the red discoloration of the stone by fire and, indeed, the drill-holes for the charges are all clearly visible. When could such a thing have been done? Clearly not before the introduction of gunpowder to the Mediterranean World in the thirteenth century, but surely prior to the depredations of Lemaire in the late eighteenth, for it resulted in the columns he sought being buried, not exposed. It seems plausible that the assault on these buildings may have been made by the Ottoman Turks during the period of their conflict (between 1535 and 1551) with the Knights of Malta, who were established in the castle at Tripoli while the Turks opposed them from a base at Tajurah. The intention would

have been to reduce the likelihood of the ruins being refortified and held by the European powers who were attempting to reassert their authority over North Africa.

Temple 'of the Gens Septimia' (8)
The dedication of the temple which overlooks the forum is uncertain: only a very small fragment of the inscription from its façade survives, enough to suggest that it included the word *concordia*, which has been interpreted as part of *Concordia Augustorum*. This would be an allusion to the harmony of the ruling house (the *gens septimia*) which was repeatedly proclaimed in public statements (on coins and inscriptions, and indeed in the sculptures of the Severan Arch at Lepcis) and so utterly negated when Caracalla murdered his brother Geta. An alternative possibility is that the temple was dedicated to the patron gods of the city, Liber Pater/Shadrap and Hercules/Milk'ashtart, who are celebrated on the pilasters of the basilica (below). The contemporary historian Cassius Dio complained that Septimius had built 'an excessively large temple to Bacchus and Hercules,' and while he does not specify where this was, the temple in the Severan Forum at Lepcis could well have attracted this criticism.

The temple has suffered greatly: probably because it stood up above the other ruins, its superstructure has been robbed out almost completely, down to the foundation-courses. However, the builders' setting-out lines which survive on the remaining blocks make the arrangement clear. The *cella* was almost exactly square, set against the rear of the podium and the outside wall of the forum in the Italian manner. The colonnade ran down either side as

Fig. 41. Lepcis Magna: reconstruction of the temple in the Severan Forum.

usual, but across the front it composed a porch three rows deep. The columns were monoliths of pink granite from Aswan in Egypt, slightly over 7 m long, and they were set on top of carved square plinths of Pentelic marble; the Corinthian capitals above, as also the frieze and the entire walls of the *cella*, were of Proconnesian marble, which probably explains the almost total disappearance of the walls. The apex-block from the rear wall has fallen outwards across the street, and may be seen lying on the ground: it is over 5 m long and its weight is estimated to be about thirty tonnes. Some of the square plinths were elaborately carved with mythological gigantomachy scenes (the Battle between the Gods and the Giants: the giants are readily distinguished by the facts that (a) they have fish-tails instead of legs and (b) they are invariably losing!). These are mostly very battered, but some are on display in the National Museum in Tripoli (Room 9C, p. 28) and others are in the Lepcis Museum (Room 11).

Various constructional details show that the design of the temple was altered as the building progressed – for instance, the podium was extended forward by 4 m – and it seems very likely that the omission of four columns from the inner part of the porch was also a change of plan. These columns, already on site, were then without a home and were made use of in the apses of the basilica (see below).

Severan Basilica** (9)

The Severan Basilica took the form of a rectangular hall, divided by colonnades into a nave and two aisles; at either end it terminated in an apse flanked by side-chapels. At the N corner, two of the columns, with their linking architrave, have stood since antiquity. They show part of the dedicatory inscription which ran along both sides of the nave, and which was repeated on the outsides of the end-walls of the building. This records that the building was begun by Septimius Severus and was completed by his son Caracalla in 216. The colonnades were of the Corinthian order, with pink granite shafts and capitals and bases of Proconnesian marble; they were two storeys high, supporting a gallery above the aisles. Above the upper colonnade there

Fig. 42. Lepcis Magna: the Severan Basilica.

pilasters on the lower level at either end was another pair, closely flanking the apse, and of purely decorative intent. The decoration on these, the work of Asiatic sculptors from Aphrodisias, consists of figure-scenes enclosed in vine-scrolls; the pilasters at the NW end show vines laden with grapes, and the motifs relate to the god Dionysus/ Liber Pater; those at the opposite end are without fruit, and are filled with scenes from the life of Hercules. These two (Roman versions of the Punic deities Shadrap and Milk'ashtart) were the patron gods of the city and of the Severan family. The brick surfaces of the apses (despite elements of decorative treatment) must always have been intended to be veneered with marble. They were also broken up by two tiers of round-headed niches, framed by projecting orders of Ionic columns with pink granite shafts. It is clear from the brickwork into which their entablature is anchored that these columns were originally intended to extend uniformly around each apse. At some point, however, the design was changed, and instead a central feature was inserted at each end, composed of two taller columns set upon high octagonal pedestals; above these (if correctly restored) was an entablature which anchored them to the wall behind, carrying two rectangular pedestals carved with the foreparts of gryphons, and then a further architrave across the top. The central columns at each end correspond in dimensions to those of the temple in the forum, where we have seen that a change of plan may

must have been a clerestory of some sort, and it is thought that the caryatid figures, some of which may be seen on the ground, may have stood at this level between the windows. The reconstruction in fig. 43 suggests that the ceiling will have been some 26 m above the floor.

The apses at either end were constructed of brick-faced concrete rubble, and carried semi-domes. They were highly ornate. The main colonnades terminated against the end walls in four square pilasters of Proconnesian marble which were decorated in high relief with acanthus scrolls enclosing protomes (foreparts) of animals springing from rosettes; the corresponding pilasters in the upper storey were simpler, with vertical fluting. Between each pair of structural

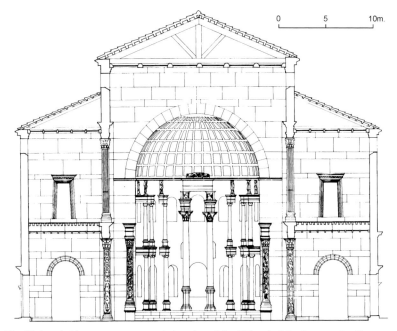

Fig. 43. Lepcis Magna: reconstructed elevation of the NW end of the Severan Basilica.

have resulted in four spare columns; this provides a plausible explanation for their late use in the basilica, and it may be noted that the gryphon-pedestals have two further counterparts in the same temple, where they flank the corners of the staircase against the temple podium.

Behind each apse is a staircase which originally led to the galleries above the aisles. That at the SE end is still accessible, and provides a fine view from above.

The floor of the basilica was paved with Proconnesian marble and the walls also were veneered with marble at the ground-floor level; within the upper galleries the absence of holes for fixings shows that they were merely stuccoed. The use of marble on the walls seems to represent another change of plan (or perhaps a failure

of communication between different teams of workmen), for the arched entrances to the flanking chapels at either end were initially provided with simple framing mouldings, which were then chiselled back to make a flat surface for the veneer.

An integral part of the design of the basilica seems to have been the street which flanked it on the NE side, and yet this is also curious and suggests some variation from the original intention. The street is terminated at either end by an archway, and the outer wall of the basilica on this side is decorated with an engaged colonnade of cipollino columns with bases and lotus-and-acanthus capitals of Pentelic marble. It seems rather over-elaborate, given that the street is not very wide and is enclosed by a plain wall on the opposite side: one could not really step back far enough to appreciate the magnificence of this façade, which is in effect identical to that in the NE forum portico on the opposite side of the building. This is one of the reasons for supposing that the original design envisaged a second porticoed piazza corresponding to the Severan forum, on the E side of the basilica.

In the sixth century, the basilica was restored for use as a church. The raised floor of the SE apse was extended forwards and the altar was placed here, enclosed by a chancel rail which was constructed from elements of the decorative order in the NW apse (evidently fallen or dismantled) together with pilasters from the Severan Arch at the entrance to the city. Two corner pilaster-capitals from that arch (now replaced in position and substituted here by replicas) were used imaginatively to build a raised ambo in the centre of the nave. In three of the four corner-chapels the former flat timber ceilings were replaced by sandstone barrel-vaults, and in the NW chapel a full-immersion cruciform font of typical Byzantine type was installed. The ground-level in each of these rooms was by now about a metre above the original floor, presumably a sign of previous long-term abandonment.

The execution of the building project
The basilica, like other parts of the Severan complex, provides interesting insights into the practicalities of executing such an ambitious scheme. In the first instance, one must imagine how the vast numbers of columns required would have been ordered from the quarries at Carystos on the Greek island of Euboea (for the cipollino) or from Aswan, far up the Nile in Egypt (for the pink granite). Weight would

have been at a premium, and the columns would therefore have been ordered to size, with limited provision for trimming and polishing on site. The Greek quarry-masons were good at this, and the cipollino columns are very uniform in length. The Egyptians were not nearly so competent, and the builders at Lepcis were faced with the difficulty of creating buildings and colonnades from columns which, when delivered to the site, varied in length by as much as 25 cm. The only practical solution was to stretch, or compress, the capitals and bases in order to achieve a level surface for the entablature above. If you look at the re-erected columns along the SW side of the basilica nave, this phenomenon will be readily apparent. The carving of these elements had therefore to be done on site, and it would have been for this reason that large raw blocks of marble (such as that displayed at the entrance to the site) would have been imported. The work was certainly done in part by Greek-speaking craftsmen, for they have left their signatures on the undersides of capitals and in various other places. Such signatures are visible on the capitals lying in the street on the NE side of the basilica.

There is also interesting evidence here of the terminal stage of the original project. One has to imagine the coffers being empty and a date being fixed for the formal inauguration. The final frantic efforts would have been devoted to making the most obvious parts look as good as possible, while no time or effort was to be expended on anything else. If you look closely at the column-bases in the basilica nave, particularly those near the centre of the NE side, it will be apparent that in several cases the final rounding and polishing of the mouldings was carried out only on the half facing the nave, while the side facing the aisle remains crudely roughed out! It was also recorded by the Italian excavators that in the street on the NE side there were many surplus architectural elements which had never actually been used. So presumably the ceremonial dedication-party, on its tour of the buildings, would have been led hastily down the centre of the basilica and would have been steered carefully away from the street alongside. We should bear in mind that, while we admire the grandeur of these buildings, throughout their actual working existence this street, with its handsome colonnade, looked like a building-site with a clutter of unfinished blocks!

Byzantine Gate (10)

The most convenient circuit now proceeds from the Severan monuments to the 'Old' or original forum which was the focus of civic life prior to the Severan development project. Follow the street which leads directly away from the N corner of the basilica and take the next turning to the R, into the *cardo maximus*. (There are some new, unpublished, excavations in the *insula* on your L.) This brings you to the Byzantine Gate, one of the entrances to the revitalized city of the sixth century. The walls, built of reused materials, stand here to a considerable height and are pierced by a single, tall, rectangular opening flanked by projecting square towers. The towers were accessed by arched entrances on the inside face, and the parapet-walk by a staircase next to the S tower. On the ground nearby are fragments of an inscription from the time of Vespasian, probably from an arch, which have been recovered from the construction of the wall.

Old Forum* (11–22)

Beyond the Byzantine Gate, one shortly reaches the trapezoidal open space of the **Old Forum (11)**, of which an enlarged plan is shown in fig. 44. It is in this area, close to both the sea and the mouth of the Wadi Libdah, that the earliest traces of occupation have been found, and it was here that a civic centre began to be developed in the late first century BC. It then acquired progressively the regular attributes of such a centre: temples to the gods of the city (and later to the Roman Imperial House), a basilica for the law courts and civil administration and a *curia* in which the Council of the city could meet. Towards the N corner of the piazza one may make out, in the paving in front of the Temple of Hercules, the hollow letter-forms of an **inscription (12)**, which record the paving of the area by the proconsul Cn(aeus) Calpurnius Piso in the period 5 BC–AD 2. The letters themselves were of bronze and have long since been prized out for their metal, but the triangular punctuation-marks (presumably too small to be worth the effort) still remain. It may be doubted that the visible paving actually goes back to this time: it is more likely that the inscription was retained when the whole area was renovated, with the installation of porticoes on three sides, in the time of Nero. An inscription on a pedestal standing in front of the Temple of Rome and Augustus (of peculiar aspect, since again its lettering was of bronze which has been prized out) records that this work was completed in AD 53/4 by Caius, son of Hanno in honour of his grandson. We are here brought face-to-face with the Punic heritage of Lepcis. This was a Punic city before it was a Roman one: the leading citizens of whom we know from inscriptions

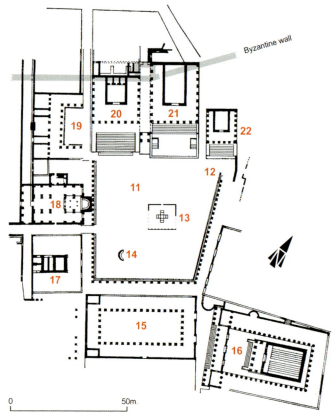

Fig. 44. Lepcis Magna: plan of the Old Forum and surrounding buildings.

11. Old Forum
12. Inscription of Piso
13. Baptistery
14. Severan exedra
15. Basilica
16. Curia

17. Temple of Cybele
18. Trajanic temple/church
19. Oriental temple
20. Temple of Liber Pater
21. Temple of Rome and Augustus
22. Temple of Hercules

retained Punic names and held Punic magistracies (the city was still governed in the first century AD by *sufetes*, not *duumviri*). Furthermore, they recorded their acts in the neo-Punic script and language (seen on the bottom of the stone) as well as in Latin.

In the middle of the forum is a **baptistery (13)** with a cruciform Byzantine font, associated with the church which was built on the SW side of the piazza. To the S of this is a **semicircular exedra (14)** of Severan date, which once provided a shady seat surmounted by statues. In front of it, a *tabula lusoria* or gaming-board is marked out on the paving.

The **basilica (15)** on the SE side of the forum is of South-Italian type (i.e. like that at Pompeii): an aisled hall with its principal axis longitudinal. Thus the main entrances were not from the forum itself but at the NE end, and the offices and the tribunals of the magistrates were at the SW end. The remains that we see, with grey granite columns surmounted by Corinthian capitals, date from a restoration in the fourth century AD, probably following the earthquake of AD 306–10 (p. 11: the porticoes of the forum were restored at the same time); the original building was constructed in the first half of the first century AD and had limestone columns, differently spaced. Their positions may be detected by the use of coarse marble mosaic to repair the floor where their bases had been.

Excavations around the basilica in recent years by a team from the University of Messina have reached some of the earliest levels of settlement on the site, with substantial structures going back to the seventh century BC. One trench has been left open with a protective cover over it, but is unrewarding to the casual observer.

The *curia* **(16)** or municipal council-house stood just beyond the SE corner of the Old Forum, facing the basilica. It was a rectangular, temple-like structure standing on a podium and with a frontal porch of cipollino columns with Corinthian capitals; within, there were the typical low, longitudinal steps of a debating-chamber, on which the seats of the magistrates would have been placed, facing across the chamber. The building was given added dignity by standing in a raised courtyard, approached by frontal steps and surrounded internally on three sides by a portico with columns of sandstone. The complex is probably to be attributed to the second century.

On the opposite side of the basilica, and opening into the SW portico of the Old Forum, stood a courtyard containing a small **temple to *Magna Mater*** or Cybele **(17)**, the Phrygian mother-goddess, dedicated in 71/2. Beyond this, across the street leading into the forum from the Byzantine Gate, stood a temple of Trajanic date, the podium of which can be made out beneath the superstructure of a **late Roman church (18)**. Paired columns of grey granite divide the interior into nave and aisles; these probably carried arcades and, above those, two barrel-vaults intersecting at right-angles. The apse projects into the former portico of the forum, and a sacristy on the NW side, with the base of a staircase, shows that there was access to the roof or to galleries above the aisles. The altar stood on a raised platform in front of the apse, beneath a *ciborium* supported by four columns. At the SW end of the church, a narthex was built across a former street, but the doorways on either side of the apse clearly indicate that the main thoroughfare was still the forum. The church was certainly built before the Byzantine reconquest of North Africa, and therefore probably in the early fifth century AD; it is equally clear that the baptistery in the centre of the forum, while associated with it, must post-date that event. This is indicated both by the particular architectural characteristics of the two structures and by the very different mortars used in their construction.

A particularly poignant note is struck here by the inscribed grave-slabs, to be seen both outside the doorway on the N side of the apse and inside the church. They commemorate, amongst others, five children of the verger (*loki serbatoris*) Stefanus: Sambas (aged 8), Demetria (3), Juliana (1), Anna (1) and Longinus (one week). Three of them died in a space of three days, probably in an epidemic. Note how here, as earlier in the Roman period, parents specify with absolute precision the ages at which their children died: so many years, so many months and so many days.

In the W corner of the Old Forum stood yet another **temple (19)**, of oriental rather than Greco-Roman design, constructed by a woman, Calpurnia Honesta, in 152/3. It took the form of a three-sided portico, paved with Proconnesian marble and with columns of cipollino, behind which a row of three separate *exedrae*, separated by passageways, occupied the full width of the rear wall. Another temple of similar design stands not far away on the sea-shore (24). The excavation of this area yielded a series of sculpted reliefs which include figures of Tyche, Liber Pater, Minerva, Roma and Mithras. It is thought that the temple was dedicated to a Punic deity, such as Tanit-Astarte-Caelestis, assimilated to Tyche/Fortuna.

The NW side of the Old Forum has been much affected by the enclosure of the area within the Byzantine defences. These run across the podia of the temples on this side, partly cutting them off and showing that they were largely collapsed and buried when the wall was built. The earliest temple in the forum area is the westernmost of these (20): it was built originally of the soft local sandstone (replaced in the second century by marble) while its neighbours are of the fine grey limestone from Ras al-Hammam, a few km to the east of the city and which began to be quarried in the time of Augustus. It stands at the rear of a high podium in the Italian manner and is believed to have been dedicated to **Liber Pater/Shadrap**, of whom a colossal statue was found nearby. The statue is now in Room 7 of the National Museum in Tripoli. Liber Pater may

have derived some additional income from small lock-up shops let into the sides of the podium of his temple.

The central temple on this side was dedicated to **Rome and Augustus (21)**, though there is some reason to believe that it may originally have belonged to Hercules/Milk'ashtart, the other patron god of the city. Hercules seems to have been displaced to the third, and much smaller temple to the right. The **Temple of Hercules (22)**, the columns of which have now been partially re-erected on modern stylobates, was completed in AD 5, and seems to have provided the model for the rebuilding of the larger temple, taken over by Rome and Augustus and completed between AD 14 and 19. Both had columns of grey limestone and of the Ionic order; the columns of the larger temple were replaced in marble in the second century, apart from the engaged half-columns at the rear, which have stood since antiquity. The top of the podium of this temple was also linked to that of Liber Pater by means of arches which spanned the narrow intervening street.

The podium of the Temple of Rome and Augustus was reached by staircases let into its sides; the front of the podium was sheer and decorated, as in Rome itself, with bows of ships (*rostra*). This provided a suitable platform for orators to address the citizenry. This temple to the ruler-cult of the Roman Empire was also embellished by many very large statues, found in the vicinity, of the first Imperial family. These are now to be seen in Room 9A of the National Museum in Tripoli.

As one leaves the Old Forum at the N corner, between the Temple of Rome and Augustus and that of Hercules, there lie on the ground to the R, just on the foreshore, three huge columns of cipollino marble. Their size shows them to have come from the Hadrianic Baths (3), far across the site. They were dragged to the shore by the French consul, Claude Lemaire, when he was exporting marble from Lepcis in the late seventeenth century (p. 87). These three escaped being shipped to France, as he found them too heavy for the barges he was using to get the material from shore to ship. They were subsequently eyed by Commander Smyth when he was loading pieces for the Prince Regent in 1817, but the Royal Navy could not manage them either!

Temple of Serapis (23)

This precinct, which occupies one end of an *insula*, belongs to the mid-second century AD as now seen. It is however built over an earlier structure on the same site, which is presumed to date from the time when this part of the city was laid out, around the turn of the era. It is entered through a passageway flanked by rooms on either side. The space then opens out into a courtyard paved in yellow limestone, containing a tetrastyle prostyle temple (i.e. with four columns across the front only) flanked by porticoes along either side; each of these is terminated by a room with an apsidal recess. The temple stands slightly forward of the rear wall of the precinct, leaving space for a passageway behind. In front of the temple steps still stands an altar, built of sandstone rubble and originally encased in Proconnesian marble. Note the pink marble veneer (from NW Turkey) on the walls of the rooms on either side of the temple.

A rich body of both inscriptions and sculpture was found in this sanctuary. Some of the inscribed statue-bases are still in position; many of the sculptures are on display in Room 7 of the museum, including a fine statue

of Serapis in black marble with head, hands and feet in white marble and Cerberus, the three-headed dog that guards the entrance to the Underworld, at his feet. The inscriptions are almost all in Greek, reflecting the Hellenistic culture of Alexandria and of the eastern Mediterranean where the cult had its greatest following. Particularly notable are two inscriptions cut on the ends of the enclosing flanks of the temple stairway. They record how the father, sister, brother-in-law, wife, children, nephews and nieces of Aurelius Dioscorus joined with him in dedicating two statues to Serapis, who had appeared to him during a serious illness and had saved his life. One of these is surely the statue of Serapis-as-Asclepius with his caduceus (staff entwined with serpents), on display in the museum. The two statues must have stood on the projecting plinths on either side of the stairway.

The temple was severely damaged in the earthquake of 306–10, evidenced by rebuilt walls, a pier inserted to support the roof of the *cella* and reinforcements to the altar in front of the steps; a number of broken statues received new bodies to support older heads. It was then definitively destroyed in the fourth century in a natural disaster, for several of the statues were lying on a thick layer of mud (responsible for their excellent state of preservation). This was probably the same disaster which overcame the Hadrianic Baths (p. 98) and which has been associated with the earthquake 'of 365' (see p. 11 f.).

Oriental sanctuary (24)

The plan of this sanctuary, very similar to that of the temple in the W corner of the Old Forum (19), clearly indicates the presence of an oriental cult. The precinct faces towards the sea: on this side it had a façade articulated by pilasters and pierced by three doorways (now barely visible, and in any case altered when the fourth-century defences were built along the foreshore here). These led into a court with porticoes on three sides, beyond which are three rooms at the same level, opening into the portico and separated by corridors which lead into the street behind. The central room is the *cella* of the sanctuary, its entrance framed by a pair of columns *in antis*. There are niches along the lateral walls, and a plinth on the side opposite to the door, framed by two stuccoed semi-columns.

The sanctuary, in local sandstone, has been attributed to the reign of Trajan (AD 98–117); it was subsequently embellished with marble. (The columns of the portico, white with dark red veins, like fatty meat, come from the Aegean island of Skyros.) Nothing has been proposed with regard to its dedication, and indeed its full publication is still awaited.

Unfinished Baths (25)
This complex is difficult to interpret, because of major changes in design, but it has been convincingly explained as a bath-complex of (probably) the first century AD, for which an ambitious enlargement and refurbishment was commenced in a later period. This project was, however, abandoned part-way through construction, and at some later date the building site was revisited and at least partly put back into service.

The original layout consisted of a colonnaded *apodyterium* next to the street on the N side (A1 in fig. 45), with a triangular latrine next to it (now buried once again beneath the sand). From there, the bather proceeded E into a *frigidarium* (F1) of which only a

cold plunge-bath now remains (CB), lined with grey marble, and then turned W again to enter the heated rooms in the centre of the later complex (T1, C1). The new, and uncompleted, project involved replacing the *frigidarium* to the E by a huge hexagonal *caldarium* (C2), with hot plunge-baths in its recesses, converting the original heated suite into just a *tepidarium*, and then breaking through the W wall of the previous *caldarium* to connect with a huge new *frigidarium* on that side (F2). The new *frigidarium* was also intended to open at either side through columnar entrances into lateral halls (*apodyteria*? A2). The whole of this late work was composed of reused building materials, incorporating many inscriptions, and there are many signs of the abandonment of the project. The external corner-blocks of the hexagon were never trimmed back into line and none of the internal hypocaust fittings were ever installed. (This is the reason for the rather curious appearance of the interior of the hexagon: the lower arched entrances in each face were actually the furnace-openings for the heating system, and the floor within would have been at the level of the doorways which communicate with the earlier structure – that is to say some 3 m above the present ground level.) Equally, the cold plunge-baths in the new *frigidarium* were built, but never lined with waterproof cement, and their drainage system was started but not completed. The foundations for the lateral hall to the N were laid, but no more; that on the S was not even started. The original *apodyterium* on the N side was, however, remodelled for some other purpose: the colonnade, which stands on its original floor surface (covered in the fourth century by yellow paving-blocks) seems to have been

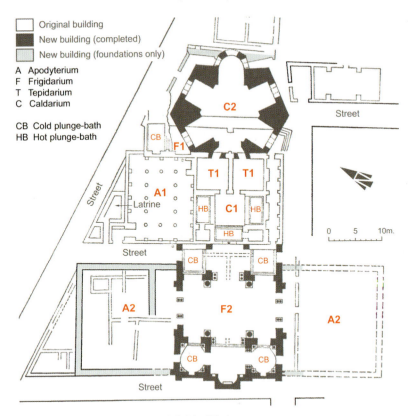

Fig. 45. Lepcis Magna: plan of the Unfinished Baths.

adapted in connection with a series of rectangular piers added around the walls – indicating a change in the form of the roofing.

The date of the late project is difficult to pin down: since it was uncompleted, naturally it was not commemorated by any inscription. The most probable time seems to be in the fourth century AD, when some people still had the means and the ambition to adorn their city with such a project. Di Vita has suggested very plausibly that the building was commenced after the earthquake of 306–10, using materials from surrounding buildings which had collapsed. A reused block with part of an inscription, incorporated in the baths, is matched by another fragment of the same inscription built into the fourth-century walls by the Oea Gate (35). The abandonment of the project has been tentatively associated with the earthquake 'of 365,' but this is not quite the end of the story. After the grandiose project was abandoned, a rough paved floor (recorded but wholly removed by the excavators) was laid in the hexagon at the level of the earlier structures, presumably in order to create a new *frigidarium* and to put the baths back – at least partly – into service.

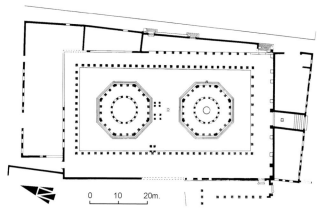

Fig. 46. Lepcis Magna: plan of the market.

Market** (26)

The functional requirement of a Roman market is to provide shaded space, and possibly counters, for market stalls. There should be sets of standard weights and measures against which those of the market traders can be verified, and preferably also water. The market building at Lepcis was provided in 9/8 BC by a wealthy citizen, Annobal Tapapius Rufus, son of Himilcho, and the rather awkward manner in which it is fitted into the layout of the surrounding streets suggests that it was built on the edge of town, before (though not long before) they were laid out. In its original form it consisted of a rectangular open space entirely surrounded by porticoes, with two pavilions, hollow circular *tholoi* encircled by octagonal porticoes, offering further provision for permanent market stalls in the centre. The southern one contained a fountain. The outer walls were of sandstone faced with stucco, and the pavilions were built in grey limestone; the main entrance was in the middle of the W side, with a dedicatory inscription cut in the stucco on the outer face.

Repairs were made in the late first century AD to the SW entrance (which quite clearly uses second-hand blocks, suggesting some haste); the northern pavilion was also rebuilt. Di Vita associates these activities with the earthquake which caused widespread damage at Sabratha in 65–70 (p. 11).

Substantial alterations were made in the Severan period. The southern pavilion (the core of which is now missing) was rebuilt in marble and the Ionic capitals (still present in its northern counterpart) were replaced with the lotus-and-acanthus type found elsewhere in the Severan buildings. The surviving grey granite columns of the main porticoes, with Corinthian capitals, also date from this time. The central entrance on the W side was blocked up, and two new arched doorways were made towards the S end of this wall, fronted by their own colonnaded portico on the outside. The principal entrance was now that from the S (from the *cardo maximus*), in the centre of the short side.

An inscription tells us that the porticoes of the market were restored

Fig. 47. Lepcis Magna: the northern pavilion of the market.

from a state of ruin c. 325 (after the earthquake of 306–10?); in the late fourth century the market had ceased to serve any public function (having been damaged again in that of 365? see p. 11 f.) and was filled by modest habitations (re-housing those displaced by the earthquake?).

Several of the counter-tops have survived; one which has been replaced in the northern pavilion is deeply scored by rope-marks, cut into it when it was used somewhere else as a well- or cistern-head. Others still bear inscriptions recording the names of the magistrates (*aediles*) who gave them, possibly in the late first century AD. The counters were supported on handsome legs decorated with dolphins or gryphons; a fine row of these used to line the S portico, but after recent damage to some of them, the remainder have now been placed in storage by the Department of Antiquities. Next to the northern pavilion are two miniature *tetrapyla* which served as plinths for statuary – presumably figures in chariots. One of these, carved with charming reliefs of merchant ships, was reused in the

fourth century (erasing its original inscription) to commemorate a certain Porfyrius, who had given the city four live elephants (*feras dentatas*). Close to this, inside the northern pavilion, now stands a replica of a block carved with the standard measures of length. (The original is in Room 14 of the museum.) Interestingly, these are the Punic cubit, the Roman foot and the Alexandrine cubit. A counter in the W portico nearby is pierced by holes of different sizes, which held the standard measures of capacity (presumably of bronze).

Arch of Tiberius (27)

Immediately to the W of the market, the *cardo maximus* is spanned by a simple limestone arch, decorated only by a moulded cornice. This is known as the Arch of Tiberius, though it is not an honorific arch in the more familiar sense. It is in fact one of a pair (with the other flanking the parallel street, next to the portico behind the theatre) which was erected in AD 35/6 to commemorate the paving of 'all the streets of the city' under the proconsul C. Rubellius Blandus.

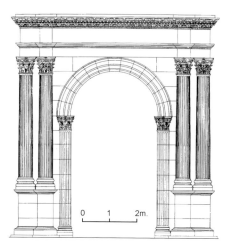

Fig. 48. Lepcis Magna: reconstruction of the Arch of Trajan.

Arch of Trajan (28)

The next cross-roads, heading along the *cardo maximus* towards the Severan Arch, is spanned by the four-way Arch of Trajan. This was erected in 109/10 by the proconsul Q(uintus) Pomponius Rufus, probably to commemorate the elevation of the city to the rank of *colonia*. The arch, built of grey limestone, was the same on each elevation, with rectangular fluted pilasters framing the opening itself and a pair of engaged Corinthian columns projecting forward from each corner-pier on a high plinth, tied back into the superstructure by a corresponding projection of the entablature above. An internal column at each corner helped to carry the weight of the vaulting above. The over-all effect was both elegant and restrained.

Tucked into one of the street-corners next to the arch is the base of a monument which carried a fine marble elephant, which is now in the Lepcis Museum and may be seen on the ground floor as you leave the building. Unfortunately, no inscription was

found, so we know nothing of its dedication.

Chalcidicum* (29)

Immediately beyond the Arch of Trajan, on the right-hand side of the *cardo maximus* as you proceed towards the Severan Arch, is an enigmatic public building which is known as the *Chalcidicum*. The name is clear, for it is so described in the dedicatory inscription and we know of other examples, for instance at Rome (built by Augustus next to the *curia*) and in Pompeii, but we have no clear understanding of what such a building embodied. It must originally have had something to do with either the Greek city of Chalcis or the region of Chalcidice, and it appears to have been a monumental entrance or portico. In the case of Lepcis Magna, it had a monumental façade and entrance towards the *cardo maximus* and it occupies the space between that and the theatre; but as a result of later modifications it is difficult to tell just how it linked the two. A flight of steps leading up to a portico runs the length of the building facing the *cardo* (see fig. 50). The steps are interrupted in the centre, where the portico projects forward to form the porch of a small shrine flanked by shops. There is, however, no obvious way through to the area behind, which may have taken the form of an enclosed market space with surrounding colonnades.

The building was constructed in AD 11/12 by Iddibal Caphada Aemilius and dedicated to the emperor Augustus. Originally of limestone, the cipollino columns and Corinthian capitals are embellishments of the late second or third century; the

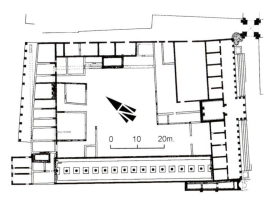

Fig. 49. Lepcis Magna: plan of the Chalcidicum.

limestone column-bases are original, as was the architrave above, now laid out on the ground. This carried the dedicatory inscription, three times, and uncertainties of both spelling ('CALCHIDICVM') and grammar in the handsome lettering show that even someone of this wealth was not confident of his Latin at the time! It is thought that the shrine was dedicated to Venus and Augustus (twin bases suggest two divinities); a statue of Iddibal was also found in the building, and is now on display in room 9A of the National Museum in Tripoli.

At the southern corner of the building is a fountain with a water-cistern behind, an addition probably of Hadrianic date. This was decorated with a figure of a lion devouring the head of a calf, now displayed on the ground floor of the Lepcis museum. If you turn the corner here and proceed towards the theatre, you will pass by an extraordinary water-cistern of the late Roman period, apparently excavated between the internal columns of a pre-existing portico, which as a result now stand on tall square piers. It is suggested that this was one of three

Fig. 50. Lepcis Magna: the approach to the Chalcidicum from the cardo maximus.

Fig. 51. Lepcis Magna: the theatre.

such porticoes surrounding the space behind the façade of the *Chalcidicum*.

Theatre** (30)

The theatre was dedicated in AD 1/2 by Annobal Tapapius Rufus, the man who a few years previously had built the market. Though superficially similar in appearance to that at Sabratha, it is almost two hundred years earlier in date, and is the earliest of its kind surviving in North Africa. It is a hybrid between the typical Greek theatre, which made use of a natural slope to support the seating, and the Roman type in which the seating is supported primarily on vaulted substructures. The lowest part of the semicircular *cavea* is cut out of the underlying rock, while the upper part is carried on a vaulted sandstone structure. The exterior of the drum is very plain, being framed by simple pilasters at ground-level, and pierced by just five arched openings which lead into the seating. The openings which lead into

the *orchestra* on either side of the stage are surmounted internally by inscriptions recording the dedication of the theatre. (One of these is replicated both in the Lepcis Museum and in the National Museum in Tripoli.) Annobal Rufus describes himself in typical Punic terms as *ornator patriae amator concordiae* ('decorator of his fatherland and lover of concord'); he holds the priestly titles of *flamen* and *praefectus sacrorum* and he is a *sufes*, a Punic magistrate equivalent to a Roman *duumvir*; the Latin inscription is also repeated in neo-Punic. The top of the *cavea* was eventually surrounded by a portico, of which a small part has been re-erected to give an idea of the height, and in the centre of the portico was a shrine dedicated to Ceres. The cult-statue, with the face of Livia, the wife of the emperor Augustus, is in the National Museum in Tripoli but the dedicatory inscription from the façade has been recomposed on the steps: the shrine was dedicated in

AD 35/6 by Suphunibal, the daughter of Annobal. Alterations to the *cavea* were carried out by a certain Ti(berius) Claudius Sestius, who in AD 91/2 paid for an altar and for the marble steps in the lowest part where the wealthy sat; they were separated from the rest of the audience by a limestone parapet on which his generosity is recorded. Someone else has made use of the outer face of the parapet as a surface on which to inscribe some lively cartoon figures.

The front wall of the stage is straight and barely articulated by small niches, in contrast to the elaboration of the stage of the Sabratha theatre (p. 64). It was framed at either end by statues of the *Dioscuri*, Castor and Pollux (now taken into store). The original form of the stage-building is uncertain, for it was remodelled in marble in a similar style to the Sabratha theatre in 157/8. The columns which now project incongruously through the wooden flooring of the stage belong to the upper storeys of this façade. Over 130 pieces of sculpture were recovered during the excavation of the theatre, and the inscribed bases which were found indicate that there were many others too! A selection are on display in the Tripoli and Lepcis museums.

Excavation beneath the stage area revealed burials of the pre-Roman period: these are explained, and the finds from them displayed, in Room 2 of the museum. The excavations also revealed that the latest occupation of the theatre consisted of a jumble of hovels built upon its ruins within the *cavea* in the first half of the fifth century AD. A small British excavation in an *insula* to the NW of the theatre in the 1990s showed that the occupation of this area did not generally extend beyond the fifth century.

Portico behind the theatre* (31)

Behind the stage-building of the theatre, an irregular quadrilateral piazza is occupied by a portico (*porticus post scaenam*) which encloses a small temple to the *divi augusti* (the deified emperors), built by Iddibal Tapapius, a member of the same family as the builder of the market and theatre, and dedicated by the proconsul Q(uintus) Marcius Barea in AD 43. As everywhere else in Lepcis, it seems, both the temple and the portico were 'upgraded' with marble in the second century: the column-shafts were replaced in grey granite, with white marble capitals and bases. The reconstruction of a section of the enclosing wall shows how this too was faced with marble, combining with the columns and the paving to create a striking and colourful effect.

In the third century, a bizarrely outsized sculpture (presumably a *quadriga*) dedicated to the Severan family was inserted into this piazza on a perforated plinth resembling four *tetrapyla* linked together. The numerous other statue-bases here include a dedication to M(arcus) Septimius Agrippa, an actor of international fame in the time of Caracalla, who was given citizenship of Lepcis Magna by permission of the emperor.

On top of the wall facing the street on the NW side of the portico is one of the most complex of the apotropaic blocks which are scattered throughout the city (see p. 95). This one has an abbreviated inscription, MAL ER, for which no satisfactory interpretation has been found. It is composed of a centaur who has not only an enlarged phallus, but also a phallic nose and apparently an 'evil eye'; he is using a trident to attack the Evil Eye, and is being assisted by a snake, a scorpion

Fig. 52. Lepcis Magna: apotropaic block near the theatre.

and a bird – a very potent combination for warding off evil!

Monument to C. Gavius Macer (32)

Returning past the *Chalcidicum* to the *cardo maximus* and turning R towards the Severan Arch, one finds at the next street corner the simple square sandstone base of a monument, which presumably supported a statue. The brief inscription, in a *tabula ansata*, proclaims that it was set up by the citizens in honour of C(aius) Gavius Macer, who was the propraetorian legate (commanding officer) of the Third Legion, in AD 29/30.

Schola (33) and Oea road

Proceeding NW along the Oea road from the Severan Arch, one is immediately aware of a very lavish building on the right-hand side of the street (33). Though built of limestone, its three entrances were arched and the façade was framed by Corinthian pilasters; its importance is also emphasized by a stepped terrace which encroaches upon the line of the street for the entire length of the building. Within is a courtyard paved with yellow limestone and surrounded on three sides by porticoes with columns of veined Skyros marble;

the side opposite the entrances has no portico but is developed into a symmetrical arrangement of niches resembling the stage-building of a theatre. This accommodated a row of statues. Behind the porticoes on either side of the building were semicircular *exedrae*. Traces of marble decoration suggest that the overall effect was highly ornate, but the absence of any sort of shrine precludes the possibility that it was a temple precinct. It has been tentatively identified either as a *schola*, a young men's meeting-place or club, or as a private building for holding receptions, belonging to a rich family living in one of the luxury villas along the coast. It was built in the early second century AD.

The re-erected columns show huge iron clamps across some of the breaks: these do not represent modern restoration but are of Roman date. It has been suggested that they relate to repairs after the earthquake of AD 306–10 (p. 11).

Beyond the '*schola*', on the same side of the road, is a bath building. The collapse of heavy cement-lined tanks from above onto the rooms below makes both the purpose of the rooms and the evident succession of modifications difficult to interpret.

The state of this ruin surely speaks of earthquake damage.

Temple on the Decumanus (34)

Proceeding further along the Oea road, there is a street on the R which leads to the theatre. It is not on a direct line, suggesting that the row of buildings along the Oea road is a late addition to the town-plan. The change of line is accommodated by a small piazza behind; in the piazza is a portico of grey limestone and a public fountain with a semicircular basin. A little way beyond this side-street is a temple precinct (34) whose frontage towards the street, like that of the 'schola', was emphasized by a shallow stairway running the whole length of the building and by three arched entrances framed by engaged columns. Within is a temple precinct similar to that of two second-century temples at Sabratha (the South Forum Temple and the Temple of Hercules). The temple itself projected from the rear wall of a courtyard, on a high podium with a frontal staircase and with an altar (now reduced to a fragmentary sandstone core) placed centrally in front of the steps. The courtyard is surrounded by porticoes with columns of grey granite on three sides, and the lateral arms terminate against the rear wall in apses. The podium of the temple is hollow, containing a crypt within (favissae), accessed from a door towards the rear on the left-hand side. The floor of the cella above will have rested upon the four piers within.

The dedication of the temple is unknown; the date of construction is surely some time in the second century AD.

Behind the right-hand boundary-wall of this temple precinct, and opening off the street behind, is an interesting but unpublished building with a wide entrance and walls built in the opus africanum technique (a vertical framework of large squared stone blocks, with the spaces between filled with much smaller blocks or rubble). Several displaced stone troughs lie in the street outside, and within are several more set into a partition-wall: the impression is of a stable. Notice also a well-head set into the thickness of an internal wall and, next to it, a narrow arched doorway in which both the upper pivot-hole for the door and cuttings in the opposite doorpost for the fastenings can be seen.

Arch of Antoninus Pius/Oea Gate* (35)

Continuing along the Oea road, one comes to the West or Oea Gate, which has been partially reconstructed. The walls and flanking towers are a fourth-century addition to an honorific arch dedicated to Antoninus Pius (138–161). This arch marks an intermediate stage between the sobriety of the Arch of Trajan (28) and the extreme emphasis on decoration (almost) without taste on the Arch of Septimius Severus (2). The structure is of limestone, but was designed from the first to be clad in marble (at least on the more obvious faces: on the outer flanks, subsequently enclosed by the defensive wall, can be made out traces of red-painted plaster). The opening was framed on either side by engaged columns of cipollino marble with Corinthian capitals, and the frieze above carried an inhabited acanthus scroll from which animals and human figures emerge. There were winged victories in the spandrels and a fine relief of a gorgon's head on the underside of the arch. (The latter is now on display in the National Museum in Tripoli: see p. 30). The figures are far more rounded and naturalistic than those seen on the Severan Arch. For the white marble, the honey-coloured Pentelic stone of Attica was used.

The fourth-century defensive wall, built largely of reused materials, may readily be traced from here northwards to the sea shore; just inside it but no longer visible was found the House of Orpheus, the source of a fine Orpheus mosaic in Tripoli. On the S side of the gate, the wall incorporates many architectural fragments from funerary monuments which must formerly have stood nearby. There is a link with the Unfinished Baths (25), inasmuch as two different fragments of the same inscription were reused in the baths and in the defensive wall. It has been plausibly suggested that the wall was built soon after the earthquake of 306–10 (p. 11), and that the outer suburbs of the city were abandoned as a result of that catastrophe.

The western suburb

Beyond the Oea Gate, extending westwards along the coast as far as the Wadi Rsaf (at the limit of the enclosed archaeological zone) was a suburban area; both aerial photography and selective excavation have shown that there was further building in this area, including tombs, farms or residences and possibly warehouses. As you proceed along the Oea road, you may see two massive square press-stones lying in the roadway. These derive from olive-presses (see p. 166 fig. 77) and are identifiable by the groove running round the edge of the upper surface, which served to collect the oil which ran out of the compressed baskets of olives in the centre.

Arch of Marcus Aurelius (36)

Some 200 m beyond the gate lie the foundations of the Arch of Marcus Aurelius. This took the form of a *tetrapylon*, like the Arch of Marcus Aurelius in Tripoli, but framed in this instance by three-quarter engaged columns at the outer corners of the four piers. The bases, in white Proconnesian marble, stand upon limestone plinths which were also originally faced with marble veneer. The column-shafts are missing. The two architraves on opposite faces which carried the dedication are preserved and are monolithic: the inscription records the erection of the arch in AD 173 in honour of Marcus Aurelius by the proconsul C(aius) Septimius Severus and his nephew, the propraetorian legate and future emperor L(ucius) Septimius Severus. The street on either side of the arch was lined with colonnades.

Hunting Baths* (37)

Also beyond the fourth-century walls lie the remarkable Hunting Baths. The path which leads to them, close to the shore, leads obliquely to the right from just outside the Oea Gate. The baths were in a remarkable state of preservation when first discovered, to the extent that it was possibly to restore the vaulted roofs and so to protect much of the painted decoration which still survived on the walls and ceilings within. At the time of writing, they are once again threatened with burial beneath mobile sand dunes and the wall-paintings are much decayed; new restorations are apparently in progress.

This bath complex is far smaller than the great Hadrianic Baths (3), but larger than those normally attached to a private residence; it seems likely that they belonged to an association of some sort, and it has been suggested (from the theme of some of the paintings) that this may at one point in its history have been a guild, either of the hunters

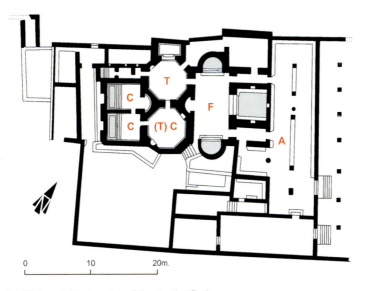

Fig. 53. Lepcis Magna: plan of the Hunting Baths.
A. Apodyterium   *F.* Frigidarium   *T.* Tepidarium   *C.* Caldarium

who fought against wild beasts in the amphitheatre (*venatores*), or of the suppliers who procured the animals. The external appearance of the baths may seem surprising on a Roman site, but that is probably a chance of preservation: we may suspect that bath-buildings not infrequently displayed the unadorned forms of their vaults and domes on the outside. The attention of the architect was directed less to the external appearance than to the arrangement of internal space. Entry was on the NE (seaward) side, through either of two corridors into a rectangular barrel-vaulted *frigidarium*; this had a semicircular basin beneath a semi-dome at either end, and (in a secondary arrangement) a larger rectangular plunge-bath between the two entrance-corridors. There are several successive layers of stucco and of painted decoration on these walls and ceilings, together with marble veneer.

The semi-dome at the SE end shows traces of a mosaic depicting a nymph suckling a kid, a sea-god and a Nilotic scene. The main vaults of the room are painted with scenes of wild-beast fights in the amphitheatre (fig. 54), in which the participants are named. Around the upper walls of the rectangular plunge-bath there are further Nilotic scenes with reeds, ducks, fishermen in boats and the like.

In the original layout, two doors led from the *frigidarium* into two octagonal *tepidaria* and thence into two parallel *caldaria* with hot plunge-baths. At a later stage the SE octagon was sealed off from the *frigidarium*, connected instead with the NW octagon, and provided with heating-flues within its walls so that it became an additional *caldarium*; a further suite of very small heated rooms was also added on the NW side. Also secondary were a portico on the street-frontage towards the

Fig. 54. Lepcis Magna: wall-paintings in the Hunting Baths.

sea and an outer room on this side fitted with benches, suggesting an *apodyterium*. The necessary furnaces and water-cisterns lay to the SW.

It is thought that the Hunting Baths were built towards the end of the second century AD; clearly, they were subsequently modified more than once, but it seems unlikely that they continued in use for long, if at all, after the fourth-century defensive wall was built to the E.

The harbour (38)

The initial establishment of a settlement at Lepcis will have been conditioned by the presence of a sheltered anchorage at the mouth of the Wadi Libdah, protected by a string of offshore islands. The early harbour installations therefore grew up close to the settlement (centred on the Old Forum), with quays and a portico of Neronian date on the W bank of the wadi, the bed of which was enlarged and encased in concrete to create a harbour-canal. It is now thought that the dam upstream on the Wadi Libdah (54), which diverted most or

all of its floodwater westwards around the perimeter of the city's defences, must have been built in the first century AD, or at least no later than the Hadrianic Baths (3). The harbour was wholly remodelled and vastly enlarged in the time of Septimius Severus (see fig. 55), to the extent that it then covered an area of 13 ha and was lined with 1,300 m of quays – making it the third largest port in the western Mediterranean, after Ostia and Centumcellae (Civitavecchia) in Italy. The Severan scheme involved the unification of the existing islands into two large enclosing moles, the creation of an outer harbour by the building of a third mole on the E side of the entrance, and the building of appropriate quays and warehouses.

The success or otherwise of this ambitious project has been much debated by modern scholars. It has been argued by some that the absence of the rope-marks which so characterize well-heads (cf. the reused counter in the market, p. 117) from the mooring-rings of the quays indicates that these facilities can barely have

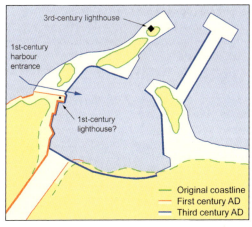

Fig. 55. Lepcis Magna: the progressive development of the harbour.

been used and that the vastly enlarged harbour probably silted up as soon as it was built; but this argument is not universally accepted. Modifications made later in its history include the conversion of the temple on the E mole (44) into a church and the construction of a Byzantine defensive wall along the rear of the warehouses on the same mole. The harbour basin (38) is now a marshy area full of reeds, occasionally wet after heavy rain, and cut off from the sea by a sand-bar across the entrance. The surrounding buildings, however, give an unusually informative impression of the facilities of a substantial Roman port.

The elements of the harbour are described in a clockwise sequence, beginning at the bottom of the Colonnaded Street (5). Those entering the area from the right bank of the wadi (i.e. from the road to the amphitheatre) may follow the same sequence, starting with the Temple of Jupiter Dolichenus (47), or may proceed in the reverse direction along the East Mole, from which the essentials of the harbour may readily be appreciated.

Flavian Temple (39)

The massive podium of the Flavian Temple, denuded down to the concrete vaults which enclosed the *favissae* within, once supported twin temples, dedicated (in an inscription which ran continuously across both façades) to Domitian and to the deified Vespasian and Titus in 93/4. (There is an explanatory display – in Italian – in Room 9 of the Lepcis Museum.) The superstructure was in the grey limestone of Ras al-Hammam; the columns of the temple façades were Corinthian, while the surrounding precinct was lined on either side with porticoes of the Ionic order. The precinct was ruined in the fourth century, probably by the earthquake of 306–10 (p. 11), after which it was partially restored for modest secular use. Not long after, in the earthquake 'of 365,' it was ruined even more comprehensively. The area is of particular interest for evidence of early Arab settlement: a pottery kiln was in use here for the production of amphorae in the ninth or tenth century. (See the display in Room 21 of the museum.)

West side of the harbour (40–42)

In front of the Flavian Temple there may already be seen quays of the Severan reconstruction. The lower level of quay is buried, but the upper level is clearly recognizable, with flights of steps at intervals which descend to the lower, and huge moulded stone brackets which are pierced by vertical holes to form mooring-rings, to which ships could be tied up. All of these features are clearer still on the inner face of the E mole. However, it is on the western side that there were already harbour installations in the first century AD: their concrete foundations were exposed when the lower end of the Colonnaded Street was scoured out by the floods of 1987, and below the Flavian Temple was found a first-century limestone portico, added in front of earlier warehouses in sandstone. Also in this area were found numerous inscribed architrave blocks recording the construction in AD 61/2 of a portico by Ithymbal Sabinus Tapapius. This was surely the limestone portico with Tuscan Doric columns which ran along here and of which the final length (40) is comparatively well preserved.

As one makes one's way around the N mole, two clefts have to be negotiated which mark the original gaps between the offshore islands (see fig. 55); the first of these (41) is still lined with a concrete revetment which protected the entrance into the harbour of the first two centuries AD. Next to its inner end are the foundations of a square building which may have been a beacon or lighthouse. At the far end, beyond a jumble of buildings which has not been fully explored, the tip of the mole is a clearly artificial construction of massive ashlar masonry which once projected further out to sea than it does now. This houses the remains of a lighthouse tower (42), which is still impressive despite the fact that two thirds of it (in plan) have already been lost to the sea. The lowest storey rises on a moulded base about 21 m square, and there is a huge doorway on the landward side. Within, there was a ramped staircase leading both down to sea-level and up into the tower, of sufficient size for a pack-animal to carry up the vast quantities of timber which were needed to keep the fire alight. From what we know of other Roman lighthouses, the tower would have risen in several receding storeys, and its height has been estimated to have been between thirty and thirty-five metres. A lighthouse is indeed shown in the background of the main processional frieze of the Severan Arch, surely representing Lepcis Magna, but its appearance may be 'conventional' rather than specific.

East mole* (43–45)

Except on the rare occasions when the Wadi Libdah is in spate, it is possible to cross the mouth of the harbour by means of the sand-bar which closes it. Close to the tip of the E mole stands a smaller tower (43), which is described in the literature as a semaphore or signal-tower. It presumably served to observe and supervise the traffic entering and leaving the harbour. A small concrete look-out was indeed built on top of it for this purpose as recently as the 1970s, as for many years the harbour was considered a strategic area to which hostile forces might wish to gain access! The next building along this mole was a small Doric temple of unknown dedication (44). The temple faced N, on a stepped platform the centre of which is extended forwards to accommodate an altar. The building was prostyle in form (i.e. with columns

Fig. 56. Lepcis Magna: the E mole of the harbour, from the semaphore.

only across the front), with a porch of two Doric columns *in antis*; in the position where the altar stood is the central pediment block, carved with a ribboned wreath (see fig. 56). The construction of the *cella* walls, with a dado of large orthostats, mirrors that of the Severan Forum. The discovery at the time of excavation of some carved brackets and a colonnette bearing crosses shows that, in late antiquity, the building was reused as a church.

The two-tier quayside is well preserved along the inner face of the E mole, with its steps and mooring-rings. The top of the quay is lined with porticoes in front of warehouses. Note how the rise in the ground from the landward end towards the former island on this side is accommodated by a tapering flight of steps, and by setting the columns of the porticoes on square plinths of gradually changing height. The rear of the warehouses is now surmounted by the Byzantine defensive wall; this gives

an inward look to the entire quay, which is not original. There are indeed tethering-rings at the base of this wall on the seaward side, together with a gently sloping paving, suggesting that vessels could be hauled up out of the water on this side. This seems at first sight surprising, but it is clear from recent underwater work by a French team under André Laronde that the Severan remodelling included a further mole (45), built of blockwork, projecting from the E mole for some 300 m, parallel to the N mole bearing the lighthouse. Most of this has been washed away over the centuries, but its foundations can still be made out. It terminated in a T at the seaward end, and the recovery of architectural and sculptural fragments from this area suggests that it may have carried a temple or some sort of colonnaded building. This mole would have protected the inner harbour from silting, have created a (deeper?) outer harbour between itself and the N mole, and have provided protection on its E side also, creating particularly comprehensive port facilities.

Eastern Baths (46)

This complex, on the foreshore just to the E of the E mole, has been under investigation since 1994 by André Laronde. It is a suite of public baths, facing the road (on its seaward side) which led from the port towards the circus and amphitheatre. It had a portico facing the street, which led through a long and irregular entrance hall ('of the four columns') to a rectangular *frigidarium*, flanked on either side by cold plunge-baths. Beyond this were the heated rooms, which rose to a height of 9 m beneath the vaults but which have still not been fully explored. The suspended floors have partly collapsed, but the flue-tiles lining the walls are readily visible, together with evidence of marble veneer. Immediately to the E of the entrance hall, and projecting partly into it, is a suite of small rooms of undetermined purpose. Between these and the *frigidarium* may be seen the opening of a huge cistern which supplied water to the baths (probably in association with another, just inside the E mole of the harbour). Sockets in the stonework indicate the presence here of a *noria*, a wheel for raising the water into the building.

The baths are built of the local limestone throughout, and the columns and the upper parts of the walls were plastered and painted. The floors and the lower parts of the walls were faced with marble. The initial construction of the complex is placed around AD 200, and abandonment c. 270, at which time the marble was stripped out almost entirely (either for reuse or to be burnt into lime): this is particularly clear in the case of the cold plunge-baths. The building then appears to have been reoccupied by squatters: various openings were crudely blocked. The squatter-occupation was terminated abruptly by the earthquake of 306–10 and further collapse occurred in that 'of 365'. After this, the ruins were engulfed by several metres of sand, but again offered shelter of a meagre kind to inhabitants between the sixth and tenth centuries. Some simple burials found close by to the N are presumed to belong to this period.

The presence of such a substantial bath-building in this position is a little surprising, and suggests a rather greater density of housing on the E bank of the Wadi Libdah than has generally been imagined.

Temple of Jupiter Dolichenus (47)
The SW side of the harbour was lined by a long tapering quay bounded on the landward side by a broad flight of steps; Laronde has suggested that this was always the shallower part of the harbour, where smaller vessels would have tied up. Behind these steps rises a monumental stairway in front of a vast denuded temple podium. An altar found in front of this was dedicated to the Syrian god Jupiter Dolichenus (originating at Doliche, now Dulluk in eastern Turkey). His presence here is likely to have been connected with Julia Domna, the Syrian wife of Septimius Severus.

Villa of the Nile (48)
On the foreshore between the Eastern Baths and the circus are scanty traces of an opulent villa. This was excavated partly in 1916, by officers of an Italian infantry regiment, and partly in 1930 by Giacomo Guidi with private American sponsorship. It derives its name from a fine mosaic depicting a personification of the Nile in a religious procession. This and other mosaics from the villa are now on display in Room 9C and the adjoining corridor of the National Museum in Tripoli (p. 29). Not all of the mosaics are contemporary: some date from the late second or early third century while others are certainly no earlier than the fourth.

Amphitheatre** (49)
The position of the amphitheatre has always been evident from a slight depression in the ground, but it was not excavated and restored until 1962–64 (by Antonino Di Vita). When approached from the car park and ticket office on

Fig. 57. Lepcis Magna: the amphitheatre from the E.

the high ground above, it opens up before the visitor in a most unexpected way, for it is almost entirely excavated beneath the original ground surface, rather than being built up above it. It was constructed initially in AD 56, almost certainly making use of a hollow created by the excavation of a quarry. Its shape is not elliptical, but composed of two semicircular ends separated by a short stretch of straight seating. Its capacity has been estimated at about 16,000 spectators. The uppermost tier of seating may have been surrounded by a portico, and in the middle of the S side this was interrupted by a temple, of which only the foundations remain. The statue of Artemis of Ephesos now in the National Museum in Tripoli (Room 9A) was found in the vicinity in 1912 and may have stood in the temple, as did an altar dedicated to Nemesis (Retribution or Fate) which lies below in the arena.

The seating area was accessed by the usual arrangement of staircases and peripheral corridors, in this case largely tunnelled through the natural sandstone. From niches in these corridors come a number of marble plaques dedicated to different gods and now in Room 10 of the Lepcis Museum (p. 138). There were two principal access routes from the city: one at the level of the arena, along the foreshore and through the circus, and the other a high-level road which crossed the first by means of a lofty bridge and led directly to the top of the *cavea*. On the upper surface of some of the lowest seats on the S side (mainly towards the SW, where they get the first shade in the afternoon) are honorific inscriptions naming prominent families or individuals of the second to fourth centuries AD, for whom, presumably, the seats were reserved. Other single letters or monograms on the blocks (often Punic) are quarry-marks, presumably indicating the output of different squads of workmen or the like. Of course an amphitheatre requires provision, not only for an audience, but also for performers (both human and animal). In the arena can be made out the outlines of the passageways, rooms and lifts which lay below (roofed over with timber) and which provided these facilities. There were also rooms opening off the main axial corridors at ground-level which could be used for this purpose. In addition to these, there were four cells for animals, flanking the main entrances to the arena on either side. That on the S side of the W entrance is most readily understood: it could be closed at both the inner and outer ends by means of a sliding shutter, so that an animal could be penned within and then released into the arena.

Reused inscriptions, employed for repairs in the fourth century, suggest that the earthquake of 306–10 caused damage here too, and the amphitheatre certainly went out of use for entertainment after that 'of 365'; it became for a while (like the theatre) an area of defended habitation.

Circus* (50)

The circus lies between the amphitheatre and the sea, and the two are linked directly by access tunnels and corridors in such a way that they appear to have been designed together. However, while the only inscription which we have from it records the building of the starting-gates in AD 161/2, it is not wholly clear whether this represents the date at which the circus was first built or the renovation or embellishment of a pre-existing structure (as in so many other parts of the city).

A Roman circus is an arena for chariot races, and the general model for circus design is that of the *Circus Maximus* in Rome (of which little detail now survives); the Lepcis example is one of the best-preserved examples. There are

a number of representations of circuses in mosaic which give us an idea of their appearance and there is a particularly good one of these in the villa at Silin (p. 145) of which there is a photograph in Room 10 of the Lepcis museum. It is likely that this is intended to portray the circus at Lepcis, but it is also clear that the artist's portrayal was 'conventional' rather than exact in detail. In its final form, the circus at Lepcis was 450 m long and 70 m wide; it had eleven tiers of seating along either side and around the curved E end, surmounted by a portico of the Tuscan order. Its capacity has been estimated at around 20,000 spectators. The seating was cut out of the hillside on the S and built up on a solid mass of concrete (now much eroded) on the N towards the sea. On the N side there were barrel-vaulted passages leading through the seating, presumably to a road along the foreshore. In the centre of the curved end there was once a monumental gate, though in this case it did not in practice lead to anywhere of significance. The four-horse chariots set out from a row of twelve *carceres* or starting-gates, set in an arc at the W end. The chariots raced up and down the arena, around a central spine (*spina*). These features are clearly visible on the ground. The arcades of the *carceres* were described as standing and so appear in a crude sketch published in 1694 by a visiting Frenchman ('M. Durand'). The upper elements now lie scattered around the bases of the supporting piers. The *spina* begins at some distance from the start, and the *carceres* are therefore set in an arc centred upon the point at which the chariots have to squeeze into one half of the track, in order to give each rider an equal chance. A glance at the plan in fig. 58 will show also that

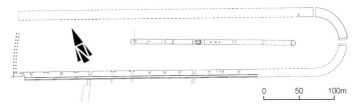

Fig. 58. Lepcis Magna: plan of the circus.

the *spina* is slightly skewed relative to the arena, in order to allow a little more space at this point. The piers of the *carceres* show various sockets, related to the gates which had to fly open simultaneously as the race began. In front of each pier stood a white marble herm: the shafts of these, with their distinctive male genitalia, are also scattered about, though unfortunately none of the heads are preserved. A study of the *carceres* in 1974 revealed a *defixio*, a lead curse-tablet, buried in the sand at the foot of one of the piers and naming four horses and their rider! The object has been dated to the fourth century.

The ends of the *spina* were marked by semicircular stone plinths (*metae*), surmounted at each end by three conical pillars 4.75 m high, with knobs in the form of stylized pine-cones on top. Several drums and one of the pine-cones may be seen on the ground near the *meta* at the western end, which also incorporated a fountain. Mosaic representations show a variety of ornament and fittings along the *spina*: water-basins with fountains, statues, possibly a shrine, and certainly lap-counting devices towards either end. There were seven laps to a chariot race, and these were marked off either by a row of seven vertical paddles in a frame, which were lowered one by one, or by figures of dolphins, so fastened to a frame that they could be tilted

downwards. No traces of these fittings survive at Lepcis (they would have been of timber), but the outline of most of the *spina* is visible and the pink waterproof cement on top shows the presence of five water-basins. There are also bases for statues, and the remains of some sort of shrine between the second and third basins.

Mausoleum of Qasr Shaddad (51)

The broad open expanse to the E of the Wadi Libdah, which now appears as a vast meadow as one drives round to the amphitheatre and circus, has not hitherto been a target for excavation at all. Even though part of it lies within the fourth-century defences and all of it within the presumed first-century fortifications, it has generally been assumed that it was not extensively covered by housing. (The discovery of the large Eastern Baths on this side of the harbour, however, implies the presence of a significant population in this area.) Part of the area was a cemetery in Roman times and therefore definitely outside the inhabited area. Traces of several mausolea have been observed here; one of these, Qasr Shaddad, still stands to a considerable height, though it is now utterly dwarfed by the electricity pylons which loom above it. It is a tower-tomb of Roman date, of which the subterranean funerary chamber and part of two storeys above are preserved. The lower storey is bounded by mouldings above and below, but is plain at the corners; the upper storey took the form of a prostyle *aedicula*. Pilasters with simple capitals and bases framed the rear wall at the corners, while in front there were engaged and free-standing columns. (Drums of the fallen columns are on the ground.) No trace remains of the roof.

Another, more elaborate, tower-tomb which formerly stood a little way to the S of the city, known as Qasr ad-Duirat, has been re-erected in front of the Lepcis Museum (see opposite).

Diversionary dam and canal (52–55)
An exploration of the Wadi Libdah upstream of the Hadrianic Baths is of some archaeological interest (see fig. 31), though this wadi, like most others in or close to modern settlements in Libya, suffers from being used as a refuse tip. About 100 m above the bridge where the wadi is crossed by the old (northerly) coast road, in the eucalyptus trees on the E bank, stands a massive rectangular water-cistern (52) faced with ashlar stonework enclosing five linked barrel-vaulted chambers. The structure is buried in sand to a considerable depth, disguising its very considerable capacity, and hiding the conduit which ran along the front and from which water fed into the interior through each of the five doorways facing the wadi. Another conduit at a lower level led northwards towards the Hadrianic Baths (3), and was presumably linked to the cisterns which surrounded the rear of that complex. The incoming conduit was linked to another cistern (53), composed of three linked barrel-vaults, some 200 m further upstream on the same side of the wadi (before the next road-bridge).

Continuing upstream, beneath the bridge of the dual carriageway which is the main coast road today, one arrives after another 250 m at the remains of the barrage dam (54) which formerly diverted the main flow of the wadi from its course. This is a massive wall of concrete rubble with four huge buttresses in the surviving part, which is over 130 m long. The function of the dam was to divert most or all of the wadi from its course through the city and into the harbour, and to send it instead along a diversionary canal to the westward, coming out to sea through what is now known as Wadi Rsaf, 1.4 km to the W of its original mouth. The course of this canal is still traceable, partly as a shallow depression in the ground and partly as a linear mound of spoil (named the 'monticelli') on the inner side. The mound is clearly visible (if you know what you are looking for) where it crosses the main dual carriageway at an oblique angle. Also, if you follow its course behind the buildings on the S side of this road, you will find a low concrete bridge of Roman date (55) where the road leading inland from the Severan Arch crossed the canal.

These structures have not been studied in detail, and their dating is based more upon the development of the buildings downstream than on any internal evidence. It is thought that the Hadrianic Baths (AD 137) and the accompanying aqueduct (AD 119/20) could not have been built while the wadi was occupying its original course. It is also clear that the canal either follows or constitutes part of a defensive circuit: a remarkable aerial photograph taken by the Royal Air Force in 1942 shows the line of the mound continuing on the E bank of the wadi all the way round to the amphitheatre (as indicated in fig. 31). It has been argued that the only justification for the construction of such defences before the late Roman period was the occasion when Lepcis was threatened by a hostile force of Garamantes in AD 69 (reported by the historian Tacitus).

The date of the failure of the dam is uncertain. Destructive fills of mud identified in the Hadrianic Baths (3) and the Temple of Serapis (23) have been interpreted as indicating that the dam was ruptured on the occasion of the earthquake 'of 365', and presumably not repaired thereafter. I am doubtful that the dam would have been retaining sufficient water by this time to have caused such a mud-flow (though a winter rain-storm subsequent to the breakage of the dam might have had such an effect): mud brought from the sea by a tsunami is another possibility. The present appearance of the dam does not in any case suggest catastrophic rupture, but rather neglect and eventual circumvention by the waters of the wadi.

The Lepcis Museum ** (56)

The present museum of Lepcis Magna was inaugurated in 1994; the objects are generally well displayed and labelled, and there are good explanatory panels in English, and sometimes Italian, in addition to Arabic. It is not on the whole, therefore, necessary to give a very detailed description of the displays. Lepcis has produced a great wealth of objects, from grandiose sculpture down to mundane everyday objects and the pottery which, at different periods, people placed in their tombs. Some of the finest are in the National Museum in Tripoli, but the display at Lepcis is also very impressive, and there is further material from Lepcis in the museums at Zlitan and Bani Walid. The spaces around the outside of the

museum also house many architectural fragments.

The visitor will naturally be struck by two monuments in the forecourt, both on the left-hand side. The first is the tower-tomb known as **Qasr ad-Duirat**. It stood originally in the countryside 2 km to the SW of Lepcis, but has been transferred here and reconstructed by the French Archaeological Mission (under André Laronde). Early twentieth-century photographs show just the lowest storey still standing, with fallen elements from the upper parts lying in the vicinity. Above a stepped rectangular podium rises an ornate tomb-chamber, framed by pilasters decorated with acanthus scrolls and surmounted by Corinthian capitals; there are four pilasters to each side and the principal face includes an opening with pivot-holes for the door, so this was perhaps not a false door as is more frequently the case. Above the doorway is the dedicatory inscription, and above that is what appears to be a bound treasure-chest (surely indicating, if we hadn't guessed it, the wealth of the builder). The wall-surface in between the pilasters recedes to form shallow niches. The frieze above the capitals takes the form of a row of grotesque male and female heads (of apotropaic intent?), the females being framed by shells which form 'heads' to the niches below. The second storey is circular with a hexagonal core surrounded by six engaged columns, which support arcuate lintels above and a Doric frieze; the six faces of the core were cut back into six curving niches. The metopes of the frieze above are decorated with the sun, the moon and signs of the zodiac. The order of the second storey is concluded by a square projecting cornice with four winged figures at the corners (the Four Seasons?).

Fig. 59. Modern bronze statue of Septimius Severus, outside the Lepcis Magna Museum.

Above this is a conical roof decorated with 'pine-cone' scales, surmounted by a Corinthian capital; there would probably have been a carved pine-cone at the apex. This remarkable monument was built by C(aius) Marius Pudens Boccius Zurgem and his wife Velia Longina for three of their children and a grandchild. It has an even more elaborate counterpart, with three storeys, at Al-Urban to the E of Gharyan (p. 159). The type may be traced back to the Cenotaph of the Julii at Saint-Rémy-en-Provence, which was built c. 30–20 BC; Qasr ad-Duirat is certainly later than that (third century?), but the publication of a full study of the monument is still awaited.

Closer to the entrance stands a bronze statue of the African Emperor, L(ucius) Septimius Severus, in Roman parade-armour (fig. 59). This is not an ancient piece but was made in 1933 and originally set up by the Italians in front of the castle in Tripoli. (The empty plinth is still there.) After a number of years in storage following the Revolution (too 'Roman'), he has found a new and appropriate home in his native city.

Inside the museum, one starts on the right-hand side and the sequence of rooms is quite clear, leading round the ground floor, up a spiral ramp to the first floor, around that in the opposite direction and so down again by a second spiral ramp to the exit. Just inside the entrance, on the right-hand wall, is a large artist's impression of the ancient city seen from the air, which gives a good idea of its size and opulence.

Room 1
This is the mandatory (but small) section on prehistory, with some stone tools, a piece of petrified wood and some casts of rock-art on the walls. The descriptive labels do not indicate where any of them were found, but it was not in the vicinity of Lepcis Magna.

Room 2: Early Punic Lepcis
This room mostly displays pottery finds from the early burials beneath the stage-building of the theatre, and panels also give information about the recent excavations of early levels in the area of the Old Forum.

Room 3: The continuity of Punic culture into the Roman period
In the first half of the room are grave-goods from a necropolis of the third century BC to the first century AD, found near the mouth of the Wadi Caam: the pottery is that which is circulating throughout the Mediterranean at the time. The burials are cremations, with the ashes contained in small rectangular stone cists with lids which

imitate a pitched roof. Also at this end of the room are finds of cinerary urns and two *stelai* from a *tophet* at Masallatah, inland from Lepcis. At the far end of the room are a number of objects bearing inscriptions in the neo-Punic script, including that from the market which records its construction in 9/8 BC at the expense of Annobal Rufus.

Room 4: Triumphal arches

Lepcis is very rich in 'triumphal' or honorific arches and this room is dedicated to them and to their decoration. The principal emphasis is naturally on the Arch of Septimius Severus. There is a model in the centre of the room which gives one of the alternative reconstructions of its appearance: note that the historical friezes are placed between the pointed broken pediments, not above them as reconstructed on site. The reliefs on the walls are panels from the inner faces of the openings in the arch (see p. 95), and include a scene of sacrifice and a scene which shows Septimius seated, as Jupiter, with his wife Julia Domna beside him as Juno (with her peacock at her feet). They are flanked by Minerva on the R (with shield and owl) and by the *Tyche* of the city on the L (with cornucopia).

Rooms 5 and 6: Religious life

These are concerned with the various temples scattered throughout the city. There is a charming tablet on the wall dedicated to Asclepius, depicting a pine-cone on a pedestal and a snake. Note the use of both Greek and Latin in the inscription. There is also a fine (headless) statue of Artemis with a hunting dog.

Room 7: The Temple of Serapis

This room is devoted to the particularly rich haul of sculpture from the Temple of Serapis (23). Note the seated cult-statue of Serapis-as-Hades in black marble, with white marble used for the extremities of the body; he is accompanied by Cerberus, the three-headed guard-dog of the Underworld. Note also a fine marble statue of a young woman with a 'melon' hairstyle.

Room 8: The Hadrianic Baths

A few of the many statues found in the baths are displayed here. There is also an informative reconstruction drawing of the inside of the *frigidarium* of the baths. The concept of such great vaulted halls was used more than once by nineteenth-century engineers when designing imposing railway termini.

Room 9: Water supply, other baths, port facilities

This room has various panels concerned with the supply and use of water in the city. There is also a panel (in Italian) describing the research of a team from the University of Pavia at the site of the Flavian Temple (39).

Room 10: Buildings for public entertainment

This large room is divided into two parts, of which the first is mainly occupied by sculpture from the theatre, including a seated figure (in the second niche on the right-hand side) of the wife of Hadrian, Vibia Sabina, as both Ceres (with flowers and poppy-heads in her hand) and Venus (accompanied by Cupid). The inscription on the wall is a cast of one of the dedications of the theatre, recording (in both Latin and neo-Punic) the munificence of Annobal Tapapius Rufus. The Aphrodite *anadyomene* (rising from the waves) on the left-hand wall was the centrepiece of a fountain on the back of the stage-building, facing the street (to the E). The centre case contains a display of miscellaneous minor objects (findspots not indicated): these include objects of bone (pins, gaming counters, dice, decorative inlay), lamps, pottery, some fragments of small sculptures and a piece of *opus vermiculatum* mosaic made of particularly tiny tesserae.

The second part of Room 10 is concerned with the amphitheatre and circus. There is a model of the amphitheatre in the centre of the room, and on the further wall is a series of marble plaques, which were placed in the second century around the main perimeter gallery at the arena level. They were dedicated to Mars, Diana and Nemesis, and were set up by M(arcus) Junius Crescens. A photograph of a mosaic in the villa along the coast at Silin (p. 143) shows prisoners being presented to a bull, who tosses them in the air: this is probably a representation of an entertainment in the amphitheatre. Other photographs in this room show another mosaic at Silin, with a fine representation of a chariot race in the circus. The Lepcis circus is surely implied, though some of the details are certainly conventional. (The larger opening in the centre of the starting-gates is typical of many circuses, but specifically does *not* occur at Lepcis. The portrayal of herms between the starting-gates is, however, accurate.)

Room 11: the fora of Lepcis

The finest sculptures from the Old Forum (those of the Julio-Claudian dynasty, from the Temple of Rome and Augustus) are on display in Room 9A of the National Museum in Tripoli (p. 26), but there are some further pieces here; also one of the 'gigantomachy plinths' from the Temple 'of the *Gens Septimia*'

in the Severan Forum, and three of the caryatid figures which are thought to have come from the clerestory level in the Severan Basilica.

Rooms 12 and 13: Portrait sculpture

The space at the foot of the ramp to the first floor is filled with typical examples of honorific statues set up to notable public citizens in the fora of the city. Heads and bodies cannot always, of course, be matched to one another!

Room 14: trade

The first room on the upper floor is dedicated to two aspects of trade. It displays how amphorae, the standard bulk containers of the ancient world, can be used to track foodstuffs of various kinds, and particularly wine and oil. Tripolitania was a major producer and exporter of olive oil, and Tripolitanian amphorae are found in many different parts of the Mediterranean. Equally, foreign amphorae found at Lepcis demonstrate the importation of wine, fish sauce (*garum*) and other goods. A case of fine red tableware, to which scholars give the conventional (and modern) name *terra sigillata*, demonstrates another class of imports. The material is, unfortunately, unlabelled; however, most of it was made in Italy (typically in Arezzo or Pisa) in the first century AD, while some pieces (of similar or slightly earlier date) come from the eastern Mediterranean, near Antioch (Antakya on the Turkish/Syrian border). The second aspect of trade demonstrated here is the management of the local market. Here you can see the standard measures of length which used to stand in the market-place (26), together with the block which once held the standard (bronze?) measures of capacity.

Room 15: Coins – the Misratah treasure
This room illustrates an extraordinary cache of 100,000 coins found in 1981 at ad-Dafniyah, between Misratah and Zlitan. The coins were found buried in the containers displayed in the middle of the room; they range in date between AD 294 and 333, and must therefore have been hidden shortly after the latter date, presumably at a moment of crisis. This amount of money is unlikely to have belonged to an individual: it is more likely that it was a consignment of pay for the troops – who evidently never received it!

Room 16: Everyday life
The cases in this room display further examples of minor objects of household use or decoration. Relatively few houses have been excavated at Lepcis (in contrast to Sabratha), but a few fragments of painted plaster on the walls give a hint of their mural decoration. A sundial in the corner (lacking its gnomon) would have adorned a courtyard or garden.

Room 17: Funerary customs
As a populous and wealthy city, it is inevitable that Lepcis was surrounded by burials and that a number of these were quite lavish. There were certainly obelisk- and tower-tombs, such as Qasr Shaddad (51) and Qasr ad-Duirat (now in front of the museum). In the early imperial period there were also substantial underground chambers (*hypogea*) which contained the ashes of entire families in rock-cut recesses. As a result of the extensive modern development of the surrounding area, large numbers of these have come to light in recent years, and some of the typical contents are displayed in this room. There are cinerary urns in limestone, alabaster and marble, sometimes inscribed with the names of the deceased (in neo-Punic or in Latin), and extensive displays of the pottery and terracotta figurines which are also deposited in the tombs as offerings for the dead. Note that the red *terra sigillata* pottery of Italian origin very frequently bears a maker's mark stamped in the centre, sometimes in the shape of a footprint. At the far end of the room are some (unlabelled) fragments of architectural decoration from upstanding mausolea (including a sleeping Eros which belongs to Qasr ad-Duirat), funerary *stelai* – effectively tombstones – and inscriptions.

Rooms 18 and 19: The frontier zone
The theme of the previous room spills over here, with a case of burial goods and an explanatory panel relating to a tomb at Gasr Gelda, near Lepcis, found in 1973. There is then a section devoted to the legionary fortress which was built at the beginning of the third century AD at Bu Ngem (Abu Njaym: p. 170) to control the Saharan frontier. Inscriptions displayed on the wall commemorate the construction there of temples to Jupiter Ammon and to Mars Canapphar, excavated by the French in the 1960s. There is also a helmeted head of a war goddess which was found in the Chapel of the Standards within the fort. At the far end of the room are panels describing the obelisk-tombs of the pre-desert region and the monumental tombs of the settlement at Ghirza (p. 182). These are accompanied by a display of architectural sculpture from the E façade of Tomb B at Ghirza, including a scene of a chieftain seated on a chair and receiving homage from his subjects. The tomb was crowned with a *sima* of paired S-spirals and

by standing winged victories at the corners.

In Room 19 are further decorated frieze-blocks from other mausolea, including a scene of camels being used for ploughing (from Tiji, in the Jafarah near Nalut). Yet more pieces may be seen outside, leaning against the wall of the museum. There is also a cast of the inscription over the false door of tomb North A at Ghirza (p. 191).

Room 20: The advent of Christianity
This room contains some carved architectural fragments from early churches, at Lepcis Magna and elsewhere in the countryside (extending from the vicinity of Tarhunah to Tarmisa in the Jabal Nafusah (p. 81: a block with a very primitive chi-rho motif in a wreath flanked by palm-fronds); they are typically recognizable by the depiction of crosses or of the chi-rho monogram with the letters alpha and omega within a wreath. There is also a panel describing the church and associated buildings near Al-Khadra, and a fragment of mosaic (presumably from a church) whose origin I have been unable to discover. A display case contains lamps and other types of pottery bearing similar Christian motifs, together with bronze frames for glass hanging lamps, which are typical of the late Roman period.

Room 21: The Arabs and the advent of Islam
Panels describe the evidence of post-Roman occupation found on the site of the Flavian Temple, with a case of early Islamic pottery from the site. There is also a display of glazed dishes which were used to decorate the underside of the dome of the tomb of Shaikh Milad

al-Aiadi at Masallatah. Some of these are Ottoman, others are attributed to the first half of the ninth century. The model is of the mosque and *zawiya* of Shaikh Ali al-Farjani near the Wadi Caam, and there is an idealized recreation of the inside of a mosque, with *mihrab* (niche indicating the direction of Mecca) and *minbar* (pulpit).

The remaining part of the upper floor is taken up with objects and displays relating to Libyan resistance to the Italian invasion and occupation in the earlier part of the twentieth century; an ethnographic display of traditional tools and jewellery with a recreation of a Bedouin tent; and gifts to the Leader of the Revolution from various sources. Modern industry is represented by a model of a projected furniture factory. A second ramp leads from here back to the ground floor and the exit. Notice in this area the marble elephant which once stood next to the Arch of Trajan (28) and a fountain-sculpture of a lion devouring the head of a calf, from the *cardo maximus*, next to the *Chalcidicum* (29). There is also in this space another gigantomachy plinth from the Temple 'of the *Gens Septimia*' in the Severan Forum.

There is a plan to open a separate mosaic museum at Lepcis Magna, in a building just behind the main museum. A number of large mosaics (including some extraordinary gladiatorial scenes from a villa discovered in recent years close to the Wadi Libdah) have already been mounted on its outside walls and may be seen (distantly) from outside the perimeter fence between the Severan Arch and the Hadrianic Baths.

Other coastal sites to the east of Tripoli

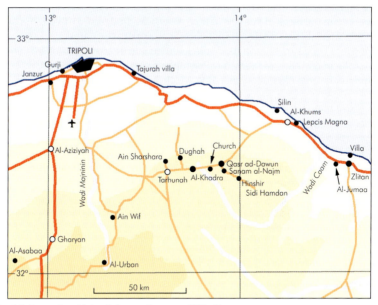

Fig. 60. Coastal and inland sites to the east of Tripoli.

Proceeding eastwards from Tripoli, one travels through a generally fertile landscape which supports cereal crops, soft fruits and olive cultivation. The coastal plain becomes steadily narrower, until eventually the road climbs through the hills where the easternmost end of the Jabal curves northwards to the coast. Beyond al-Khums and Lepcis Magna, one comes successively to the conurbations which have grown up around the oases and palm groves of Zlitan and Misratah (see fig. 1). At Misratah, the main road turns S, skirting to the W the Tawurgah flats into which the Wadi Sawfajjin feeds, and which used to be malarial before big agricultural schemes were introduced here in the mid twentieth century. The terrain rapidly becomes more barren and desolate; the road rejoins the coast at the abandoned settlement (briefly important as an anchorage during the Second World War) of Buayrat al-Hasun and then traverses the marshes at the mouth of the Wadi Bayy al-Kabir. Beyond this point, settlements are modest and widely separated. Surt has been promoted in recent years as a centre of government for Libya, and for the African Union, but without the necessary transport infrastructure it is something of a ghost-town.

The ancient settlement of this coastline showed a similar pattern to that of today. There were coastal villas of very rich landowners stretching all the way from Tripoli to Misratah, of which the examples at Tajurah, Silin and Zlitan are typical: over a hundred have been identified altogether. These villas will have communicated with one another and with the cities by sea as much as by land, and mosaics show us how they had their own jetties and landing-stages. (See, for example, the mosaics

141

from the Villa of the Nile at Lepcis, in Room 9C of the National Museum in Tripoli.) To the E of Lepcis there was certainly an ancient harbour of some significance at Qasr Ahmad, close to Misratah, which may have been known as *Thubactis*. This is evident from the block of Pentelic marble which was dredged up there some years ago and which is now on display at Lepcis (p. 93): both the harbour and the road linking it to Lepcis must have been adequate for it to be used in the third century AD for the importation of heavy building-materials.

Itineraries and navigation manuals which have come down to us from the Classical period give us names of settlements and anchorages along this coastline, but few of them have been identified with certainty and there is nothing to attract the cultural tourist today. The one exception is Madina Sultan, which traces its origins back to the Punic period and which gained particular importance after the Arab conquest. The visible remains are modest, but the historical interest of the site is considerable and it would surely repay further archaeological investigation. The small museum there displays finds from a number of locations along the coast, including Surt and Bin Jawwad.

The entries in this section of the gazetteer are all on, or close to, the main coast road; they are listed from west to east.

TAJURAH

Coordinates: N 32° 50.512', E 13° 29.030'
Directions: The villa described below is at km 30 of the Tripoli–Misratah road, 11 km E of the modern village of Tajurah. It lies close to a radio station and is in a military zone, which unfortunately makes it inaccessible at the time of writing except by special permission from the Department of Antiquities.

Villa of the Nereids

Part of a wealthy coastal villa was discovered here in 1964, and excavations were carried out in that and the following year. As elsewhere, a considerable part of the complex had already been lost to coastal erosion, but two peristyles, a considerable number of rooms and a bath-complex were uncovered. The finest mosaic, with a head of Amphitrite in the centre, is now on display in the National Museum in Tripoli (Room 9B); the name given to the villa derives from a motif in the bath-building depicting Nereids competing in various games. The construction of the villa is closely dated because it made use of stamped bricks imported from central Italy, mainly from the brickyards of Domitia Lucilla Minor, the mother of Marcus Aurelius; these were all produced between 155 and 160. The best mosaics are probably contemporary with the initial construction, but there are others in a poorer style which were probably laid in the early third century. The villa was destroyed in the fourth century, and modest squatter occupation (probably attracted by a good spring of sweet water on the spot) is datable before the end of that century. It is likely therefore that the main phase of occupation was terminated either by the earthquake 'of 365' (this coastal position would have been extremely vulnerable to any tsunami) or by the devastation of the Tripolitanian countryside around the same time by the *Austuriani* (p. 6).

SILIN

Coordinates: N 32° 42.552', E 14° 10.651'
Directions: Turn towards the coast off the main road from Tripoli to Lepcis Magna at N32° 38.383' E14° 9.033'. (There is a police post at this junction, marked from either direction by a cut-out figure of a traffic policeman on the central reservation.) Follow this road, forking L at N 32° 41.250' E 14° 9.625' and R at N 32° 42.270' E 14° 9.150'. (If approaching from the centre of al-Khums, take the coast road westwards, past the container port and naval base, and then turn right at the first of the two forks listed above; the rest of the route is the same.) The site is at the end of the road and is guarded but has no ticket office. It is therefore necessary to obtain entry (and camera) tickets at Lepcis Magna. The tickets may be dated, so make sure that you are buying them for the right day if you are not going there immediately. (In 2008, the site was entirely closed for restoration work: ticketing arrangements may of course change when it reopens.)

Villa***

The Roman villa at Silin (note that 'Silin' is a local place-name, not strictly the name of the villa) is the most striking example of its type that the tourist can see in Libya. It is only one of a succession of wealthy Roman seaside residences which stretched all the way from Tripoli to Misratah. Other examples (the 'Villa of the Nereids' at Tajurah, the 'Villa of the Nile' at Lepcis Magna and the Villa of Dar Buk-Ammara at Zlitan) are represented by fine mosaics on display in the National Museum in Tripoli, but this is the one place where you can see mosaics of the same quality *in situ*, accompanied by walls which are painted, stuccoed or panelled with veneers of marble. These are the residences of very wealthy people, and

their only close counterparts are to be found around the Bay of Naples in Italy. The villa probably grew and evolved over an extended period, but the publication of a definitive study is still awaited. All that can be said at present, based upon the layout and the style of the mosaics, is that the earliest part was probably the *atrium* (1) and the rooms surrounding it; that it was probably at its most magnificent in the second or third century AD, when Lepcis itself was at its most prosperous; and that it did not survive into the late Roman period.

The complex was exposed by winter storms in 1974 and was subsequently excavated and consolidated by the Department of Antiquities. What you can see is part of the domestic range (*pars urbana*) of the villa, built on the foreshore and facing NE towards the sea. It is likely that there were also facilities related to farming activity (the *pars rustica*), but these are not visible. The numbers in brackets below refer to the plan in fig. 61.

The villa is now approached from inland by passing around the western end and entering the colonnaded peristyle around which the principal rooms are disposed. Part of this peristyle (and certainly some additional rooms) has been lost through coastal erosion, but it may be doubted whether the fourth side was ever closed: the open prospect towards the sea would surely always have been appealing. The modern wooden walkways, constructed over the central garden area, enable the visitor to enjoy the mosaics within the colonnades without causing damage. On the SE and NW sides, between the columns, are charming scenes of pygmies doing battle with crocodiles and storks, surrounded by luxuriant foliage and quacking ducks. Many of

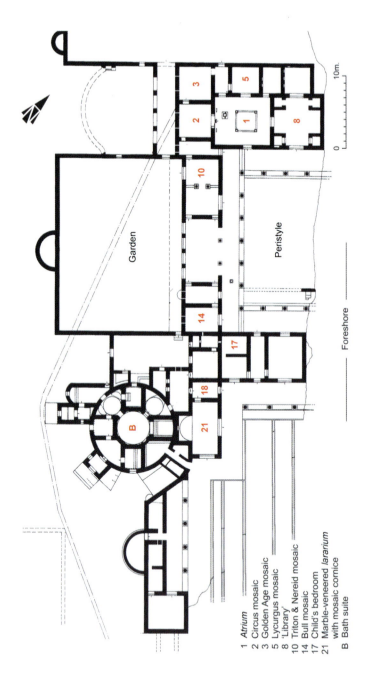

1 *Atrium*
2 Circus mosaic
3 Golden Age mosaic
5 Lycurgus mosaic
8 'Library'
10 Triton & Nereid mosaic
14 Bull mosaic
17 Child's bedroom
21 Marble-veneered *lararium*
   with mosaic cornice
B Bath suite

Garden

Peristyle

Foreshore

Fig. 61. Plan of the Roman villa at Silin.

Fig. 62. Villa at Silin: detail of the peristyle mosaic.

the pygmies are using pieces of broken amphorae as helmets or shields and the so-called 'Nilotic' scenes are full of humour. Note on the SE side, near the S corner, a pygmy anxiously heaving on the legs of his companion, a large part of whom has already disappeared into the jaws of a crocodile! The SW side of the peristyle shows best the more formal scheme of squares containing a rich variety of coloured geometric patterns which extended round the peristyle inside the colonnades.

On the NW side of the peristyle, a doorway leads into an atrium (1) with a central water-basin (*impluvium*). The room, which is now entirely covered, would originally have been open to the sky in the centre, with the rainwater draining into this basin. The floor is paved with a geometric mosaic, and the walls show well-preserved hunting scenes together with images of buildings in a rural landscape. From this room, it is possible to see into room 8 on your right. Because of the cupboards built into the corners, it has been suggested that this room

may have been a library. The floor is decorated with a geometric mosaic set out in small square panels containing masks and other figural motifs.

Room 5, seen through the doorway opposite the entrance to the *atrium* from the peristyle, is a small *triclinium* (dining room) with a fine central mosaic panel depicting the myth of Lycurgus. There are various versions of this, but the essence is that he was a Thracian king who opposed the god Dionysus and attacked him and one of his female adherents, Ambrosia, with an axe. Ambrosia was transformed into a vine which then took him captive. He is portrayed here dropping his axe as he is ensnared by the vine.

Room 2, which may not be entered but which may be viewed both from the atrium and from the adjoining room 3, is mainly taken up with a magnificent mosaic showing a chariot race in the circus. (We may assume that the circus at Lepcis Magna is intended, though not all the details correspond.) The arcaded starting-gates are clearly depicted at the end nearest to the *atrium* and the chariots race around the central *spina*, upon which are basins of water, statues on columns and two lap-counters (frames carrying seven paddles which are lowered one by one as the laps are completed). Room 3, in the corner, has a central panel with a curious allegorical scene which has been interpreted as Aion ('Time') holding up a hoop representing the zodiac; through this the Four Seasons pass somewhat reluctantly into the Golden Age. The scene is witnessed from above by Apollo (as the Sun), rising out of the sea in his chariot (representing the Dawn of the New Age) and by a winged flautist. Behind Aion sits Venus, with Cupid fluttering behind her head.

Returning to the peristyle, the colonnaded opening in the centre of the S side (12) has been interpreted as a summer *triclinium* (an open dining room, facing north). It is decorated partly with geometric mosaic, and partly with marble slabs; it has windows in the rear wall which once looked out onto an enclosed garden. Two small pairs of rooms open off it to either side, each decorated with mosaic flooring. In the centre of room 10 is an *emblema* in very fine tesserae, showing a triton and a sea-nymph disporting themselves together. In room 14 at the opposite end of the range is a representation of victims being presented in the amphitheatre to a bull, who tosses them in the air: their dress suggests that they are oriental (Iranian or Arab?) captives. The inscription in the mosaic, FILOSERAPIS COMP(OSUIT) – 'Lover of Serapis organized (this event)' – has been taken as evidence that the originator of the mosaic lived in the time of the emperor Caracalla (AD 211–217) and wished in this way to show his loyalty. (Caracalla was known to be a devotee of the Greco-Egyptian god Serapis; he was also campaigning in the Orient in 216, and may well have brought back captives such as those depicted here.)

The rooms on the E side of the peristyle can now be entered only from the E: it is necessary to pass around the seaward end of the range onto a mosaic-paved terrace bordering what appears to be a formal garden, with flower-beds separated by low walls entirely covered in mosaic: here is a real display of luxury! As you approach the buildings again from this direction, the third door on the right opens into a vestibule with a floor of *opus sectile* (cut marble shapes) surrounded by mosaic. The inner room (17) has a mosaic floor with a meander pattern, but is chiefly striking for its painted wall-decoration, preserved virtually up to the ceiling. On a white background, panels are delicately picked out with red borders, enclosing representations of cupids equipped for hunting; there are also borders with festoons of foliage inhabited by ducks. This was surely a child's bedroom.

Fig. 63. Roman elegance: marble veneer in the villa at Silin.

Returning to the terrace and continuing towards the circular bath suite (B), one enters a small lobby (18) off which another remarkable room (21), usually barricaded off, may be glimpsed through a doorway. It is not the mosaic floor which catches the eye here, but the grey marble panelling which is still intact, held in place by its original bronze clamps, and covering the walls up to head-height (fig. 62). Above this, there is painted wall-plaster, and at ceiling-height in one or two places are traces of a coving decorated in coloured mosaic. The room is T-shaped, and originally had a semi-dome over the focal recess; high on the wall in the centre of the recess (not readily visible from the doorway) is a pedimented niche, also elaborately framed in marble. This was surely the *lararium*, where the images of the family gods (*lares*) were kept and venerated. The room has an axial doorway from the terrace, facing the niche, and this would have been the normal route of approach.

Continuing straight ahead now from room 18, you enter the remarkable circular bath suite of the villa. The core of the complex is the octagonal central *frigidarium*, which has a typical mosaic of the head of Oceanus surrounded by sea creatures. There is a cold plunge-bath and stucco decoration on the walls, which survive here up to the springing of the dome. A niche on one side has a mosaic of boxers above a hole for a fountain. Off the *frigidarium* are various small heated rooms with hot plunge-baths. Note the hollow flues which are sometimes visible in the walls: in these rooms the walls as well as the floors benefited from the heat of the furnace outside.

Beyond the baths, towards the E, are further rooms, less well preserved and of uncertain function, though they too have painted walls.

WADI CAAM

Coordinates: N 32° 29.971', E 14° 26.673'
Directions: The main road between Lepcis Magna and Zlitan crosses the Wadi Caam on a long bridge at a distance of 21 km from Lepcis. The Roman hydraulic works are next to the old road immediately downstream (N) of the present bridge and below the monument to Libyan resistance.

Hydraulic works

The Wadi Caam is one of the places where the remains of Roman hydraulic engineering are both accessible and broadly intelligible. Below the modern bridge is a deep rock-pool fed by a perennial stream which comes to the surface at this point. Above, on the eastern bank, is a massive concrete retaining wall which incorporates rectangular tanks at its upstream end (next to the old road, where it descends to ford the wadi). There are also tumbled ashlar blocks on the slope above, which must have formed part of an imposing building. On the western bank, down among the eucalyptus trees and opposite the point at which the retaining wall on the other bank (housing a water-channel) turns across the wadi, can be seen part of the aqueduct which carried water from here to Lepcis. Because of erosion, it is possible to see both the vaulted channel of the aqueduct (in small rubble masonry) and one of the inspection shafts which formerly led down from the ground surface for maintenance purposes: it now stands bizarrely in the open air, like a tall chimney. If you clamber up the bank, you will see the next shaft projecting above ground in the adjoining field, and while many others have doubtless

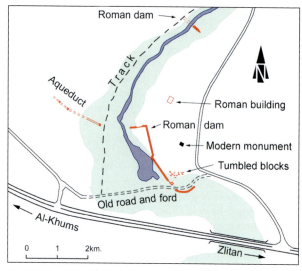

Fig. 64. Plan of water-control works in the Wadi Caam.

disappeared over the years, almost the whole course of the aqueduct between here and the city has been traced. A further 350 m downstream (to the N) is the concrete mass of a dam, which appears to incorporate a spillway and which must once have crossed the wadi bed and enclosed the reservoir from which the aqueduct drew its supply.

There would have been two purposes to fulfil here. On the one hand, the perennial source of fresh water needed to be enclosed and fed to the city; while, on the other, it would have been desirable to prevent this valuable source from contamination by the muddy floodwaters which would rush down from the hills with violence – and at short notice. We may suppose that the various walls were designed to control and to separate both sources of water. Only partial studies of these works have been carried out, but the system is complex. In addition to the aqueduct heading westwards, there are three water-channels of different sorts which

emerge from the retaining wall on the E bank and which may be associated with farm buildings some 500 m to the E. These works will have had a lengthy history, but it is reasonable to associate their initial construction with epigraphic evidence at Lepcis Magna for the provision of a water supply in AD 119/20 by a certain Q(uintus) Servilius Candidus (see p. 98).

AL-JUMAA (EL-GIUMA)

Coordinates: N 32° 28.121', E 14° 28.985'
Directions: At 5 km E of the Wadi Caam or 7 km W of the Zlitan junction on the main coast road (N32° 28.856' E14° 29.601'), turn off to the S, past the E side of a filling station. Follow this road to its end and then turn R; the mausoleum stands amongst the houses in its own enclosure, about 100 m further on your L.

Mausoleum
This is a massive rectangular tower tomb, restored in 1927. What remains is a low,

stepped podium in fine ashlar masonry, covering the funerary chamber, and a very plain first storey above, crowned by a narrow cornice but otherwise undecorated. In the N face is a door-frame which originally surrounded a false door (long since destroyed, and now replaced by an iron gate); above this is an uninscribed frame for an inscription. Only a few courses remain of the upper storey above the cornice, which appears to be of rougher build: maybe this is secondary, for fallen elements around the mausoleum clearly indicate the presence of an engaged colonnade at the higher level. The funerary chamber is unusually large and sumptuous: it is approached through an ample doorway directly beneath the false door and is vaulted within; there are five recesses, each large enough to accommodate a sarcophagus.

ZLITAN

Directions: The Zlitan Museum is in the centre of the town, at N 32° 28.424' E 14° 34.023'. For the villa of Dar Buk Ammara, go past the Zlitan Hotel and take the next turning on the R. Fork L after 2 km at N 32° 29.430' E 14° 34.136'; the villa will be found in a gated enclosure on the R at N 32° 29.877' E 14° 33.517', between recent buildings.

Museum

The Zlitan Museum now occupies the ground floor of the former Italian *Albergo delle Gazelle*; it faces a little piazza which also houses the former *municipio*, and is recognizable by the ceramic gazelles on its façade. Its modest displays include some casts of statue-heads which seem to recur in other museums also (e.g. Sabratha): I have ignored these in the description which follows.

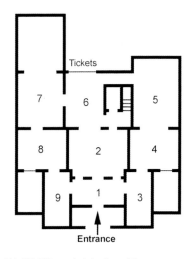

Fig. 65. Zlitan: sketch-plan of the museum.

In **Room 1**, three statues stand within the openings to room 2 beyond: they have been brought out of storage at Lepcis Magna and are (L) a figure of Asclepius, (C) a draped, headless female figure of the second century AD and (R) a satyr. The carved limestone cornice-block attached to the pier left of centre is attributed to the third century, but no provenance is indicated.

On the right-hand wall of **Room 2** is a funerary inscription, said to have been found about 20 km E of Zlitan, and formerly kept in the old *municipio*. It records the erection of a monument by M(arcus) Domitius Celer and his wife Cassia Iuliana Namgyddus to their three dearest children; it is attributed to the second century. Also in Room 2 are various architectural fragments, all unlabelled. Noteworthy are a *stele* with the symbol of Tanit carved in relief, and a fluted sandstone column-shaft with a grape-vine winding around it. This is surely a pair to a column in the Bani Walid museum from Wadi Merdum (p. 178).

Rooms 3 to 5 are devoted to wall-paintings and a mosaic from the villa of Dar Buk Ammara at Zlitan; the finest of the mosaics from this villa are of course on display in the National Museum in Tripoli (Rooms 1 and 9A). In **Room 3** are a plan of the villa and several fragments of Nilotic scenes (water-life and fishing in the reeds of the Nile delta). **Room 4** has a large fragment of wall-plaster with an architectural composition, and several small fragments showing human figures. **Room 5** has the most impressive items of the collection. On the floor is a pleasing geometric mosaic composed of swastikas and roundels (end of first or early second century AD) and on the walls are various further fragments of painted wall-plaster, including a winged victory with a palm, a flying Pegasus in a roundel, a gorgon's head, a seahorse, Tritons and Nereids, and a (green) bronze statue of Mercury.

In the corridor between Rooms 5 and 6 are three small stone cinerary chests with pitched lids: these are old finds formerly kept in the *municipio*. **Room 6** contains two cases of pottery and other small objects from tombs. That on the R was found in 1966 in a family tomb at Rumaia to the W of Zlitan; the material belongs generally to the middle or the second half of the first century AD. That on the L is of similar date: it was found in 1977 at Asdu, a little to the E of Zlitan. The small amphorae around the edges of this room form part of the Rumaia find.

Room 7 contains the usual ethnographic display of items representing the pre-modern life of the region. **Room 8** contains a photographic display of old buildings in the Zlitan area and **Room 9** is devoted to Achievements of the Revolution.

Villa of Dar Buk Ammara

The Roman villa of Dar Buk Ammara was one of the first to be excavated by the Italians, in 1914, and the finest of its mosaics are deservedly on display in the National Museum in Tripoli. The position, on a low cliff overlooking the sea, will have made it a very desirable residence indeed, but has not assisted its preservation since it has been exposed. Its appearance is also not enhanced by the red plaster coating which is intended to preserve the walls.

On entering the site (from the S), one first encounters a bath-building with a bewildering arrangement of curvilinear walls. A circular room looks as though it should have had a raised, heated floor, but for the presence at low level of mosaic in one of its doorways, showing a pair of sandals. Beyond the bath-building is a rectangular courtyard, originally paved with clay tiles laid in a herring-bone pattern; beneath the centre of it is a long barrel-vaulted cistern, with a draw-hole at either end. At the W end of the courtyard, most of the rooms shown on the plan are no longer visible, but the curious quadrant-shaped room can still be made out, in which was found the very fine mosaic in *opus vermiculatum* which is now in Room 9A of the National Museum (p. 26).

The westernmost wing of the villa contained the most prestigious rooms, though again, little of the detail is now visible. A range of rooms was bounded by corridors on both the N and S sides: only the N corridor is now visible, and this still retains a fine black-and-white geometric mosaic. It was fronted on the N side by an open colonnade, which presumably looked out onto a garden terrace above the sea; at some point this was partially walled up, leaving

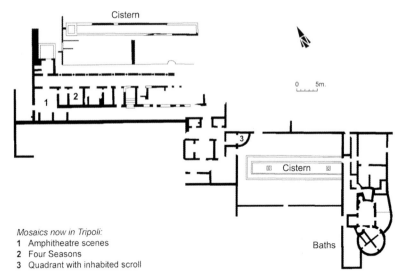

Fig. 66. Zlitan: plan of the villa of Dar Buk Ammara.

windows in the intervals between the columns. A staircase in the same range of rooms, entered from the S corridor, implies the former presence of an upper storey. The terrace was extended forwards by the construction beneath it of a long vaulted cistern, which is still well preserved.

Because of the early date of the excavation, no direct dating-evidence for the history of the villa was recovered: we are therefore dependent on scholarly opinion on the style of the mosaics. The received wisdom is that the villa was built in the last quarter of the first century AD or the first quarter of the second; however, this is now by no means universally accepted. Subsequent discoveries (e.g. at Silin) have shown that it could even be as late as Severan.

MISRATAH (MISURATA)

Coordinates: N 32° 22.947', E 15° 5.115'
Directions: The coordinates given are those

of the museum, which is located on the second ring-road, next to the Quz al-Tik Hotel.

Museum

The museum in the futuristic Borj Quz al-Tik was closed in 2008 for renovation. It has not therefore been possible to verify the details of the display, nor indeed is it certain that the previous display will be unchanged when it reopens.

Room 1 contains finds from a Roman shipwreck discovered during enlargement works at the port of al-Khums (immediately to the W of Lepcis Magna). *Room 2* is dedicated primarily to finds from burials. In the two recesses on the R are amphorae and cinerary urns from ad-Dafniyah, about half-way between Misratah and Zlitan; on the left is a reconstructed Punic burial with its grave-goods. In the corridor beyond there are various explanatory panels: these describe recent archaeological work carried out

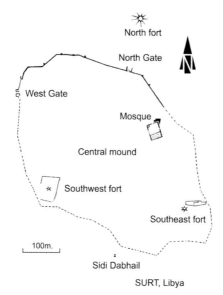

North fort

North Gate

West Gate

Mosque

Central mound

Southwest fort

Southeast fort

100m.

Sidi Dabhail

SURT, Libya

Fig. 67. Madina Sultan: plan of the medieval town.

by the French mission at Lepcis Magna and the glories of prehistoric rock-art in the Wadi Matkandush and the Tadrart Acacus. In the circular *Room 4* is displayed more Roman pottery and part of the Misratah horde, a cache of 100,000 Roman coins of AD 294–333 which was found in 1981. Part of the horde is also displayed in Room 15 of the museum at Lepcis Magna (p. 138).

MADINA SULTAN

Coordinates: N 31° 7.303', E 17° 6.051'
Directions: The entrance to the arch-aeological enclosure is through a green metal gate on the N side of the main coast road, about 50 km to the E of Surt. (The coordinates given are for this point.) The centre of the medieval city is about 1 km to the N. (There is not usually any objection to one taking a vehicle inside.)

Ancient town
The site may be identified as Punic *Charax*, Roman *Iscina* and Arab *Sort*, which last fell into decline after the Hilalian invasion in the mid eleventh century. Of the medieval town, a circuit of walls and two prominent forts, at the SW and SE angles of an irregular polygon, can be made out. In each, a mound of rubble suggests the presence of a redoubt. There is also a mound outside, to the N, representing another fort. The W and N gates have been exposed, and an extensive stretch of the city wall is visible between the two. Within the walls, the Fatimid mosque has been excavated (see below), as has an elevated area a little way to the W of it, though the visible remains of the latter are not readily intelligible. A cemetery on the S side surrounds the whitewashed tomb of Sidi Dabhail (or Dakhail). The medieval city had a port, but it is not clear where this was: it may have been as much as 5 km to the E.

Aerial photography in 1952 showed extensive and regular enclosures to the

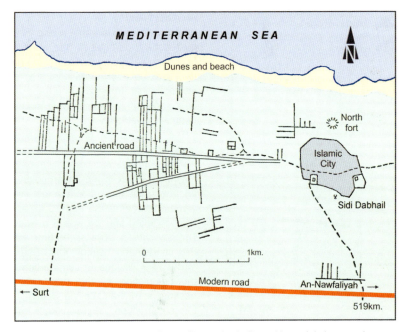

Fig. 68. Madina Sultan: outlying (Roman?) remains indicated by aerial photography.

W of the medieval town (see fig. 68), which are virtually indistinguishable on the ground. These may be medieval, or may relate to the earlier Roman settlement.

The mosque

The mosque was excavated and consolidated in 1963–4; its walls survive only to a low height, but the plan is easily understood. The main entrance (in Phase II: see below), on the W side, was originally double and led into a courtyard surrounded by porticoes and provided with a large water-cistern beneath the centre. The building is aligned almost N–S, and on the S side five doorways opened into the prayer-hall. The large niche on the right-hand side of the central doorway held a water-jar, which was found in position. The prayer hall was divided into three aisles parallel to the qibla wall, with a cross-axis between the central doorway and the *mihrab*, embellished by engaged semi-columns framing the piers of the vaulting. The marble bases used here were probably taken from a Byzantine building, whereas the capitals which have hitherto been found are of limestone and are of Islamic manufacture. The solid square foundation in the NW corner of the courtyard is the base of the minaret; there is slight evidence that its superstructure was octagonal.

A later phase (III) in the history of the building is marked by the strengthening of the outside wall on three sides of the building, the blocking of one of the doorways on the W side and of three of the entrances to the prayer-hall; the porticoes surrounding the courtyard were also divided into ranges of rooms by transverse walls. The work is inferior and suggests a belated attempt to

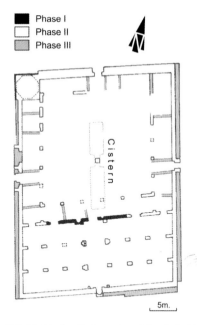

Phase I
Phase II
Phase III

Fig. 69. Madina Sultan: plan of the Fatimid mosque.

shore up an already partly ruinous building.

Later investigations in 1977 suggested that the visible remains incorporate fragments of an earlier and much smaller mosque (Phase I), which is detectable only in the N wall of the later prayer-hall, where the small niche to the left of the central doorway would have been the original *mihrab*; the cistern must also have existed in this phase. This building is not readily datable, but would probably not have been earlier than the eighth century AD. Phase II is represented by a complete rebuilding and enlargement of the mosque, almost certainly carried out by the Fatimid caliph Al-Mu'izz between 953 and 965. Phase III probably represents secular reoccupation of the ruins after (long after?) the invasion of the Bani Hilal in 1051.

Arco dei Fileni*

While really outside the scope of a guidebook to antiquities, the remains preserved at Madina Sultan of the Arco dei Fileni, built by the Italians, present an irresistible attraction, and have not been accurately portrayed in recent popular guidebooks.

The construction of an asphalted road between the Egyptian and Tunisian frontiers of Libya was certainly a major engineering feat of the Italian colonial administration. It was built in just over a year, between 1935 and 1936, and the asphalted surface was 5 m wide. The governor of Libya at the time was the charismatic aviator Italo Balbo, and it was his idea to commemorate the completion of the road (which became known as the Via Balbia) by the construction, approximately half-way along it and in the most barren stretch of desert, of a great triumphal arch (fig. 70). The arch was designed by Florestano di Fausto, the architect responsible for a substantial part of Italian official building work in the colony; it took the form of a single tapering pylon 30.85 m high, with an opening 15.75 m high and 6.50 m wide. In style, it had much of the severity of the Fascist architecture of the period and was said to combine Egyptian, Phoenician, Hellenistic and Roman influences. The arch was built of concrete, faced with 350 tonnes of travertine, which was quarried at Tivoli (this was ferried from Civitavecchia to Ras Lanuf in sailing-ships, a journey of 15–20 days); its construction occupied two hundred men for six months and it was completed in February 1937.

Across the three-tiered attic of the arch was inscribed in huge letters a quotation from the *carmen saeculare* of the poet Horace, written in 17 BC and lauding the achievements of the

Fig. 70. The Arco dei Fileni at Ras Lanuf, from a postcard made shortly before its demolition in 1972.

emperor Augustus: ALME SOL POSSIS NIHIL URBE ROMA VISERE MAIUS ('O fostering Sun, may you never see anything greater than the City of Rome!'). Beneath this, on either side of the arch, was a long rectangular recess in which was placed a huge bronze figure, lying on its side and evidently writhing in distress. The allusion is to the legend of the Philaeni, which has come down to us in different forms through various classical authors. The essence of the legend concerns the fixing of the boundary (in the fifth century BC?) between the respective spheres of influence of the Phoenicians of Tripolitania and the Greeks of Cyrenaica. It is said that after long and fruitless conflict, it was decided to settle the matter by a race, in which two pairs of runners were to set out simultaneously from Carthage and from Cyrene, the boundary to be set at the point where they met. This point proved to be near the bottom

of the gulf of the Greater Syrtis, near Ras al-Aali, about half-way between Ras Lanuf and al-Uqaylah. (The Italians actually built their arch at Ras Lanuf, about 30 km to the W.) A glance at the map shows instantly that the Carthaginians (reported as the Philaeni brothers: 'lovers of fame') had run more than three times as far as the Greeks, and they were accused of cheating. In proof of their good faith, they offered (or were challenged) to be buried alive on the spot, and so the frontier came to be fixed. For the latter-day Romans of Fascist Italy this was a crowning example of devotion to one's country, fit to be commemorated on their arch; and so the Philaeni were represented, one on either side, in the act of being buried alive!

After Libyan independence, the Latin inscription across the crown of the arch was replaced by verses from the Qur'an (as seen in the photograph, which dates to about 1970, immediately after the Revolution), but the structure as a whole could not long be allowed to coexist with the Republic, and it was demolished in about 1972. The foundations can just be made out in the road surface, close to the W end of the airstrip at Ras Lanuf. The Department of Antiquities was, however, allowed beforehand to take down the principal sculptures. The two vast bronzes are now set on plinths just inside the entrance to the Madina Sultan antiquities zone (within an enclosure on the left-hand side of the track). A few metres further on, lying on the ground on the opposite side of the track and gradually disappearing beneath the vegetation, are fragments of carved travertine reliefs. These originally formed two tall panels, facing one another across the inside of the arch. Their themes were the Construction

Fig. 71. Figures in the sand: Mussolini salutes the King-Emperor Vittorio Emanuele III to mark the foundation of the (new) Roman Empire.

of the Road and the Foundation of the (new Roman) Empire respectively. The first of these panels showed the land surveyors with their pith helmets and their drawings in the foreground; behind/above them were Arab workmen with sledge-hammers, stone-crushing machinery and the mineral-railway trucks used for moving the soil; and in the far background could be seen a camel-train bringing water in barrels to the waterless wastes of the Syrtica. On the opposite side, the foreground was occupied by the Duce (Mussolini), at the head of his troops, saluting the Re Imperatore (Vittorio Emanuele III, with the moustache); behind the king were the Hills of Rome with their monuments (fig. 71). Above was a farmer ploughing the land (swords into ploughshares, making the desert bloom etc.) and the scene was solemnized in the upper corners by angels blowing trumpets. The arch also carried inscriptions on the E and W faces in both Italian and Latin, commemorating the completion of the road and the establishment of the (new) Empire, the great gift to the world of Fascism. There were two further tablets bearing quotations from 'historic' speeches by Mussolini: one of these may also be seen, in pieces, on the sand.

The effect now, of this preposterous monument, built 'for all time' but demolished some thirty-five years after its construction and with its fragments lying discarded in the sand, is a compelling revisitation of the fallen glories of the Egyptian pharaoh Rameses II, and of Shelley's Ozymandias:

And on the pedestal these words appear:
'My name is Ozymandias, king of kings:
Look on my works, ye Mighty, and despair!'
Nothing beside remains. Round the decay
Of that colossal wreck, boundless and bare
The lone and level sands stretch far away.

Museum

On your R as you enter the archaeo-logical zone is a small museum built around a courtyard (with toilets on the outer side of the N wing). Though a little dusty, its cases are worthy of a brief visit: start by entering the right-hand (S) wing, and make your way round anticlockwise.

The first case inside the door displays prehistoric stone tools from five different sites in the locality. The remaining cases in this wing, including those in the corners, contain finds from a late Roman cemetery at Bin Jawwad, some 80 km to the E. The second island-case contains Tunisian and Tripolitanian dishes in red slip ware of the fourth and fifth centuries AD, and the next two cases contain similar dishes of the sixth and seventh centuries. A dish with an impressed cross in the centre (in the fourth case) is a sixth-century import from Phocaea in Asia Minor. The corner-case beyond contains a variety of non-ceramic objects from the burials: coffin-wood and nails, bone pins and glass items, including Byzantine hanging lamps.

The six cases in the central wing of the museum are devoted mainly to ceramic lamps. The first two (in the row of four) contain lamps from the same Tunisian and Tripolitanian potteries as the dishes already seen (also found at Bin Jawwad): note the Christian crosses and chi-rho monograms. The third case in this row contains late Roman lamps from Surt (where a Christian catacomb has been found); the fourth case contains some bronze bracelets and pins, and some Islamic lamps of the ninth century from Madina Sultan. Of the two inner cases in this wing, the first contains some much earlier lamps of the first to third centuries AD, some of them certainly imports from Italy. These allegedly come from sites on either side of Madina Sultan, at Al-Uqaylah and Al-Qardabiyah. The second case contains further lamps from Surt, and some coins.

The N wing of the museum is devoted to medieval finds from Madina Sultan: the corner-case and the island-case in front of it contain unglazed buff pottery of the eighth and ninth centuries AD and the next two island-cases contain decorated glazed pottery of the tenth and eleventh centuries. The final island-case on this side contains three coins and some fragments of glass. Against the wall to the R of this are some Arabic inscriptions, two in the monumental script known as Kufic, from Madina Sultan, and the third from Umm al-Barakim. In the corner-case are some fragments of architectural decoration, presumably from Madina Sultan, though no provenance is indicated. On the end wall is another fragment of a Kufic inscription from the site, some column-capitals and some further architectural fragments.

The Eastern Jabal
and the Tarhunah plateau

This is the part of Tripolitania which enjoys the highest rainfall and the best agricultural land: it was intensively cultivated in the Roman period and, as a result of Italian colonial activity, it is once again cultivated for cereals and olives today. The terrain is hilly and rolling, extending from the heights around Gharyan (up to 837 m), past the plateau of Tarhunah and down to the coast. In Classical antiquity there were no major settlements here, and indeed it is a particular feature of Tripolitania which contrasts strongly with the distribution of small Roman towns in Tunisia, that the three *emporia* of the coast seem to have dominated their hinterland to the extent of preventing the development of other urban centres. The road built in AD 15/16 by Aelius Lamia from Lepcis Magna into the hinterland for 44 miles (*in mediterraneum*: see p. 93) would have stretched almost as far as Tarhunah and may well have signified the extent of the *territorium* controlled by the city. In any case, the wealth in olive oil implied by the tribute imposed upon Lepcis by Julius Caesar (p. 90) is amply reflected in the traces of Roman olive farms which have been identified in this area. I have mentioned just a few in this guide which may be easily located (al-Khadra, Hinshir Sidi Hamdan, Sanam al-Najm).

The rural inhabitants of these farms certainly required market centres of some sort, and such centres are probably identifiable at Madina Dugha and Ain Wif – where there are also signs of a military presence. Neither of these sites has been investigated extensively, and indeed it is evident that much has been ploughed out or built over on both sites since they were first described. The olive farms, though sometimes very extensive, do not on the whole seem to have included the residences of their owners; it has been suggested that they were occupied and run by managers or tenants, on behalf of owners who lived in comfort on the coast. None the less, the discovery of mosaic floors at Ain Sharshara and the survival of monumental tombs such as those at al-Urban and Qasr Dughah show that there was indeed some display of wealth in the countryside.

The fortunes of the district in late antiquity and in the medieval period are unclear. The advent of Christianity is marked by the church to the east of al-Khadra, and this implies (through features definitely assignable to the Byzantine period) that there was still a sufficient population to maintain and refurbish it in the sixth century. After that, however, there appears to be practically nothing prior to the Italian colonization of the twentieth century; at the end of the nineteenth century, there was no permanent settlement on the Tarhunah plateau, and its seasonal inhabitants lived in underground houses or in tents.

The sites listed below are shown in fig. 60 on p. 141; they are described in order from west to east.

AL-URBAN (ES-SENAMA)

Coordinates: N 32° 2.904', E 13° 19.953'
Directions: The mausoleum stands on high ground, immediately to the N of the southern road between Tarhunah and Gharyan, and is easily visible from a distance; it is within a fenced enclosure, accessible through a turnstile. It is approximately 63 km by road from Tarhunah.

Mausoleum*

The mausoleum has been referred to in the past (by Haynes) as es-Senama; the locality is also known as Bir al-Waar. The solid core of this mausoleum has stood since antiquity, though consolidation and reconstruction carried out in the nineties by the Department of Antiquities has repaired cracks which may have been due to earthquake damage, and has partly restored the columns of the second storey. The structure is 4.64 m. square at the base and now stands to about two thirds of its original height of some 20 m.

The tomb-chamber itself is below ground-level and contains three recesses for the dead; above this is a solid, square podium. The first storey, above this, is adorned with four pilasters on each side, with Corinthian capitals. Above the two central pilasters on each side are funerary portraits in relief, while there are stylized acanthus leaves at the corners. In between the pilaster-capitals are linking arcades in shallow relief, each one framing a shell; above these is a frieze of square panels (not exactly metopes, since there are no triglyphs!) carved with a variety of rosettes, and a decorated cornice (best preserved on the rear of the monument). On the SE side (facing the road) the pilasters are interrupted

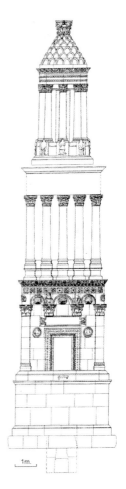

Fig. 72. Reconstruction of the Roman mausoleum at Al-Urban.

by the elaborate frame of a false door. The door itself must have been smashed by tomb-robbers, probably in antiquity: it has been restored in cement. The doorway is framed on either side by *clipei* (roundels) containing portraits (presumably) of the deceased couple; above is a *tabula ansata* frame for an inscription, which may have been painted, since it was not carved.

The second storey was also square, but with a smaller core enclosed within a free-standing Corinthian colonnade, five to a side. The details of the attic of this storey are unclear, though decorated blocks have been found which must belong to it. The third and final storey was smaller again, composed this time of eight Corinthian columns in a circle, supporting an entablature and cornice, above which was a conical pine-cone roof with a final Corinthian capital at the apex. The columns of the third storey stood on a continuous plinth, with a female figure in relief beneath each column: some of these blocks have been set on top of the reconstructed monument, behind the columns of the second storey, presumably for safe-keeping.

Collected together on the ground, to the right of the monument, are many pieces from the highest part of the structure: the circular cornice of the third storey and blocks of the pine-cone roof can be made out. The fenced enclosure also encompasses a more recent cemetery: the dragons' teeth are markers of Muslim burials, presumably placed here because of a belief that the Roman mausoleum either had magical power or contained the remains of a Muslim holy man.

This elaborate monument, with its crowning circular *tholos*, is partly paralleled by the two-storey Qasr ad-Duirat near Lepcis Magna (now reconstructed in front of the museum there, p. 135), and belongs to a type which can be traced back to the Cenotaph of the Julii at Saint-Rémy-en-Provence (c. 30–20 BC). The mausoleum at Al-Urban probably belongs to the (early?) third century AD.

AIN WIF

Coordinates: N 32° 14.526', E 13° 22.214'

Directions: The site is at a road junction, with roads northwards to Souk al-Khamis, eastwards to Tarhunah and southwards to al-Urban and Gharyan.

Roman settlement

The site occupies a narrow ridge between the wadis Wif (to the W) and Hammam (to the E): the palm-fringed springs of Ain Wif below provide sufficient justification for the establishment of a settlement here in Roman times. It is undoubtedly to be identified with *Thenadassa*, named in the Antonine Itinerary as lying on the Jabal road 30 miles to the W of *Mesphe* (Madina Dughah: see p. 162). The site, characterized by 'a low heap of rubble, in which lines of walls are dimly recognizable, and occasional standing-stones indicate orthostat-and-rubble constructions,' has never been excavated. Brief surveys were made in 1948 and in 1981. The main part of the site, on the ridge, has now been totally obliterated by levelling and modern building. Below the main site and close to the springs have been found the remains of a substantial bath-house. An inscribed altar found on the main site and an inscription found in the bath-building both testify to the presence of Roman military officers, indicating that a detachment of the *Legio III Augusta* was stationed here in the early third century; traces of a substantial enclosure towards the S end of the site, still just detectable in 1981, have been interpreted as part of the associated fort. Pottery collected on the surface has indicated occupation from the late first or early second century AD, while the identification of a church suggests continuation at least until the fifth.

AIN SHARSHARA (AIN SCERSCIARA)

Coordinates: N 32° 27.984', E 13° 37.270'
Directions: From the main square in the centre of Tarhunah, head N (to the L of the mosque); fork L after 2 km at N32° 27.050' E13° 37.911' and descend through trees, past a football field on the R and a walled enclosure on the L; the road ends (after a further 2 km) at a waterfall.

Roman pottery kiln and villa

The perennial spring here used to be an admired beauty spot, but the water is now reduced to a trickle as a result both of diversion and of a falling water-table. It would have been equally desirable in antiquity, and the former presence of a residence of some pretension is attested by the discovery, in a road-cutting some 50 m W of the cascade, of a portico with a Roman mosaic floor. No trace of this now remains, nor was the associated villa located in the restricted excavations which took place in 1947. At that time, however, signs of pottery-making were discovered 100 m along the track to the N of (i.e. beyond) the cascade. One small and two large pottery-kilns were identified: one of the latter was sufficiently well preserved to be consolidated and left open to inspection.

The kiln is now surrounded by a new enclosure fence and wall, and cannot be missed as you look at the hillside on the far side of the waterfall. It consists of the lower part of a circular structure over 6 m in diameter (and therefore one of the largest known of its type), enclosed by a wall of partially-fired clay blocks; within is a perforated floor upon which the vessels to be fired were

stacked; the floor is supported by arches which radiate from a central pillar. The stoke-hole arch in the perimeter wall was found in the excavations, but is no longer visible; it showed that the combustion-chamber, in which the fire was placed, was originally 4.50 m deep. It is not possible to say whether the firing-chamber would have had a permanent superstructure, or would have been built up and then broken down for each firing of the kiln. The angular outer wall within the present enclosure is modern and is all that remains of a previous consolidation of the area. There has been little study of the products which were fired here, but they certainly included amphorae (for oil) ranging in date from the late second to the late fourth centuries AD.

The ancient name of the settlement here (or in the vicinity) was *Cercar*; the distance is slightly more than 44 Roman miles from Lepcis Magna (the length of the road built by Aelius Lamia in the first century AD: p. 93) and this may therefore have represented the easternmost settlement under the control of Oea.

DUGHAH (DOGA)

Coordinates: N 32° 29.271', E 13° 41.933'
Directions: Leave Tarhunah eastwards on the road to Qusbat/Al-Khums and turn left after 7.5 km at N 32° 26.283' E 13° 42.728'. Follow this road northwards through huge olive plantations. The mausoleum will become visible on high ground ahead of you, across a wadi. Follow the road round to the left into the modern village, and then turn right (6 km from the junction with the main road) at N 32° 29.212' E 13° 41.647' onto an unmade track (uninviting, but passable in a saloon car) which leads down to the mausoleum.

Qasr Dughah (Gasr Doga) mausoleum*

This imposing rectangular mausoleum was originally three storeys high. What remains is a solid mass of ashlar masonry, 9.30 m high out of an estimated 15 m, far more elongated than usual, as the sides are drawn forwards in the form of two massive piers flanking a deeply recessed façade. The two existing storeys are each framed by simple pilasters at the corners and bounded by a base-moulding below and a cornice above. The third storey was embellished with a Corinthian colonnade in a basic arrangement of nine by six, recessed to the third row of columns across the front. There are fragments of these columns and capitals on the ground around the monument and they presumably enclosed some sort of *cella*, but of this no identifiable trace remains. At ground-level, a corridor between the flanking piers (probably originally a manhole in the paving) leads down into two vaulted burial-chambers. The inner chamber has two low stone benches against the rear wall, and niches in the opposite wall which may have been intended for lamps.

Excavations carried out around the monument in 2003 have exposed a variety of (ostensibly) post-Roman structures built up against it, which make use of fallen elements from the superstructure.

As usual with monuments of this type, there is no direct dating-evidence, and there is no associated inscription. In comparison with some other monumental mausolea of the Tripolitanian hinterland, what this one lacks in richness of decoration, it makes up for in sheer mass. It is unlikely to post-date the third century AD, and from the style of the column-capitals it

Fig. 73. Reconstruction of the Roman mausoleum at Qasr Dugha.

is also unlikely to be earlier.

Madina Dughah (Doga) settlement

About 2 km to the S of the mausoleum, in a large olive plantation, are occasional traces of Roman masonry and scatters of Roman pottery. This has been identified as the site of a village or road-station during the Roman period, at a point where up to five roads converged. It is almost certainly *Mesphe*, recorded in the Antonine Itinerary as the first station to the W of Lepcis Magna on the Jabal road, at a distance of 42 Roman miles. A colonnaded building and two bath buildings were detectable on the surface in 1949, together with a large enclosure built of ashlar blocks (possibly military?). Very little is now visible, and much has probably been destroyed in the intervening years by ploughing.

AL-KHADRA (BREVIGLIERI)

Coordinates: N 32° 26.619', E 13° 45.887'
Directions: The former Italian colonial centre of Breviglieri, now al-Khadra, is 12 km due

E of Tarhunah on the road to Qusbat and Al-Khums.

Olive farm

The old colonial centre of Breviglieri is now a few metres to the N of the main road, and faces onto an irregular piazza with a wired enclosure which is strewn with rubbish. This encloses the square, grooved, pressing-slabs and uprights of two Roman olive-presses ('Sanam at-Thubah'), demonstrating the presence here of an olive farm in Roman times.

Sanctuary of Jupiter Ammon

About 800 m to the NW of the piazza, on a low hill-top, were found in 1947 the foundations of a small country shrine. This was the source of an inscription, found many years earlier, recording the construction of a shrine to the Libyan god Jupiter Ammon in the proconsulship of L. Aelius Lamia (AD 15–17).

Church and fortified building

The ruins described below lie 8 km to the E of al-Khadra and 400 m to the S of the road; when travelling eastwards from Tarhunah, cross the Wadi al-Farjan and stop outside a school on the S side of the road at N 32° 27.011'

E 13° 50.677'. Walk up the track on the left-hand side of the school, and the ruins will be visible on the crest of the ridge to your R, at N 32° 26.795' E 13° 50.687'.

This complex of ruins (see fig. 74) was excavated by Giacomo Caputo between 1939 and 1942, and a more extended study was made by another Italian team in 1967. The excavation was left open, with the result that the existing walls have deteriorated substantially and little of the detail which was recorded is now visible. The church faces towards the W, and immediately beyond it in this direction is a complex of ruins around a late Roman fortified building. An inscription in Latin characters, but in the Libyan language and therefore not fully understood, at least makes it clear that the building was a *centenarium* (whatever that was: see the glossary). This inscription must have been placed above the entrance to the building and was found nearby. The walls are in roughly-coursed rubble masonry, and their solidity suggests a tower-type structure with an internal courtyard; the former presence of three internal staircases is surely unique and perhaps confirms its military character (giving rapid access from the courtyard to look-out or fighting platforms above).

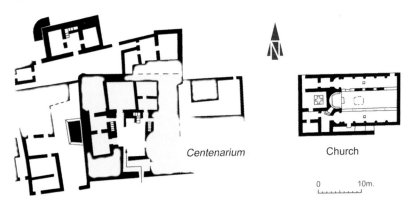

Centenarium   Church

0   10m.

Fig. 74. Plan of the church and centenarium to the E of al-Khadra.

During the excavations, a Vandal coin of the fifth century was found embedded between two blocks. Around the original core of the fort (?) are traces of further outbuildings.

It has been disputed whether the church went through two phases, having been built initially in the fifth century AD and subsequently enlarged in the sixth (Ward-Perkins and Goodchild), or whether it is entirely Byzantine (i.e. of the sixth century: Caputo, De Angelis and Farioli). Since none of the detail is now visible on the ground, the arguments need not detain us. The basic structure consists of a nave and aisles, separated by two rows of columns carrying arcades (the voussoirs of one of these are laid out on the ground). Engaged semi-columns against the outer walls, corresponding to those of the nave arcades, suggest that the aisles may have been vaulted; the nave almost certainly had a timber roof above a clerestory. There is a raised apse at the W end, and behind this is a baptistery with a cruciform font, which is typical of the Byzantine period. The interior of the church was adorned with elaborately decorated architectural fittings in carved limestone: the surviving pieces, most of which are now on display in Room 13 of the National Museum in Tripoli, include window-frames, which probably came from the clerestory, and impost blocks and brackets, the original positions of which are uncertain. Their chip-carved ornament consists mainly of geometrical and foliage patterns.

QASR AD-DAWUN (GASR ED-DAUUN)

Coordinates: N 32° 27.397', E 13° 54.388'
Directions: This lies on the Tarhunah–Qusbat road.

Settlement

The Roman road from Lepcis Magna to the Tarhunah area passed through this area and there are scattered traces of ancient settlement, including the remains of several ancient dams (one of which may have carried the road) in the bed of the Wadi al-Mayy below the road. (Traces may be made out just below both of the modern bridges across the wadi; another may be seen upstream of the village from the small Turkish fort which overlooks the area from high ground to the W, next to the filling station.) The construction is uniformly of boulders set in mortar. There are wells here, and this has probably always been a market-centre or gathering-point of some sort. No excavation has been carried out, and there are no signs of a formal layout or of any military presence, but the settlement is probably to be associated with the name *Subututtu* which appears on the ancient map known as the Peutinger Table. High on a spur to the E of the village, where the main road and the wadi diverge, are traces of a substantial enclosure resembling the late Roman fortified farms of the pre-desert. A survey made c. 1950 showed a trapezoidal enclosure with entrances on opposite sides and rooms around an internal courtyard; excavation in the gateways showed that the walls were standing in places to 3 m. in height. Late Roman pottery was found in association with it.

SANAM AL-NAJM

Coordinates: N 32° 25.919', E 13° 55.140'
Directions: The site is 3 km by road to the SE of Qasr ad-Dawun, on the road to Wadi Taraglat. It stands immediately above the road on the right-hand side.

Olive farm

Close by the road here are the tumbled orthostats of a Roman olive farm, with three pairs of uprights for olive-presses still standing in position. A few kilometres further down this road (which leads past Hinshir Sidi Hamdan) the remains of a similar farm may be seen a little way off to the L.

HINSHIR SIDI HAMDAN

Coordinates: N 32° 24.016', E 13° 59.490'
Directions: Turn off the Tarhunah–Qusbat road at Qasr ad-Dawun and head SE towards Wadi Taraglat. The site is just to the R of the road at a distance of 11 km by road from Qasr ad-Dawun.

Olive farm*

This is the site of one of the largest olive farms in the hinterland of Lepcis

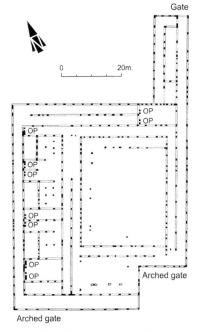

Fig. 75. *Plan of the olive farm at Hinshir Sidi Hamdan. OP = Olive Press.*

Magna. The buildings used the *opus africanum* type of construction, with walls given a sturdy framework of massive upright stone blocks (orthostats), set quite widely apart and then infilled between with small rubble masonry, concrete or mud-brick. The orthostats may be monolithic, or they may (as mostly here) be in the form of massive ashlar piers. As a result, such buildings, when ruinous, give the impression of a vast spread of tumbled stone with dragons' teeth projecting from the rubble at regular intervals.

At Hinshir Sidi Hamdan, the orthostats allow one to identify the basic outlines of the layout: a regularly planned rectangular building measuring about 58 × 52 m, with an internal courtyard, off which may have opened rooms for the resident labourers. Along the NW side of the building was a row of pressing-rooms housing seven olive-presses, in between which cuttings in the openings (no longer visible) suggested the presence of bins or hoppers for the olives, which could be shovelled out through a hinged flap at floor-level. Close examination of the uprights of the olive-presses shows that when the fulcrum bar was withdrawn from the lowest anchorage holes, it could rest in a slot in the adjoining block (see fig. 77). Two more presses are housed in a separate room in the E corner of the principal courtyard. None of the grooved pressing-slabs or counterweights are visible, but the present ground-level is probably a metre or more above the original floors, so they may remain buried. At the E corner was a substantial rectangular extension, with its own entrance from the outside – perhaps living-quarters, though this cannot be established without excavation. (A scattering of

Fig. 76. Orthostats of the Roman olive farm at Hinshir Sidi Hamdan.

mosaic tesserae in the vicinity may support this inference.) A principal (arched) gateway at the S corner led into a subsidiary courtyard, in which the presence of stone water-troughs suggests that animals may have been housed. The water-supply for the establishment was provided by a cistern excavated on higher ground about 130 m to the S.

The potential output of the farm (or 'oilery') at Hinshir Sidi Hamdan has been estimated at up to 100,000 litres in a good year and, though it is larger than the average for the Tarhunah region, it is not the largest; the farm at Senam Semana 35 km to the NW, where seventeen presses were counted in 1897, could have supported double that output. For lack of excavation,

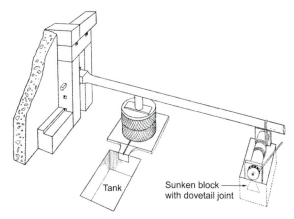

Fig. 77. Reconstruction drawing of a Roman olive-press, based on examples at Hinshir Sidi Hamdan.

The Eastern Jabal and the Tarhunah plateau

there is little direct dating-evidence for the life-span of these farms. The robust outer wall, some 5 m high, will have deterred uninvited intruders, as one would wish to do anyway with the kind of capital investment which the installation represents; but it does not suggest that defence was given the same priority as in the late Roman *qsur* of the pre-desert. It is also of note that these farms practically never show signs of the domestic comfort which ought to accompany the wealth that they represent. It is therefore likely that they were owned by absentee landlords, living at Lepcis Magna or in the luxury villas along the coast (such as that at Silin), and that the residents of the farms were essentially tenants, managers or slaves. Their heyday therefore probably coincides with that of Lepcis, covering more or less the first three centuries AD.

The pre-desert zone

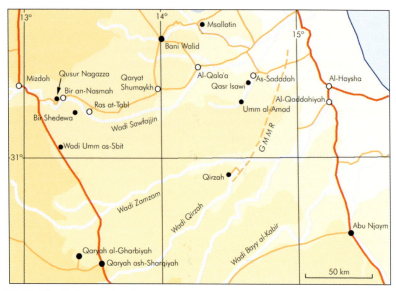

Fig. 78. Sites in the pre-desert zone.

Much of this region is technically pre-desert: barren stony wastes are dissected by wadis of all sizes which have flat alluvial flood-plains. These are capable of supporting agriculture when the seasonal rains come. Such agriculture was practised in the Roman period through careful water management; this involved building low walls across the wadis in order both to detain the rushing waters of occasional spates, encouraging them to sink into the soil, and to prevent the soil itself from being carried away by the torrent. Cisterns were also dug and water draining off the higher ground was channelled into them, providing a reserve for watering flocks in between the rains. Field survey over the last fifty years has shown a density of occupation of this zone in Classical antiquity which is only now being matched again. One of the areas which gives the best impression now of how these wadis would have appeared in, say, the fourth century AD is at Bani Walid, shown in fig. 79: the wadi floor is dissected by walls which retain small lakes after the rains have passed, and in these stand olive trees; later on, cereals will be grown beneath them. Meanwhile, the habitations of those who live here cluster along the banks of the wadi on the higher ground.

In this landscape, which is treeless except low down on the wadi floors, the fortified farms of the late Roman period stand out as solid masses of masonry, sometimes still three storeys high and even preserving doorways bridged by wooden lintels which must be original. They caught the attention of early travellers and are still remarkable today. Scholars at first thought that their solidity and regularity indicated a military origin, and this was reinforced by occasional Latin inscriptions (as at Qasr Duib, p. 201) which refer to them as *centenaria*. It was concluded that they were the homes of the *limitanei*, military personnel settled in the frontier zone in the late Roman period in order to support the Roman provincial administration as soldier-farmers. Now, however, it is clear that these late Roman fortified farms (known as *qsur*, castles, like the communal granaries of the Jabal Nafusah) are in many cases successors to open (i.e. less defensible) farms with buildings assembled around courtyards, which start in the second and possibly even in the first centuries AD. Likewise, scholars no longer feel impelled to regard these buildings as the habitations of immigrants or colonists. Where there are tombs with inscriptions, what we see are the indigenous people, choosing to adopt to a greater or lesser extent Roman ways.

The settlements in this landscape naturally congregate in those areas which are most susceptible of cultivation, but on the whole (as for instance in the Bir Shedewa basin, p. 180) this results simply in scattered buildings within sight of one another. Ghirza (p. 182) is exceptional in being a more concentrated settlement which could be described as a village or tribal centre. In 1817, Commander W.H. Smyth visited this site, having heard elaborate tales about it, and was offended at what he saw as primitive attempts to build and to decorate in the Classical style; in the 1930s, the Italian Lieutenant Guido Bauer proposed the construction of an airstrip, so that tourists might come to admire these tokens of penetration of the desert margin by the civilizing force of Rome. Thus are we inevitably conditioned to see the monuments of antiquity through the perceptions of our own time. There seems no reason now not to regard them as part of an entirely Libyan heritage: there are many more such monuments in the pre-desert zone than I have listed here (including ruined churches), but I have attempted to describe a representative selection that is reasonably accessible.

To the S of this zone lies true desert, and two of the traditional routes across the Sahara. These were controlled for a while in the third century AD by legionary forts at Qaryah al-Gharbiyah and Abu Njaym. The discovery at the latter of numerous *ostraca*, ephemeral records of camp life and administration written on potsherds, has given us a remarkable insight into the realities of military duty in this zone.

There seems no order in which to describe the sites in this region which might correspond to a tourist itinerary; the arrangement of this section is therefore purely alphabetical.

Fig. 79. Wadi Bani Walid after winter rain.

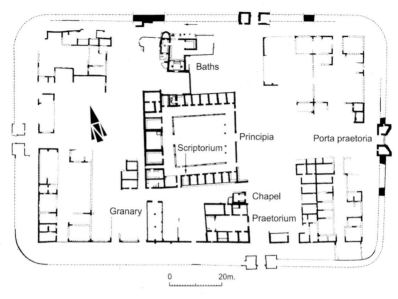

Fig. 80. Abu Njaym: plan of the legionary fort.

ABU NJAYM (BU NGEM)

Coordinates: N 30° 34.586', E 15° 24.166'
Directions: The modern agglomeration lies on the road which leads southwards from al-Haysha to Waddan and Fazzan at about 80 km from al-Haysha. The abandoned Italian colonial fort (to which the given coordinates refer) is visible to the left of the road and to the S of the oasis; the Roman fort is visible against the horizon 1 km to the E.

Fort*

The strategic realities of the little oasis at Abu Njaym are reflected in the presence of both Roman and Italian forts at the same spot, where they could regulate traffic between Fazzan and the coast. The troops entrusted with the building of the Roman fort of *Gholaia* arrived on site on 24 January AD 201, and the latest definite evidence that we have for military occupation is in 259. (It had certainly ended by 263.) The garrison would have been around 500 men and for part of that time it included a cavalry component. There was clearly also a civil component to the local population, for an extensive scattered settlement around the fort is evident from aerial photographs. Occupation of parts at least of this settlement (including the fort itself) persisted after the formal withdrawal of troops, as late as the fifth century AD.

The N gate of the fort was standing to its full height when seen and drawn by G.F. Lyon in 1819 (fig. 81); our knowledge is otherwise derived principally from the work of a French team which carried out excavations under the direction of René Rebuffat between 1967 and 1976. At the time of those excavations, tops of walls were consolidated with cement and two of the most interesting buildings (the *scriptorium* in the *principia* and the main baths) were provided with protective roofs. The wind and the sand have long since reasserted their

Fig. 81. Abu Njaym: the North Gate as drawn by G. F. Lyon in 1819.

pre-eminence: the roofs are smashed and the hollows filled with sand. Much is visible, none the less, and this will doubtless vary in character from one time to another.

The fort has the typical 'playing-card' outline of a rectangle with rounded corners, measuring 138 × 93 m – just half the size of the contemporary fort at Qaryah al-Gharbiyah (p. 196). It conforms to the normal type for the period, being divided internally into three more-or-less equal parts. The principal entrance, the *porta praetoria*, faces E and has chamfered external walls (fig. 82). Note the slot and socket for the beam which fastened the double doors, and which could be withdrawn into the guardroom on the N side. On entering the fort from this direction, one encounters four barrack blocks (two on either side) and then the headquarters building (*principia*), flanked on the right by a bath-building and on the left by the commandant's house (*praetorium*) and the granary. The third part of the fort, behind the *principia*, also contained barrack-blocks, though the layout on the northern side is not entirely certain. There were four gates, two interval towers, and probably curving towers at the corners like that which still survives at Qaryah al-Gharbiyah. The construction was mostly of small rubble masonry, with large ashlars of the local hard grey limestone used for the lower parts of the gates, and for piers and orthostats elsewhere. It is interesting, and a little surprising, that the dimensions of the fort correspond exactly to 270 × 180 Punic cubits, rather than to some measure in Roman feet. It seems also that a surveying error in laying out the N gate (which is not opposite to the S gate) was responsible for the skewed alignment of several of the internal buildings.

Fig. 82. Abu Njaym: the porta praetoria.

The *principia* had a large central courtyard surrounded by porticoes, still marked out by their surviving orthostats; in the centre of the side opposite to the main entrance was the Chapel of the Standards, with access through a trap-door in the NE corner to the strong-room beneath. (A head of a helmeted war-goddess, found here, is on display in Room 18 of the museum at Lepcis Magna.) The southern end of the portico in front of this range terminates in a raised tribunal, and the first room in the S range, close to this, was a *scriptorium* (a very rare discovery) with a central stone writing-desk and benches. The other rooms around the courtyard will have been offices, storerooms and armouries. A remarkable aspect of the excavations at Abu Njaym has been the discovery, in the southern part of the *principia* and in a dump against the outside wall near the *scriptorium*, of hundreds of inscribed sherds, or *ostraca*, recording many different aspects of the fort's daily life during the last three years or so of its occupation. Because of the lack of other writing materials, all kinds of records were written on broken potsherds; it seems that when

these were no longer of interest, they were simply dumped outside. It is very possible that thousands more such texts lie in the huge unexcavated midden which is clearly visible to the SW of the fort. Those which have been read and published consist entirely of administrative records: lists of strengths of units, indicating duties to which soldiers were allocated and those off sick; records of deliveries of supplies (mostly by camel); letters recording the despatch of supplies etc. We can even read of the arrival at the fort of a party of Garamantes bringing letters (of introduction?) for the commandant, four donkeys, two Egyptians and a runaway slave!

The *praetorium* is composed of rooms around a courtyard, with the dining room (*triclinium*) on the W side, opposite to the entrance. Attached to the N side of the *praetorium* is a two-room chapel, with benches along the walls of the outer room; the *cella* within was found to contain an altar dedicated to the *Genius* of *Gholaia*, and a later dedication to the *Numen Praesens* (the 'present spirit', a similar concept). The space immediately behind the *praetorium* has not been excavated, but beyond that the two piers in the centre of the two-aisled granary may be made out.

The baths on the N side of the *principia* were approached by a descending flight of steps, and were preserved up to roof-level when excavated. Despite the provision of a cover building, the structure is once more entirely buried. The baths were entered from the S side through a stepped lobby flanked by columns, where was displayed an inscription commemorating the completion of the building in 202/3. This handsome stone (which deserves to be on display) carries eighteen lines of verse, dedicating the baths to *Salus* (Health) and to her refreshing waters, which are so crucial to those living under the flaming sun amidst the dunes of sand. This inscription is at first sight anonymous, but it is in fact an acrostic: the first letter of each line spells out the name Q(uintus) Avidius Quintianus! The lobby led down into the main *frigidarium*, from which opened a meeting-room lined with benches to the right, and a second *frigidarium* with a cold plunge-bath in an apse to the left. From this lesser *frigidarium* one passed into a small *tepidarium* and into the

hot rooms beyond. The contemporary sketch of the fort reproduced in fig. 83 was scratched into the plaster on the apse of the lesser *frigidarium*: whilst simplified in certain respects, it shows clearly the great height of the towers. Another verse inscription, found in pieces in the bath-building and concealing the name of its dedicator in a similar acrostic, commemorates the restoration of one of the gates of the fort in 222 and tells us specifically that the towers had four floors.

Aerial photography, and indeed a walk over the landscape, shows that the fort was surrounded by a scatter of small buildings, representing the civil settlement that grew up around it. A building which stands on a slight eminence some 400 m to the E is composed of a rectangular room with an external apse and four internal stone piers; there were raised benches for worshippers along either side. An altar found here showed it to be a Temple to Mars Canapphar. On the northern side of the oasis, a temple to Jupiter Ammon was found. Dedicatory inscriptions relating to both of these temples are on display in Room 18 of the museum at Lepcis Magna; there

10cm.

Fig. 83. Abu Njaym: the appearance of the fort in a contemporary graffito scratched on a wall in the baths.

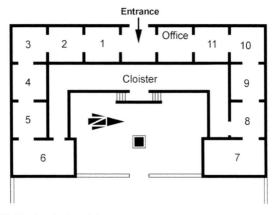

Fig. 84. Bani Walid: sketch-plan of the museum.

is also an inscription from one of the gates in the National Museum in Tripoli (between Rooms 10 and 11).

BANI WALID (BENI ULID)

Coordinates: N 31° 45.318', E 14° 1.072'

Directions: The coordinates are those of the museum, which stands close to the present pastiche of the former Turkish castle that overlooks the wadi-crossing on the S side. After crossing the wadi (from the N) fork L at the top of the rise: the museum is on the L after another 100 m, readily identified by re-erected sandstone columns on either side of the gate and by ancient Corinthian capitals on top of the boundary wall.

Museum*

Bani Walid exemplifies the kind of prosperity which can be derived from pre-desert wadi-agriculture, with handsome, mature olive trees growing in profusion in the bed of the wadi (see fig. 79); from here eastwards along the wadi (see below under Msallatin, p. 195) are plentiful signs of occupation in Roman and post-Roman times. It is ' therefore fitting that this should have been chosen as the location for

a museum dedicated principally to illustrating the monuments of Roman settlement in the pre-desert from here southwards. (Beware, however, of items from Tripoli and Lepcis Magna!) The museum, which was opened in 1999, is arranged on three sides of a courtyard and is entered in the centre of the W side; the visitor should proceed to the R after entering the lobby, which is flanked by re-erected columns.

Room 1

This contains the obligatory display of prehistory, with photographs and casts of rock-art in the Tadrart Acacus in the extreme SW of the country. The case on the left-hand wall contains flint implements and quern-stones for grinding corn, but no provenance is indicated. The entrance to the next room is framed between two Punic amphorae from a tomb in Tripoli.

Room 2

In the centre of the floor are five small stone cinerary chests with neo-Punic inscriptions on their lids. These are from a tomb at Lepcis Magna ascribed to the early third century AD. On the left-hand wall is a carved stone doorframe from a Punic temple in Wadi Marsit (to the S of the Bir Shedewa area). There are portrait-heads on the lintel and standing figures on the uprights. The figure on the right is interpreted as that of a priest or god; there is a triangular symbol of Tanit above. A wall-case on this side of the room contains small objects from tombs: two bronze mirrors, some unslipped dishes on pedestal feet, often used in religious rites, and some late Hellenistic and early Roman *unguentaria*.

On the opposite wall is a reproduction of an Egyptian tomb-painting showing Libyans in procession; to the right is a wall-case containing *lagynoi* (squat narrow-necked flagons) from tombs in Tripoli and ovoid jars used as cinerary urns for animal-offerings in the tophets of Sabratha (see p. 71) and Masallatah. The second case on this wall contains examples of black-slipped tableware, whose provenance is not indicated. These pieces are of the second or first centuries BC (the label incorrectly attributes them to a later date) and they are therefore likely to have been found in tombs in the coastal region, rather than inland. In opposite corners of the room are two displays of amphorae, showing a variety of Greek and Punic types of the late Hellenistic or Roman periods found in tombs in Tripoli.

Room 3

Going clockwise around the room from the entrance, the first three pieces of sculpture are blocks from a tomb in Wadi Migdal, which is illustrated to the L of the archway. They show women in mourning (with their hands on their heads), a lion chasing a deer (or the like) and a fish. The end wall is occupied mainly by part of an obelisk-

tomb from the Wadi Khalbun. The single reconstructed storey is framed by engaged Corinthian columns supporting a frieze and a projecting cornice. On the face towards the room is an unframed inscription recording the names of the deceased and of the constructors of the monument (showing the usual mixture of native and Latinized names). Below this is a tiny figure of Hercules, with club and lion-skin, and above is another standing figure; on the frieze is a lion chasing a donkey. The left-hand face is very battered, but is filled by a false door with indeterminate reliefs (busts?) between the capitals and animals on the frieze. To the left of this monument is another frieze-block from Wadi Khalbun, showing a man leading a yoke of oxen pulling a cart; the two blocks on the right-hand side of the room are from the same wadi.

The wall-case on the left-hand side of the room contains coins from Lepcis Magna and elsewhere (not sympathetically displayed). On the right-hand side are two wall-cases: the first contains plain and red-slipped cups and beakers of the first century AD. No provenance is indicated: they are probably from either Tripoli or Lepcis Magna. The second case contains fragments of architectural ornament from Wadi Khanafis and Wadi Antar.

Room 4

This room is filled with sculpted blocks, many carved in very high relief and mostly from tombs in Wadi Antar. Notice in particular, immediately on the L as you enter this room, a very lively Winged Victory, carrying a palm and wearing the most enormous boots! A case of fine pottery on the right-hand wall comes from Lepcis Magna. The pieces are Italian imports of the first century AD, from Tuscany and Campania.

Fig. 85. Bani Walid Museum: part of a richly carved tomb from Wadi Khanafis.

Room 5

In the centre of this room are two Corinthian capitals surmounted by pine-cones, which are examples of the finials which topped most of the obelisk-tombs in the pre-desert. (See also the example in the courtyard.) The more complete example is from tomb South A at Ghirza (p. 194) and the other is from tomb A in Wadi Umm al-Ajrim. On the left-hand side of the room, the charming carving in the wall-case of a man climbing a date-palm is from Wadi al-Binaya. The rest of the material on this side is from Ghirza: there are columns, capitals and arcuate lintels from tomb South F, a cast of the inscription flanked by eagles from

tomb North A (also shown in the photographs on either side of it) and, at your feet, a selection of offering-tables and columnar tomb-markers from lesser burials in the south cemetery.

The architectural elements on the right-hand side of the room are from Wadi Umm al-Ajrim and the two lions which flank the archway between this room and Room 6 are from Wadi Antar. In the first wall-case on the right-hand side are figs, olives and almonds found in a tomb in Wadi al-Binaya; above is an amphora from a tomb at Lepcis Magna. The second wall-case contains a display of pottery lamps from Lepcis and the surrounding area; the examples on the bottom shelf are Hellenistic, those on the middle shelf are of the first and second centuries AD (probably from Italy and Tunisia), those on the top are Tunisian and Tripolitanian lamps of the fourth and fifth centuries.

Room 6

The last room in the S wing is devoted entirely (apart from the wall-cases) to finds from Wadi Khanafis (the wadi 'of the beetles'). It is dominated by the fine tomb which has been reconstructed at the left-hand end (fig. 85). This is thought to portray a priest or chieftain, who is represented in the round, standing within a shell-headed niche flanked by engaged columns with exotic capitals. The whole façade is framed by larger engaged columns with Corinthian capitals, above which is a composition, carved entirely in the round, showing a lion and a lioness, heraldically opposed about the head of a bull. (This motif occurs also on friezes in the south cemetery at Ghirza: one such block is on display in Room 19 of the Lepcis Magna Museum.) The monument is attributed to the third century AD. On the long wall between the two doors is part of another tomb-façade, with a false door, a dedicatory inscription which has overflowed two *tabulae ansatae* provided for it, and part of an ornate vine-scroll pilaster on the left-hand side.

The other long wall contains three wall-cases. The right-hand one houses four small amphorae (provenance not stated); the central case contains three stone cinerary urns from Lepcis Magna and the left-hand one contains four glass cinerary urns, partly encased in lead, from Tripoli.

Cloister

The second door in Room 6 leads into the cloister surrounding the courtyard. On the S side are further fragments of relief-carving from tombs in the pre-desert zone; the first four blocks are from Wadi Khanafis, the others from various other wadis. On the W side of the cloister are reassembled blocks from the sima (parapet) of one of the Ghirza tombs (probably South C, though in that case the central palmette has been interpolated from another tomb). On the N side of the cloister are reassembled blocks from the frieze of a tomb in Wadi al-Binaya, including lively hunting scenes (note the man on horseback pursuing an ostrich) and the usual scenes of ploughing (one with a camel) and reaping.

Courtyard

The courtyard is reached by steps from the centre of the W range of the

Fig. 86. Bani Walid Museum: reconstructed obelisk-tomb from Wadi Umm al-Ajrim.

cloister. The centrepiece here is an entire obelisk-tomb from Wadi Umm al-Ajrim (Agerem: fig. 86). The tomb stands on a plain square plinth, above which the first storey is contained between a broad base-moulding and a corresponding cornice. There are plain pilasters at the corners, with simple capitals; above these is a frieze of rosettes, which also includes on the principal face a *tabula ansata* with the dedicatory inscription (containing Libyan and neo-Punic names). The second storey is framed by engaged columns at the corners, supporting curious basket-like capitals and a frieze with a continuous vegetal scroll. Above this is another broad cornice, a tapering obelisk and a finial in the form of a stylized Corinthian capital surmounted by a pine-cone. The inner and outer courtyards contain many further decorated architectural blocks and elements of tombs; particularly charming is a fluted sandstone column with a vine spiralling round it. This was found in Wadi Merdum and its twin (surely) may be seen in the museum at Zlitan (p. 149).

N wing

Returning to the cloister, one enters the N wing. Rooms 7–9 are devoted to an ethnographic display of traditional dress, agricultural and domestic tools and other objects. Room 10 displays testimonials and gifts made to the Leader of the Revolution and shows some of the local achievements of the Revolution, including a model of Bani Walid hospital and its associated residential facilities. The final room, 11, has a model of a woollen factory on the left and of a hardware factory on the right; examples of their products are also on display.

BIR AN-NASMAH (BIR NESMAH)

Coordinates: N 31° 21.385', E 13° 15.658'
Directions: The coordinates given are those of the first (and more prominent) building described below. To reach it, take the main road S from Mizdah, and turn L at N 31° 20.181' E 13° 3.839', about 15 km from Mizdah. Follow this road for 25 km along the course of the Wadi Sawfajjin. After a long loop southwards, the two *qsur* described here will be seen on the L, framing a tributary wadi. Qasr Nagazza W is about 350 m from the road (at N 31° 20.951' E 13° 15.209'), with a reasonable track leading directly past it; Qasr Nagazza E is about 500 m from the road, and unless you have a 4-wheel-drive vehicle is best approached on foot.

Qasr Nagazza East*

About 8 km upstream from Bir an-Nasmah is a group of monuments of the Roman period, dominated by two large farm buildings set about 1 km apart, on the N bank and on either side of a tributary wadi; they are known jointly as Qsur Nagazza (or perhaps it is uncertain to which one the name should apply?). Qasr Nagazza East is the better preserved, being a solid structure about 20 m square and still standing to

Fig. 87. Qasr Nagazza East from above.

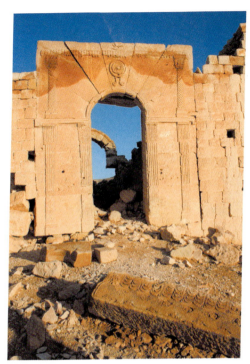

Fig. 88. The ornate entrance to Qasr Nagazza East.

an eagle grasping a hare in its talons. There is further elaboration at the inner end of the entrance passage: voussoirs of an arch with a decorated keystone (motif now unidentifiable) standing upon engaged columns with Corinthian capitals. (The right-hand column, which was unfluted, has disappeared since 1981: the fact that the pair did not match one another suggests that this was already a secondary use for them.) The fallen debris, both inside and in front of the monument, includes a number of other fragments of elaborate architectural ornament. Within the building, there was a central courtyard surrounded by perhaps four rooms, but the detail is obscured by the masses of fallen masonry. There is a staircase leading to an upper floor on the R, within the entrance passage; there is a carved tethering-ring on the outside of the right-hand wall of the building, towards the front. This farm must have belonged to someone of considerable wealth; pottery found in the vicinity ranges between the third and fifth centuries AD.

Qasr Nagazza West

This is built in similar masonry to the upper parts of its neighbour, and it too has an entrance framed by large dressed voussoir blocks, but it was less elaborately decorated. A rosette within a cable-wreath above the entrance is now fallen; but in front of the entrance lies a fragment of a frieze with dolphins on it. The inner entrance, into the courtyard, is set at ninety degrees to the outer one (for easier defence); but it is composed

a considerable height in places. The building stands high above the valley floor on a spur of rock, from which it is cut off by a rock-cut ditch (fig. 87); this must have cost considerable labour to construct. The masonry is ashlar, with massive blocks and squared corners in the foundation courses, smaller stones and rounded corners above. The entrance is set within a huge rectangular frame, elaborately decorated with two tiers of pilasters (fig. 88): the four below have flat, fluted shafts and rather stylized capitals and bases; the two above are rather rounder, spirally-fluted and with Corinthian capitals. They support a laurel-stave which runs across the top. There is a ribboned rosette on the keystone of the arch, and the lower part of another motif above the laurel-stave which was probably

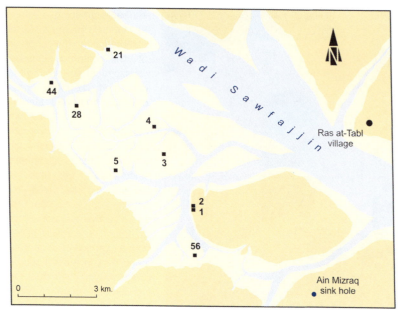

Fig. 89. *Plan of the Bir Shedewa basin, showing the locations of late Roman qsur (fortified farms).*

of much more impressive blocks, with an arch set within a rectangular outer frame. This can hardly have been seen to full advantage here and one cannot help wondering whether the door-frames were obtained from a specialist mason elsewhere and then erected in the wrong positions by the local builder! Within, there is a scatter of decorated architectural elements and the vaults of some of the rooms survive. The over-all structure is approximately 26 m square, with rounded corners. It is surrounded by a rock-cut ditch which is crossed by a plaster-lined aqueduct channel; this can be traced snaking across the higher ground behind for about 100 m, at which point it opens out into two low walls which funnelled the run-off from the hillside behind into a cistern within the building.

The surrounding area shows other signs of intensive activity in the Roman period: closer to the wadi are traces of an open courtyard-farm which has yielded pottery of the second to fourth/fifth centuries; there are cross-wadi walls designed to hold up the flow of flood-water and so improve fertility, and there are at least two separate cemeteries, marked either by cairns or by traces of more substantial mausolea. A cistern in modern use, by the wadi edge, is almost certainly ancient in origin.

BIR SHEDEWA (BIR SCEDUA)

Coordinates: N 31° 18.003', E 13° 24.816'
Directions: The area described is in a broad but dissected part of the Wadi Sawfajjin, roughly 10–15 km SE of Bir an-Nasmah. **A 4-wheel-drive vehicle is most certainly required for its exploration.** Follow the asphalt road eastwards from Bir an-Nasmah,

for a distance of about 12 km, and then fork R at N 31° 23.176' E 13° 27.045'. Follow this road until it comes to an end in the village of Ras at-Tabl (another 10 km: N 31° 18.527' E 13° 30.352'). (Along this stretch it is possible to see a number of fortified farms across the wadi to the R.) Turn R through the village; it is then necessary to find a route across to the opposite bank of the Wadi Sawfajjin, and to make your way W towards the main concentration of Roman farms. Be warned that the name Shedewa or Shedwa is no longer recognized in the area!

Fortified farms*

The Bir Shedewa basin is an area of dissected ground where a number of tributary wadis, dropping from the rocky plateau of the Hamada al-Hamra to the S, join the main valley of the Wadi Sawfajjin, resulting in the outcropping of a number of more or less isolated rocky bluffs. This was an area of quite intensive settlement in Roman times, and surface survey in 1981 identified a large number of ancient features, including cross-wadi walls for agricultural purposes, open farm sites, tower-like *qasr*-farms and cemeteries. The open farms occupy low-lying sites close to the alluvium of the wadi bed and appear mainly to have been occupied from the late first until the early third century AD; the *qsur*, on the other hand, seem to have succeeded these, being datable from the third until the seventh centuries (and possibly later). There are at least nine of these and they are placed in prominent defensible positions. They are numbered in fig. 89 according to the 1981 survey: the best-preserved *qsur* are BS 1–5 and 28. The coordinates given above for the area as a whole are those of Qasr BS 4, from which one can get a good idea of the lie of the land. BS 28 (also particularly worth a visit) is not directly in sight but may be found at N 31° 18.085' E 13° 22.842'.

These *qsur* form a homogeneous group in terms of design and construction. The faces of the walls are formed of fairly small but tidy ashlar masonry, with larger blocks externally at the corners; the core is formed of loose stones packed with mud. The buildings range in size from 8 × 10 m to 13 × 14 m; each has a single entrance, arched and framed by large, well-cut blocks of limestone. In elevation, they rise to either two or three storeys (BS 2, 4), with a small central courtyard surrounded by rooms on two, three or four sides. Fig. 90 shows some typical

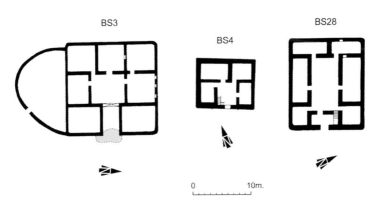

BS3

BS4

BS28

0   10m.

Fig. 90. Typical plans of fortified farms in the Bir Shedewa basin.

ground-plans. Stone staircases provide access to the upper floors. Sockets in the walls facing the courtyards, occasionally with surviving timbers (particularly evident in BS 28), and doorways opening at upper levels towards the central space, indicate the provision of wooden balconies. Light and air entered the rooms through their doorways or through small vents in the stonework; there is only one instance (in BS 4, at second-floor level) of a window in an external wall. At about 1.5 m above ground-level, mostly outside on either side of the door but occasionally also inside (BS 2, 4), there are stone tethering-rings for animals projecting from the walls. This is a type of architecture that is well suited to hot, dry climates, providing plenty of shade and stable temperatures within. There is no reason to suppose that the occupants were anybody other than the local elite, who had probably lived previously in the more open farms, but who, in the less settled circumstances of the later Roman period, found it preferable to live in something that offered more physical protection.

The buildings are surrounded by numerous roughly-built structures of irregular blocks: these were probably stock-enclosures and the like. At least one olive-press has been found in this area, but it seems likely that the economy was mostly pastoral. As in other settlements in the pre-desert, there are, of course, also cemeteries. There are no examples here of obelisk-tombs or tower-tombs, but a variety of burial types have been recorded, from simple circular cairns to more substantial structures of squared masonry. An example of such a cemetery lies immediately to the N of Qasr BS 4. Some 10 km to the W of this area, close to the springs of Bir ed-Dreder in the Wadi Dreder, is an extensive cemetery which includes carved upright *stelai*: some of these portray soldiers, eagles, palm trees, rosettes etc., while others are inscribed in Latin characters, but in a Libyan language, giving the names and particulars of the deceased. (Many of the inscribed stones have been transported to Tripoli for safe-keeping.) This cemetery does not lie close to any settlement, but may represent a kind of boundary-marker on the edge of the tribal lands belonging to the inhabitants of the Shedewa basin.

While in this area, the visitor may find a nearby natural feature of some interest. About 7 km to the SW of Ras at-Tabl, at N 31° 15.896' E 13° 27.455', lies a sink-hole in the limestone known as Ain Mizraq. It is a cylindrical hole (entirely unprotected!) some 50 m in diameter and 150 m deep, with water at the bottom. Hoisting-platforms have been built around the perimeter for drawing water, but this must always have been a very arduous (not to say perilous) occupation!

Fig. 91. Qasr BS4 in the Bir Shedewa basin.

GHIRZA (QIRZAH)***

(I have preferred the English/Italian spelling

Fig. 92. Ghirza: the southern part of the settlement.

of this name, since it is used almost universally in previous literature and in museum labels.)

Coordinates: N 30° 56.846', E 14° 33.144' Directions: From the coast road south of Tawurgah, at approximately 82 km from Misratah, turn R at the flyover junction at N31° 38.924' E15° 6.972', onto the road to as-Sadadah. After a further 18 km, at N 31° 35.228' E 14° 56.656', turn L at a cross-roads, onto the (unsurfaced but good) road which runs beside the pipeline of the Great Man-made River ('GMMR' in fig. 78). Follow this for 80 km and turn R at N 30° 56.533' E 14° 36.556' where an oil-drum constitutes the signpost for Ghirza. The modern village of that name is reached after 4.5 km, and the main cluster of ancient ruins (readily visible to the L when approaching the modern settlement) is 2 km to the SW. **The final approach to Ghirza (from the pipeline and particularly between the modern village and the ancient settlement) is rough and requires a 4-wheel-drive vehicle.**

In the wadi Qirzah/Ghirza, about 10 km upstream from its confluence with the wadi Zamzam, may be found a concentration of some forty major buildings with attendant cemeteries, a number of monumental tombs and extensive traces of agricultural activity belonging to the late Roman and early medieval periods. Whilst other concentrations of late Roman farms are known (for instance in the Bir Shedewa basin, p. 181), the settlement at Ghirza certainly constitutes the densest known agglomeration in the pre-desert region. Fanciful tales told to early modern travellers of a petrified city in the desert may well have derived their original substance from this place. The first modern European traveller to visit Ghirza was Commander W.H. Smyth, who in 1817 was at Lepcis Magna loading onto his ship pieces of architecture which the Pasha of Tripoli, Yusuf Karamanli, was sending to Britain 'as a present for the Prince Regent.' On his way to Ghirza he was repeatedly assured by those whom he met of the petrified marvels that he would see, but his previous acquaintance with the refinements of the very highest Classical Art caused him to be both disappointed and offended by the 'very indifferent taste' of what he found. He complained bitterly of 'ill-proportioned columns and clumsy capitals,' 'vile imitation of arabesque decoration' and of the carving of human and animal figures which were 'miserably executed.' Today we can appreciate the material evidence for a thriving, and surely native, community living on the edge of the Roman world and taking from it only that which it wanted. The most thorough

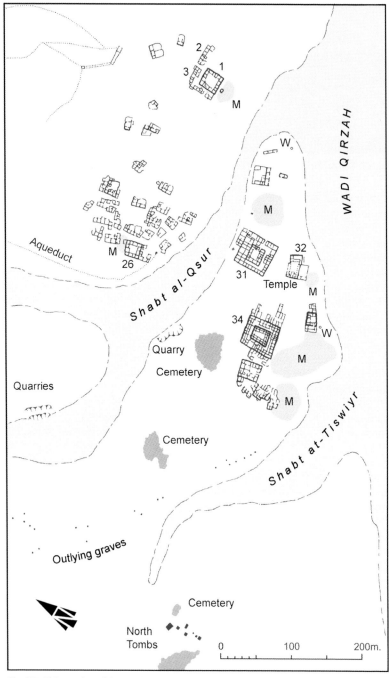

Fig. 93. Ghirza: plan of the settlement. M = midden, W = well.

examination of the settlement to date was made by a British team under the direction of Olwen Brogan and David Smith in 1955–57, when all of the significant buildings were surveyed and limited excavations were carried out in what turned out to be a Semitic temple (Building 32) and in the surrounding middens which proved to be rich in organic remains, including textiles. The numbering of the buildings used here refers to their study. At that time also, one of the tombs in the S Necropolis (South G), which had collapsed in an earthquake in the 1930s, was transported to Tripoli: it has now been re-erected inside the entrance to the National Museum (p. 21).

The main settlement is split into two parts along the N bank of the wadi Qirzah (fig. 93), on either side of the tributary Shabt al-Qsur. It is surrounded by several cemeteries, mostly of simple form but including one group of monumental tombs (the N Tombs). About 2 km further upstream, on the S bank of the wadi and at the limit of the former cultivated area, stands another group of monumental tombs (the S Tombs). The buildings in the Ghirza settlement include typical fortified farms of *qasr*-type, of one or more storeys and sometimes with internal courtyards or ancillary buildings grouped around them; also simpler rows of connected rooms and two quite exceptional rectangular complexes (Buildings 31 and 34), each measuring some 47 m square. The evidence of inscriptions, some in Latin characters and language and some in Libyan, shows that the population was essentially Libyan. The presence of the two exceptional building-complexes, perhaps representing communal storage facilities (precursors of the Berber granaries in the Jabal Nafusah?),

and of two groups of monumental tombs, has been interpreted as suggesting the presence of two distinct families or clans. The settlement has yielded a few artefacts of the first or second centuries AD but no structures of this date. What is visible now belongs mainly to the fourth to sixth centuries. Building 32 (see below) was destroyed by fire in the first half of the sixth century, and was then reoccupied between the middle of the tenth and the middle of the eleventh century; some of the other buildings also show signs of reoccupation in the same period.

The settlement is characterized also by a number of large middens or refuse tips, which have yielded evidence for the agricultural economy and diet: these, together with the scenes of daily life vividly portrayed on the tombs (in such profusion that there are slabs from Ghirza in Tripoli, Lepcis Magna and Bani Walid: pp. 21, 24, 139, 176), teach us that, in addition to practising pastoralism, the inhabitants cultivated barley, wheat, olives, vines, figs, almonds, dates, pulses and possibly watermelon. The uprights of an olive-press have been found in the NE corner of Building 31, and the intensive cultivation of the bed of the wadi Qirzah during the period of occupation is clear from the evidence of water-control measures (see below).

The ancient name of the settlement is not known. The modern name appears first on a map of 1802, and the English spelling 'Ghirza' originates with Smyth in 1817. However, the sixth-century writer Corippus reported that the Tripolitanian Moors of his time worshipped a god named *Gurzil*; and the tenth-century geographer Al-Bakri wrote of a stone idol called *Gurza*, located somewhere in this very region, which was still worshipped by the

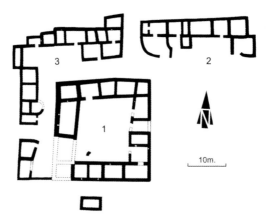

Fig. 94. Ghirza: plan of Buildings 1–3.

Berbers of his day. The present name may therefore have a genuinely ancient origin.

The farm buildings*

The state of preservation and visibility of the various buildings varies widely; unfortunately, it is the largest and potentially the most interesting (Buildings 31 and 34) that are the most ruinous. In each of these two cases, the plan suggests a two-storey courtyard-farm of regular layout with an equally regular outer court around it, lined with ancillary buildings. Of the same general type, but in a less developed form, is Building 1 (fig. 94), the first major structure to be seen as one approaches the settlement from the modern village. This is a courtyard-building with a single wide, arched entrance in the E side. In the SW corner of the courtyard, the remains of a flight of stairs indicate access to an upper storey. Inside the room to the R of the entrance, where the walls still rise to a considerable height, may be seen a recessed ledge for the beams supporting the upper floor, and above that, stones projecting inwards on either side of one corner, which would have

provided footholds for climbing up to the roof above. This feature may be seen in a number of buildings, and made a convenient substitute for a ladder. The extra thickness of the walls enclosing the room at the NW angle suggests that there may have been a tower here rising to three storeys. Outside the building, on the N and W sides, were further structures (Buildings 2 and 3) built around it but probably only of single-storey height. These probably fulfilled for Building 1 the same function as the fully-developed outer courts of Buildings 31 and 34.

Building 26 (fig. 95) is another particularly well-preserved courtyard-farm in this first group of buildings on the N side of the Shabt al-Qsur; it still stands to a height of some 7 m on the W side. Close examination of the masonry shows that in a first phase it consisted only of a single-storey range of rooms along its (later) W side; subsequently these were extended into the large courtyard-building now visible and upwards to encompass a second storey with a tower at the SW corner and possibly another over the entrance. The entrance, in the E side, is set externally in a rectangular frame of large blocks enclosing an arched doorway; behind this is a massive flat stone lintel in which can be seen the pivot-holes for the single-leaf door with which it was closed. (The inner entrance, on the other hand, was closed by double doors.) This building serves to illustrate several features which are common to the Ghirza farms. Note the rectangular niches in the walls, which may have served as cupboards; projecting corbels and other traces of a timber balcony around the courtyard at first-floor level; occasional small windows, high in the external walls; footholds in the internal corners of both towers which provided means of climbing to their upper floors or roofs; pierced tethering-stones projecting from the E and W external walls at a convenient height for tethering an animal. (Such tethering-stones may also be seen in the *qsur* of the Bir Shedewa basin and elsewhere.) Building 26, like Building 1, has an additional complex of rooms added to its exterior, mainly on the S side; but here they look more like a secondary dwelling than storerooms.

Apart from the developed courtyard-farms and the temple (see below), there are a considerable number of well-built but lesser buildings, particularly in the area around Building 26. These ranges of rooms, which sometimes include towers or upper floors, tend to be characterized by projecting, unfinished ends: the evidence of Building 26 suggests that they may have been built with the unfulfilled intention of later extension into fully-fledged courtyard-structures.

Building 32 (the temple)

Building 32 was chosen for excavation by the British team in order to establish the relative chronology of the different types of masonry used in the buildings at the site. In this it was not wholly successful, but the building did turn out to be of exceptional interest in that it proved to have been a temple of Oriental (Semitic) type. (There are two such temples, 19 and 24, at Lepcis Magna.) In its first phase (Period 1A in fig. 96), it consisted of a courtyard with porticoes along the N and S sides and a range of three rooms across the W end. The central room in this range was vaulted and had a raised floor, approached by three worn steps. To this 'chapel' were subsequently added an ante-chapel in front, while next to the ante-chapel on the N was added a further chapel, and a third was established in a second courtyard on the S side of the original structure (Period 1B). Few finds could be associated directly with these phases of the building, but its occupation, terminated by fire, seems to have extended between the fourth and sixth centuries AD. A final phase of occupation, clearly of a domestic nature, was more readily datable to the tenth and eleventh centuries, but

Phase 1

Phase 2

Fig. 95. Ghirza: plan of Building 26.

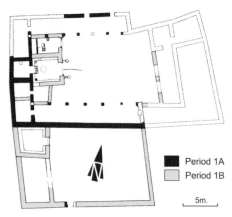

Fig. 96. Ghirza: plan of Building 32 (Semitic temple).

amongst the finds of this period were a large stone basin (the base of which still lies in the southern courtyard), which had almost certainly stood in the centre of the earlier ante-chapel, and over twenty small, rectangular decorated stones which had clearly been altars, 20–30 cm high, associated with the building in period 1. Other finds included stone offering-tables in the form of small rectangular blocks with a row of circular hollows in one side: one of these, with seven hollows, is also visible lying on the surface.

The characteristics of Building 32 – the artificially raised 'high place' set at the rear of a sacred precinct, the stone basin in the ante-chapel, the columns flanking the entrance, the little altars – all point to the practices of a Semitic cult, still being venerated in the fourth and fifth centuries AD. To whom was the temple dedicated? Some of the altars are inscribed, but in Libyan characters which unfortunately cannot yet be understood. It has been 'plausibly contended' that the cult was that of Ba'al Saturn in his dual role as god of earthly fecundity and as lord of the Nether World. Another possibility

(depending on whether or not this was the only temple in the settlement) must be that it was dedicated to the Gurzil mentioned by Corippus.

Water-control/agriculture

The Ghirza settlement, like most of the agricultural communities of the Roman period in the pre-desert region, depended for its existence on the maximization of the rain which fell on the surrounding landscape. Studies have shown that the climate in Roman times was not so very different in this region from what it is today. The ability of the landscape therefore to sustain a large settled community was affected by the skill of the inhabitants in two respects. One was to draw off some of the rain that fell into cisterns, to provide sustenance for flocks and people in the long dry months. The other was to hold up the run-off of rainwater from the stony plateau so that its rush should not carry away the alluvium in the wadi bed, but should remain long enough to soak into the soil and so to be of benefit to arable crops and other vegetation growing there. The employment of both techniques at Ghirza is clearly visible.

Fig. 97. Ghirza: the monumental tombs of the N group.

Between the position of the S Necropolis, about 2 km upstream of the main settlement, and a point about 200 m downstream of the settlement, the wadi was until recently crossed by some 35 walls. The most substantial were some 2 m wide, and their purpose was undoubtedly to arrest the flow of storm-water down the wadi after rain, thereby enhancing the fertility of the alluvium in the wadi bed. This system is typically also accompanied by walls along either side of the wadi and running parallel to it: these may have been intended to control the run-off from the plateau into the wadi bed and/or to prevent stones from being washed into the cultivated area.

Two wells have been identified, one of which, on the extremity of the spur between the Shabt al-Qsur and the Wadi Qirzah, is choked with sand; the other, immediately to the S of Building 33, was still functional in the 1950s ('the water is foul but the animals drink it apparently without ill-effect'). Five cisterns have also been located. Some of these (to the N of Building 5 and to the S of Building 26) are stone-built, lined with pink waterproof cement and fed (via settling-tanks) from hillside run-off, channelled into them by low catchment-walls. (The aqueduct behind Building 26 is clearly traceable.) Others (in the edge of the Shabt al-Qsur below Building 31 and in the middle of the Wadi Qirzah, refurbished in modern times) are rock-cut and would have been filled directly by storm-water rushing down the wadi. Some of the farm buildings certainly also had cisterns constructed within their walls, as is clear from the presence of the typical pink cement render and the absence of doorways: these may have been fed by rainwater from the roofs or by catchment-walls on the neighbouring hillside.

The monumental tombs

The form of burial accorded to the majority of the population is largely uniform. The individual tombs are rectangular structures with enclosing walls of small coursed masonry, set simply upon the cleared rock surface of the plateau; the internal dimensions are sufficient to accommodate an extended body and one or two votive objects, and the whole was covered by flat stone slabs. Scattered stones, rarely *in situ*, show that a few of the graves had simple columnar 'headstones' and that many were accompanied by 'offering-tables' – stones with a row of hollows carved out of the top surface into which offerings for the dead could be placed. Examples of both types of object are on display in Room 5 of the museum at Bani Walid (p. 189).

There are also at Ghirza two groups of monumental tombs which are more akin to those found in other parts of Tripolitania, though the concentration of numbers and the decorative detail of the Ghirza tombs are quite exceptional. The design of these monuments falls into two classes: obelisk-tombs (South A only) such as are found elsewhere in Tripolitania (e.g. Msallatin, p. 195; Wadi N'fid, p. 203) and temple-tombs, which are otherwise rare (cf. Qasr Banat in Wadi N'fid, p. 203; also the *asnam* of Ghadamis, p. 85). The temple-tombs show considerable variety in design according to their size, ranging from those which are large enough to have a (real or virtual) chamber within the surrounding colonnade (North A, North B) to those in which this is reduced to a small, solid pier which may or may not be embellished by the addition of a false door on the principal face. They make use of classical design forms and decorative details, interpreted in a manner which suggests that the lack of the stonemasons' familiarity with 'the real thing' was more than made up for by the imagination and vitality with which they were executed. The figured friezes with which they were decorated, while again showing no great technical competence, offer a fascinating insight into the lives of the people who lived here.

The presence of offering-tables associated with the simpler burials, and of libation-ducts in the monumental tombs, demonstrate that the people who lived here believed in a continuing relationship with their dead ancestors, acted out (presumably) in regular rituals. Some of the inscriptions on the more elaborate tombs include instructions that the children and grandchildren of the departed are to visit the tomb and to perform such rites. One inscription actually records such an event, in which 51 bulls and 38 goats were sacrificed! This must have been a major tribal gathering and suggests that we are here in the presence of a strong ancestor-cult.

We can glimpse a further aspect of an ancestor-cult amongst the Libyans through two ancient writers of the Classical period: both Herodotus (writing in the fifth century BC) and Pomponius Mela (first century AD) tell us that the Libyans would seek guidance from their ancestors by sleeping in or on their tombs. They would then regard any dreams that came to them as oracular. It is possible that there is direct evidence for this practice in the Ghirza cemeteries (see tombs North G and South B below).

The North Group**
The N group (fig. 98), situated some 350 m from the settlement, consists of six or seven tombs, standing more or less in a row facing the settlement; behind them is a denuded cemetery of 'ordinary' burials. Three of the tombs (A–C) are well-preserved, including their surrounding colonnades; the others are reduced to their cores or foundations. Various considerations suggest that their physical order (A–F) corresponds also to their chronological sequence, from the third century to at least the fifth. **'Tomb G'**, between and in front of Tombs B and C, is of a somewhat different design, being semi-subterranean and composed of a simple outer and inner chamber in small rubble masonry and without architectural pretension. It also has a stone bench in the outer chamber, and the interesting hypothesis has been advanced that this is in fact a 'vision chamber' in which one would sleep in order to communicate with one's ancestors.

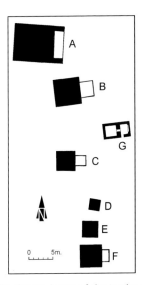

Fig. 98. Ghirza: layout of the tombs of the N group.

Tomb A, the largest of the Ghirza tombs, takes the form of a classical peripteral temple with a colonnade of 4 × 5 columns enclosing the *cella* (fig. 99). It stands on a moulded podium approached by a frontal flight of steps; the columns have 'Ionic' capitals (apart from one on the rear which is a more conventional Corinthian!) and they are spanned by flat architraves carrying a Doric frieze. The metopes of the frieze are decorated with alternating rosettes and plainer roundels. The roof above was flat, so there were no pediments, but it was bordered at either end by a *sima* (parapet) decorated with opposed pairs of S-spirals and upright palmettes. These blocks now lie on the ground around the building. This tomb has two burial chambers. The lower one is cut into the rock and is entered through a low-level passageway on the S side of the podium; within is a square chamber with a slightly pitched ceiling, supported by a central pillar. The upper chamber is within the *'cella'* of the temple, but was never accessed from the front. Rather, there was a false door (now completely gone) in this position and access to the upper chamber was through an opening high up in the S wall. This arrangement seems to be a secondary feature, perhaps introduced after repairs had been made at some point to the tomb. Above the false door, on the E side, is an inscribed panel flanked by a pair of eagles clutching hares in their talons. The inscription identifies the building as the tomb of M(archius) Nasif and of M(archia) Mathlich, built for them by their sons M(archius) Nimira and Fydel. (There are casts of this panel in the museums of Lepcis Magna and Bani Walid.) To the L is a sacrificial scene (a bull held by one man, about to be struck with a mallet by another), to the R a lion chasing another animal. Just around the corner to the L, on the first block on the S side, are two female portrait busts in high relief.

Tomb B is composed of the same basic elements, but the *'cella'* is a solid central pier with a masonry facing and an elaborately carved false door on the E side; as with Tomb A, the podium is approached on this side by a flight of steps. The podium, more ornate than that of Tomb A, is framed at the corners by stubby pilasters and is encircled by a vine-scroll frieze. The sepulchral chamber was entered from beneath the S side of the podium, where a small rock-cut passage leads into a vaulted rectangular room. In the E wall of this room is the lower opening of a libation-duct, through which offerings to the dead would have been poured from an aperture in the paving in front of the false door. The colonnade is composed of 5 × 5 columns and the order is Corinthian; a pair of extra columns is

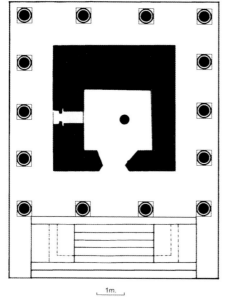

Fig. 99. Ghirza: plan (at top of podium) and elevation of Tomb North A.

lintels which survive *in situ* are decorated simply with rosettes in the spandrels, but those which spanned the E face were more elaborately decorated with figure scenes (now in the Lepcis Magna Museum). The arcades in turn supported a decorative frieze, the blocks of which are now mostly on display in Tripoli or at Lepcis Magna, though a few were removed in the nineteenth century to Istanbul. Above this, as in Tomb A, was a *sima* of opposed S-spirals with a palmette in the centre of the E and W faces, and upstanding winged victory figures at the corners. The inscription which stood above the false door (part now in Istanbul, part in Tripoli) indicates that the tomb was built for M(archius) Fydel and F(lavia) Thesylgum, the parents of M(archius) Metusan.

Tomb C is the best-preserved in the North Group. It is closely similar in all details to Tomb B, except insofar as it is smaller again, with only four columns to each side. The funerary chamber is entered from beneath the S side of the podium, and it is connected to the space in front of the false door by a libation-duct. The frieze around the top of the podium is noteworthy for the variety of subjects enclosed within its scrolls, and the heads sculpted on the Corinthian capitals of the colonnades should also be noted (e.g. a cat at the SE corner). The figured frieze above the colonnade is partly *in situ*; other blocks are in the National Museum in Tripoli and in

squeezed in against the *cella* wall on the W face. In this tomb (and the remainder of the temple-tombs, where the evidence survives) the columns are surmounted, not by a flat architrave, but by arcuate lintels. (Since each interval is spanned by a single block, the structural effect is identical to that of a flat lintel, but the visual effect is that of an arcade.) The

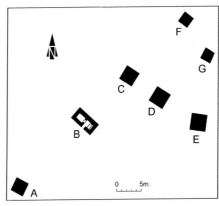

Fig. 100. Ghirza: layout of the tombs of the S group.

Istanbul. The figures are much smaller than those which decorated Tomb B, which allows for more crowded scenes, of hunting, ploughing, attendance on a seated chieftain (in Istanbul) and the like. Fragments found in the vicinity suggest that Tomb C had a similar crowning *sima* to Tombs A and B. The dedication of the tomb stands above the false door. It reads:

M(archius) Chullam and Varnychsin, father and mother of Marchius Nimmire and Maccurasan, who made for them this memorial. We have calculated the expenditure exactly. There was paid out in wages in coin 45,600 *folles* of *denarii simplices*, besides food for the workmen. May our sons and grandsons visit the tomb in good fortune.

Tomb D is entirely fallen. It was the smallest of the group, with a colonnade of only 2 × 2 columns, but otherwise conformed to the same type as Tombs B and C. **Tomb E** was again of the same type, with a colonnade of 3 × 3 columns. The carving of the ornament is of poorer quality, and the capitals resemble closely those found in the church at al-Khadra (p. 163); it has

been inferred that this tomb belongs to the fifth century. **Tomb F,** ruinous apart from its core, belongs also to the same sequence and is surely the latest in this group; despite an attempt at grandeur (5 × 5 columns), the carving of the stonework is extremely rudimentary.

The South Group*
This group stands at the southern limit of that part of the Wadi Ghirza which was terraced, and therefore presumably cultivated, by the inhabitants of the settlement. It is 2.5 km as the crow flies from the main settlement, and on the E side of the wadi, at N 30° 55.730' E 14° 32.505'. The most prominent member of the S Group is the partially collapsed obelisk-tomb A. This is the only example of this familiar pre-desert type here; the remaining tombs in this group are small examples of the temple-type seen in the N group, with three columns per side (C, D, E) or two (F, G), apart from '**Tomb B**', which is a two-chamber structure in small masonry, closely similar to Tomb North G and arguably another 'vision chamber'. Tombs A and C of the S group were almost intact when photographed in 1933, but suffered serious damage in

style of carving at Lepcis Magna in the Severan period, and the fact that this tomb alone belongs to the Punic tradition of the obelisk-tombs, suggest that this is probably the earliest of the monumental tombs at Ghirza, to be dated around the middle of the third century AD. Comparison with the sequence in the N group suggests that Tombs C–G probably belong to the fourth century: none of them seems to be as late as North D, E or F.

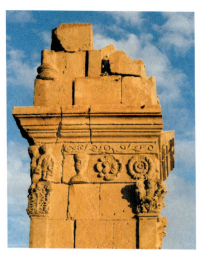

Fig. 102. Ghirza: detail of the ornament on Tomb South A.

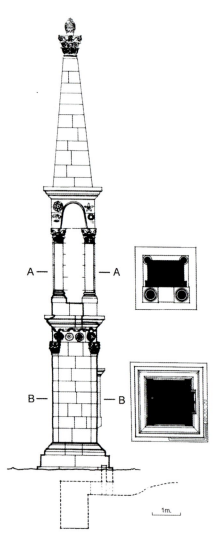

Fig. 101. Ghirza: reconstruction of the obelisk-tomb, South A.

an earthquake, which must have been that of 19/20 April 1935. Tomb G was transferred in 1958 to Tripoli, where it may now be seen in the entrance to the National Museum (p. 21).

The decoration of Tomb South A is of a high standard, superior to that of Tomb North A; it has echoes of the

Tomb A (fig. 101) is built of ashlar masonry throughout and stands, as usual, above a subterranean funerary chamber which was entered from the N side (facing the settlement). Unusually, there is a channel running round the edge of the low podium above, from the centre of the E face (usually the principal face of a tomb, as shown here by the *aedicula* on the second storey) to the entrance to the funerary chamber on the N side: this is a libation-duct. Above the podium rises a solid, square first storey, framed by Corinthian pilasters at the corners. The capitals are carved in high relief and have a variety of heads or busts projecting between the acanthus leaves. The frieze which runs round the monument above the capitals (fig. 102) is also richly decorated with a bizarre profusion of non-matching motifs in equally high relief, which contrasts strongly with the generally flat relief of the later tombs. The false door, carved on the N face, is the finest at Ghirza, with a lion-headed knocker on the right-hand leaf. The second storey was, curiously, rotated 90° with regard to the storey beneath: the E side took the form of an *aedicula* framed by two Corinthian columns supporting a tall, rather elliptical, arch. On the left-hand part of it were carved the apotropaic symbols of a phallus, a scorpion and an eye. Fragments of both male and female statues in the round have been found nearby: these presumably represented the deceased couple and stood within the *aedicula*. The rear corners of this storey were framed by smaller engaged columns. Both of the lower storeys were terminated by boldly projecting cornices; above that of the second storey rose the usual obelisk, carrying at its apex a fine Corinthian capital surmounted in turn by a pine-cone finial. This is on display in the museum at Bani Walid (p. 176): the topmost block of the pyramid itself, enclosing a long stone peg which anchored both the pine-cone and the capital to it, is still lying on the ground by the tomb.

Of the remaining monumental tombs, only the small **Tomb F** has any of its superstructure (the central pillar and two of the four enclosing columns) still standing above the podium. Other elements are on display in room 5 of the museum at Bani Walid (p. 176).

Fig. 103. Obelisk-tombs at Msallatin.

MSALLATIN

Directions: Take the road eastwards from Bani Walid along the floor of the Wadi Mardum (which is known as the Wadi Bani Walid in the vicinity of the town). Follow this for 33 km, noting the considerable density of Roman fortified farms (amongst medieval and modern structures) lining the high ground on either side of this fertile wadi. At the road junction at N 31° 49.758' E 14° 16.978', turn left to cross the wadi for the mausolea (towards Zlitan: the maps misleadingly show this direction as being straight on!) or continue straight on for Qasr Bularkan.

Mausolea*

Having crossed the wadi, the extensive but much-collapsed ruins of a Roman fortified farm known as Qasr Faschiat al-Habs are to be seen immediately to the R of the road. From here, the needles of two obelisk-tombs are visible about 1 km across the rough ground to the E. They may be reached in about 15 minutes on foot, or slightly more quickly in a 4-wheel-drive vehicle. Close to, it is clear that they mark an extensive cemetery: a third obelisk-tomb nearby has collapsed and 33 cairns corresponding to simpler burials have been counted. The two surviving tombs (which still stand 18 m and 15 m high respectively, despite the efforts of earthquakes to twist off their apexes) show differing degrees of elaboration. Each is three storeys high, set upon a plinth and with projecting cornices marking the tops of the lower two storeys; in the more elaborate example these storeys are decorated with corner-pilasters or engaged columns and a vegetal scroll in relief forming a frieze above, whereas the simpler tomb is entirely plain. In either case the topmost storey is a tall, plain obelisk. (If either of them had a crowning finial, it is now gone.)

The antecedents of tombs of this kind go back to the pre-Roman period (see the Punic-Hellenistic Mausoleum B at Sabratha, p. 42), and in many instances they are demonstrably associated with farm buildings of the first and second centuries AD.

Qasr Bularkan

Continue past the junction (previously mentioned) with the road to Zlitan, for 1.6 km; the ruins of Qasr Bularkan, immediately recognizable by its projecting bastions, will be very evident on the left-hand side, just between the road and the wadi, at N 31° 49.321' E 14° 17.874'. The building consists of a substantial walled enclosure 22 m square, with square bastions bonded into the corners and in the middle

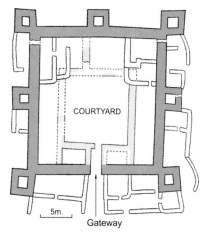

Main walls of fort
Interior walls-visible faces
Arab huts

Fig. 104. Plan of the Roman fortlet (or farm?) of Qasr Bularkan.

of three of the sides (fig. 104). The fourth side has a gateway in the centre, leading into a courtyard 10 m square, which must have been surrounded by rooms. The walls survive to a maximum height of about 3 m, which is probably not far short of their original height. The details of the interior are obscured by fallen rubble and an accretion of later structures.

There is no dating-evidence for this structure, and while the plan resembles that of fourth-century military installations in other parts of North Africa, it is decidedly small in comparison to other examples; on the other hand, it seems unnecessarily elaborate for a fortified farm. It could not have been more than a police post.

QARYAH AL-GHARBIYAH (GHERIA EL-GARBIA)

Coordinates: N 30° 25.236', E 13° 25.119'
Directions: Leave the main road S from

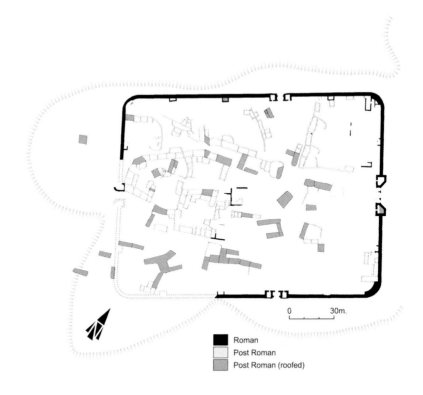

Fig. 105. Qaryah Al-Gharbiyah: plan of the legionary fort. Not all of the post-Roman structures are shown.

Mizdah to Fazzan in Qaryah ash-Sharqiyah, turning R at N 30° 22.627' E 13° 35.135'; at a junction 700 m along this road, take the L fork. Follow this road westwards (in the direction of Dirj and Ghadamis) for 17.5 km, and turn R at N 30° 21.941' E 13° 24.473'; after 6 km this road comes to an end in the modern village of Qaryah al-Gharbiyah. The ruins of the legionary fort and pre-modern village give a jagged profile to the skyline above you to the R. If you drive past the ruins, an easy path up the slope will be found next to the football pitch.

Legionary fort**

This site has been known since 1850, when Heinrich Barth recognized the unmistakable gateway to a Roman fort.

Examination of the surface remains by Richard Goodchild in 1953 and by the UNESCO Libyan Valleys Survey team in 1981 has identified the presence of a substantial enclosure of regular playing-card type, measuring 181 × 137 m. Three quarters of the wall-circuit are traceable: the construction is mostly in small rubble masonry. The interior of the fort is largely obscured by the Berber village (now abandoned) which grew up within it in post-Roman times, but all four gates of the Roman fort are identifiable, and two of the eight interval towers still stand over 9 m high. The most imposing gate is still the principal one, the *porta praetoria* in the centre of the NE side (furthest

Fig. 106. Qaryah Al-Gharbiyah: the legionary fort from the N.

from the modern village). This was composed of a triple arch in fine ashlar masonry (equal to the best Severan work at Lepcis Magna), with flanking towers, chamfered back on their inner faces (see fig. 107, a reconstruction of its appearance by Derek Welsby). The voussoirs of the wide central span survived in position until 1980, but now lie tumbled on the ground (apparently following vandalism by a road-builder!). The lower parts of the flanking towers are also in large ashlars, but of less careful construction, while the upper parts (which survive to about two thirds of the original height in the left-hand tower) are in the same rubble masonry as the rest of the walls. Windows in the upper part of the surviving tower, as also around the N corner of the fort, indicate the level of the rampart-walk. This is also marked out in places by an external string-course. The NW and SE gates had single openings flanked by square towers, and on the SW side traces have been recognized of a gate protected by D-shaped towers, which may imply a reconstruction at a date subsequent to the rest of the design. No trace of the enclosure wall remains in the S corner, but this has probably been robbed down to the bedrock in the course of building the Berber village. In contrast, the area between the W corner and the edge of the wadi scarp shows extensive remains of what was probably the civil settlement associated with the fort (*canabae*). Within the fort, the now-ruined mosque makes use of Roman columns and capitals which may originally have belonged to the headquarters building (*principia*).

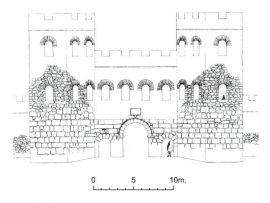

0   5   10m.

Fig. 107. Qaryah Al-Gharbiyah: reconstruction of the NE gate.

Fig. 108. The fine masonry of the Roman fortlet at Qaryah Ash-Sharqiyah stands out from its enveloping Italian successor.

About 1 km (15 minutes' walk) across the stony plateau to the NE of the fort stands a circular watch-tower with a panoramic view over the wadi systems to the N. From here it is possible to see the Roman outpost at Qaryah ash-Sharqiyah.

The oases at al-Qaryah have until modern times fulfilled an important function on the route directly south from Oea/Tripoli to the Fazzan: this was the last point at which the traveller could stock up with water, dates and other foodstuffs before embarking on the crossing of the stony plateau of the Hamada al-Hamra. They have for the same reason been important to the military control of the region. Inscriptions have shown that the fort at Qaryah al-Gharbiyah, which is closely similar to that at Abu Njaym on the more easterly route to Fazzan (p. 170), was likewise built at the very beginning of the third century AD; it probably went out of use by the end of the same century.

The construction of the watch-tower is dated by an inscription to AD 230–5.

Investigations in 1981 showed other traces of occupation at Qaryah al-Gharbiyah during the Roman period, including a small bath-house on the W side of the oasis, which may represent evidence of Roman military activity prior to the construction of the third-century fort.

QARYAH ASH-SHARQIYAH (GHERIA ESH-SHERGIA)

Coordinates: N 30° 23.485', E 13° 35.429'
Directions: Turn R off the main road S from Mizdah towards Fazzan just after the rise on entering the modern village of Qaryah ash-Sharqiyah (at N 30° 22.627' E 13° 35.135', the turning for Dirj and Ghadamis); fork R at the next junction, after 700 m, and follow this through the village until you come to the abandoned Italian Forte Baccon. The Roman building is entirely within the twentieth-century fort.

Fig. 109. Qasr Wamis: the tower above the entrance, seen from the inside.

in Wadi N'fid (opposite), with which it shares the neatly rounded and inset external corners. It is surely earlier than the third-century forts at Qaryah al-Gharbiyah and Abu Njaym. The question of whether or not this quality of work has to signify a military structure remains open.

QASR DUIB

Coordinates: N 31° 39.139', E 12° 28.067'

Directions: See fig. 23. Qasr Duib stands on a low spur beside the Wadi Duib; beside it lies Saniet Duib, an important spring and water-point in the upper Wadi Sawfajjin. **There are only unmade tracks in the area: a 4-wheel-drive vehicle is essential and the site is not easy to find.** It is 20 km as the crow flies (about 25 km on the ground) to the W of Qasr Wamis and approximately 36 km to the SE of az-Zintan.

Fortlet (?)*

Part of the perimeter wall of a fortified building, approximately 38 × 26 m and built in fine ashlar masonry, may be seen above the oasis of Qaryah ash-Sharqiyah, where it has been much altered by its incorporation into an Italian redoubt of 1928–43. Three sides still stand some 7 m high, and the presence of two massive sill-stones in the entrance to one of the offices of the Italian fort may indicate the position of the entrance on the fourth side. The building overlooks the oasis of Qaryah ash-Sharqiyah, and has intervisibility with the watch-tower near the legionary fort at Qaryah al-Gharbiyah, 16 km to the W (p. 199).

The building is undated but is very similar in construction to Qasr Isawi

Fortlet

This is a typical fortified courtyard-building in coursed rubble masonry, and it still stands two storeys high in parts, though it is now very ruinous. Some of the rooms were vaulted, others had flat wooden ceilings. On the upper floor they opened into one another: only one here opens towards the courtyard, and access must have been by means of a ladder or wooden stair. The solidity of the walls suggests that, as in many other such buildings, there was a tower rising yet higher above the entrance. The building has been occupied over a long period, and both the nature of secondary modifications and the presence of cable-patterns on

Fig. 111. Qasr Isawi.

and third centuries AD (indicated by pottery picked up in the vicinity).

About 300 m to the E of Qasr Isawi, across a small re-entrant in the bank of the wadi, there is a substantial mausoleum known as Qasr Banat, which was surely associated with it. This a temple-tomb like Tomb North A at Ghirza (p. 191), but it has lost its surrounding colonnade almost completely. What remains is a substantial podium, formerly approached on the W side (towards Qasr Isawi) by a flight of steps. There is a lower funerary chamber set within the podium, which is approached through a sloping passage beneath the frontal steps. The *'cella'* of the temple is also preserved: this constitutes a second, upper, funerary chamber, since it was closed not by a door but by a stone slab which slid down from above into slots in the door-frame. The roof is supported on two stone beams which rest on corbels at either end; there are also projecting brackets on the walls at

a lower level, perhaps intended for urns or lamps. There is carved decoration on the brackets and on the undersides of the roof beams. A few fragments of the decoration above the colonnade survive on the ground round about, and the frieze contained the dedicatory inscription, the style of whose lettering has been attributed to the third century AD. The inscription identifies the tomb as that of Aurellius Nazmur and his wife, set up by their sons Aurellius Maior, Magnus and Arcadius.

Umm al-Amad*

Some 17 km upstream from Qasr Isawi (on unmade tracks), the course of the wadi is framed by a pair of obelisk-tombs, one on either bank. That on the S side, 13 m high, has stood since antiquity; the other was restored by the Department of Antiquities in 1992–93.

The N tomb (at N 31° 21.814' E 14° 37.103'), now reconstructed, rises from a single square foundation-course.

Fig. 112. The Wadi N'fid, looking upstream from the N tomb at Umm al-Amad; the needle of the S tomb is just visible a kilometre away on the opposite bank.

There was no funerary chamber directly beneath the monument, but two stone cist-graves immediately in front (to the E). The first storey is framed by pilasters decorated with vegetal or palmette scrolls and supporting Corinthian capitals. Above these is a Doric frieze composed of pointed rosettes between triglyphs, succeeded by a projecting cornice. The second storey has engaged columns at the corners, with Corinthian capitals and a frieze above in the form of a continuous vegetal scroll. At this level there is a (reconstructed) false door on the E face, with an uninscribed *tabula ansata* for an inscription above. Above the cornice of the second storey rises the obelisk; no terminating finial survives.

The S tomb (at N 31° 21.258' E 14° 37.151', exactly 1 km to the S) is essentially similar, but differs in some details. The podium is higher, and encloses a partly subterranean funerary chamber. The first storey is framed by plain Corinthian pilasters at the corners, above which is a Doric frieze containing a variety of rosettes and including a pair of male and female portrait busts on both the N and S sides, with a cornice above. The second storey is similar to that of the other tomb, with again an empty *tabula ansata* above the false door on the E face.

The tombs have been attributed to the third century AD; small differences between them suggest that they are not exactly contemporary, and indeed it was noted that mortar had been used in the construction of the S tomb, but not in that of its twin. There are two ruinous courtyard-farms on the N side of the wadi, at the mouth of a small tributary, to the WNW of the N tomb. These have yielded pottery of the second and third centuries AD and may therefore be contemporary with the tombs. It is noteworthy, however, that there is an almost total absence of wadi cross-walls for some distance downstream of this point (until one reaches the vicinity of Qasr Isawi), whereas they begin again precisely here and are frequent for the next 15 km upstream: it is possible therefore that, as with the S tombs at Ghirza (p. 193), these monumental tombs were placed as markers on the edge of a tribal or family domain.

WADI UMM AS-SBIT MAUSOLEUM

Coordinates: N 31° 4.861', E 13° 15.873'
Directions: This is on a spur which overlooks the road from Mizdah to Qaryah al-Gharbiyah at about 50 km S of Mizdah. It is immediately to the E of the road and is readily visible from a distance, about 2 km after passing the ruins of a Roman fortified farm on the same side of the road.

This is a collapsed obelisk-tomb, standing in a prominent position and probably associated with the nearby fortified farm (or its predecessor: obelisk-tombs seem generally to have been going out of fashion as the fortified farms were coming in, but there are often traces of an open courtyard-farm nearby). The funerary chamber was excavated or constructed beneath the monument, and the opening into it is clearly visible on the S side. This would have held a cinerary urn rather than an inhumation. The surviving first storey is simple in design, with little attempt at curved mouldings for either the base or the cornice. The square core is framed by flat pilasters at the corners with simple capitals, above which is a frieze of very simple rosettes. The second storey and the crowning obelisk have collapsed since the monument was recorded by Heinrich Barth in the 1850s

Fig. 113. The mausoleum in Wadi Umm as-Sbit, as seen by Heinrich Barth.

(fig. 113), but the blocks remain scattered on the ground. The second storey was framed by three-quarter columns with Corinthian capitals; it appears to have been decorated on one side with busts of the deceased couple.

The mausoleum did not stand alone but, as usual, is surrounded by other burials. There are a number of simple ring-cairns, and about 30 m to the S of the principal tomb is a pair of large table-tombs, built of ashlar masonry with flat cover-slabs, now broken apart and scattered.

Glossary

Aedicula: A niche or recess with an architectural frame, such as a pediment supported on a pair of columns.

Agora: The civic centre and marketplace of a Greek city.

AH: Dates in the Muslim calendar (*Hijrah*), which are in lunar years, starting from the flight of the prophet Muhammad from Mecca to Medina in AD 622.

Ambo(n): A pulpit in a church, with the distinction that in the early Church this was used for readings from the epistle and gospel rather than for preaching, and it was provided with two flights of steps, one towards the altar and the other towards the nave.

Amphitheatre: A place of entertainment (usually oval), with tiered seating all around a central arena (like a football ground), for watching gladiatorial combats and wild-beast fights. NOT to be confused with a theatre!

The Antonine Itinerary: A list of routes of the Roman Empire, probably compiled in the reign of Caracalla (211–217). It gives lists of roads, the settlements along them and the distances between them.

Apodyterium: Part of a Roman bath-building: the changing-room.

Apotropaic: An adjective used to describe objects or carvings intended to avert evil, such as an amulet worn around the neck or a carved phallus at a street-corner.

Architrave: The horizontal lintel which spans a doorway or the space between columns in a colonnade.

Arcuate lintel: A single block which is carved as an arch but which (not being composed of multiple elements) is structurally no different from a flat lintel. Typical of the colonnades of Tripolitanian temple-tombs (e.g. at Ghirza).

Ashlar: Masonry cut in regular rectangular blocks and laid in horizontal courses; a block of such masonry.

Asnam: See **Sanam**.

Atrium: The central hall of a Roman house of Etruscan type.

Attic: The box- or plinth-like uppermost element of a Roman building or triumphal arch, above all other architectural ornament.

Breccia: A geological term used to describe a rock which is formed of large irregular fragments of one or more rock-types, cemented together in a matrix of a finer-grained material, often resulting in a veined appearance.

Byzantine: A cultural and chronological term used to describe the culture of the Roman World during the period when it was ruled from Constantinople (the former Greek city of *Byzantium*) rather than from Rome. Where North Africa is concerned, this means essentially the period following its recovery from the Vandals by Justinian in 533 until its loss to the Arabs between 642 and 698. It should be noted that the term is a modern construct: the people we describe as 'Byzantine' never thought of themselves as such, but as 'Roman.'

Caduceus: A winged sceptre entwined with snakes, the exclusive attribute of two gods, Hermes/Mercury and Asklepios/Aesculapius. (The association with Asklepios, the god of healing, is responsible for its use in modern times to identify a pharmacy.)

Cal(i)darium: Part of a Roman bath-building: a hot, humid room with hot plunge-bath(s).

Canabae: Plural, literally 'huts', used to denote the civil settlement which tended to grow up immediately outside the gates of a Roman fort.

Cardo and **Decumanus:** Terms freely employed by modern archaeologists (on the authority of ancient surveyors) to name the streets of Roman towns. The **cardo** (pl. *cardines*) should run N–S and the **decumanus** E–W; the principal street in either direction would be the **cardo/decumanus maximus**.

Cavea: The auditorium of a theatre or amphitheatre.

Cella: Of a temple, the central chamber, housing the cult statue.

Centaur: A mythical being composed of the upper part of a man with the body and legs of a horse.

Centenarium: Theoretically, a small military post intended to house a century (nominally a hundred men). However, the buildings identified as *centenaria* by inscriptions differ widely in size and character, and may not always be military.

Chi-rho monogram: A Christian symbol composed of the first two letters of 'Christos' in Greek (XP), often accompanied by the letters alpha and omega (symbolizing Christ as the Beginning and the End).

Ciborium: A regular architectural feature of early churches, in the form of a canopy supported on four columns which enclosed the altar.

Cipollino: A type of marble, quarried in antiquity at Carystos on the Greek island of Euboea and widely used in Roman buildings. It has alternating stripes of green and white colour and has a high content of mica, which sparkles in the light.

Circus: A track with spectator seating for the presentation of chariot-races. Identical to a hippodrome.

Cist: A coffin-like grave, lined with stone slabs; also a small stone chest, for the burial of ashes.

Clerestory: That part of the nave of a colonnaded basilica (sacred or secular) which rises above the aisles and is pierced by windows (often the main source of light for the interior of the building).

Colonia: Initially a term for a new settlement of Roman military veterans, this came to symbolize full assimilation to the administrative structure of Rome itself, a status much sought after by pre-existing communities and *municipia* (q.v.).

Comes: A widely-used title under the late Roman Empire, whence the English title 'Count.' The *Comes Africae* held military command over the forces stationed in the former province of Africa.

Corinthian: An order of architecture for Greek and Roman public buildings, in which the capitals of the columns are formed like the base of an acanthus plant, with three tiers of leaves. The columns usually have narrow vertical flutes and the entablature above is decorated with a frieze based on a continuous acanthus scroll.

Cornice: A horizontal projecting moulding which crowns a roof or a lower storey of a classical building.

Cryptoporticus: A partially underground portico, designed to provide protection from the heat of summer.

Damnatio ad bestias: Condemnation to death by exposure to wild beasts in the amphitheatre.

Damnatio memoriae: The erasure of a name from public inscriptions and documents, as if the individual (or body, since it was applied in AD 238 to the *Legio III Augusta*) had never existed.

Decumanus: See Cardo.

Decurio: A member of a Roman town-council (a position of prestige, held for life, but one in which one was expected to use part of one's private wealth for the public good).

Doric: An order of architecture in Greek (and occasionally Roman) buildings identified by the absence of bases beneath the columns and by very plain capitals in the form of squat inverted cones. The columns have wide vertical flutes and the frieze above takes the form of alternating metopes and triglyphs (q.v.).

Duumvir: One of the two supreme magistrates in the administration of a Roman town (corresponding to the two consuls at Rome itself).

Dux: A military title under the late Roman Empire, subordinate to the *Comes Africae*. The title is the origin of the English 'Duke.'

Emblema (-ata): A small mosaic panel, usually not more than about 60 cm. square, with a picture in fine mosaic (*opus vermiculatum*). This would have been assembled in a workshop as a complete panel, which a less skilled craftsman could then place in the centre of a floor with simpler (and coarser) decoration around it.

Emporium (pl. emporia): A trading-post.

Engaged (column): See under Pilaster.

Entablature: The totality of the architectural elements which properly surmount a colonnade, composed therefore of an architrave, a decorative frieze and a projecting cornice.

Exedra: A semicircular or rectangular recess ('for sitting out in').

False door: A decorative device on many tombs: the appearance of a wooden double-door, carved in stone on the face of the monument, while the genuine entrance to the burial chamber is located elsewhere.

Favissa (-ae): A room inside the raised podium of a Roman temple, equivalent to a crypt and often used as a strongroom under the protection of the relevant deity.

Forum: The civic centre and marketplace of a Roman city.

Frieze: A horizontal band above the architrave (q.v.) in a colonnade, usually decorated in relief with either some sort of vegetal scroll or with figure scenes.

Frigidarium: Part of a Roman bath-building: the cold room, usually with a cold plunge-bath.

Funduq: A building for travelling merchants which combined the provision of accommodation for people and animals with that of warehousing (Arabic).

Genius: A spirit (of a place); also, decoratively, a winged figure used in classical art in much the same way as angels and cupids are in later periods.

Hellenistic: Conventionally, the period between the death of Alexander the Great (323 BC) and the Battle of Actium (31 BC) which confirmed Augustus as the first Roman emperor. Most of the Mediterranean world shared a similar culture at this time, and the term may be used in both a cultural and a chronological sense.

Herm: A rectangular pillar surmounted by a male bust (originally Hermes) and with genitalia indicated on the front. Often used decoratively, but also as a boundary marker.

Hinshir: Farm (Arabic).

Hippodrome: A track with spectator

seating for the presentation of chariot-races. Identical to a circus.

Hypocaust: An under-floor Roman heating system, used particularly in bath-buildings and (in colder climates) for general room-heating. The floor of the room is raised on small piers, and the exhaust gases from an external furnace are conducted beneath the floor and up flues set behind the wall-surface.

Impost block: A moulded or decorated block at the top of a pier and beneath the springing of an arch, similar to the capital of a column.

In antis: Of columns, when placed between projecting stub-walls; typically at the front of a temple, where the flanking walls of the *cella* extend forward as two wings (*antae*).

Inhumation: The burial of an intact corpse. This term is used by archaeologists to distinguish the practice from that of cremation, which may involve either the digging of a grave in which the corpse is burnt before it is filled in, or the burial of the ashes (gathered from a pyre elsewhere) in an urn.

Insula (-ae): Conventionally used by modern scholars to indicate a city block bounded by streets.

Ionic: An order of architecture for Greek and Roman public buildings, in which the capitals of the columns are decorated like a scroll which is rolled up (or rather, downwards) on either side of a 'cushion'. The columns usually have narrow vertical flutes and the entablature above is decorated with a frieze based on a continuous acanthus scroll.

Kouros: A sculpture of a standing male figure with the arms hanging straight by the sides and with one foot slightly in front of the other. This is the typical pose of formal Egyptian statues, adopted by the Greeks (and Phoenicians) and gradually made less stiff and more realistic.

Laconicum or **sudatorium:** Part of a Roman bath-building: a particularly hot room without plunge-baths, intended to generate a dry heat for sweating.

Late Roman: A rather loose chronological term, to describe the Roman period after the crises of the mid-third century AD: partly (but not invariably) synonymous with 'Byzantine.'

Libation: A liquid offering, to a god or to the spirits of the dead.

Libation-duct: A channel incorporated into a tomb, so that liquid offerings may be poured to the dead within.

Limes: Frontier, used of the borders of the Roman Empire.

Loculus: Niche or recess.

Jupiter Ammon: The god worshipped at the oracle in the oasis of Siwa in Egypt, often represented as a man with ram's horns.

Legion: The largest single infantry unit in the Roman army, nominally about 5,000 strong.

Madrasa: A school for Islamic studies.

Metope: Part of the frieze above a Doric colonnade: a more-or-less square panel with relief decoration (typically either a rosette or a human figure).

Mihrab: A niche, usually semicircular, in the *qibla* wall of a mosque, indicating the direction of Mecca. An additional *mihrab* is often provided externally in a courtyard wall so that those outside the mosque may also know the direction of the Holy City.

Minbar: In a mosque, the pulpit from which the Friday sermon is delivered.

Monolith: A term for an architectural element (such as a column or pier) which takes the form of a single block of stone.

Municipium: A town in the Roman Empire enjoying local autonomy under a municipal charter, whose citizens had the status of Roman citizens.

Narthex: Vestibule or outer room at the entrance to a church.

Neo-Punic: A cultural descriptor used of those aspects of Punic culture which persist through the Hellenistic and Roman periods (thus, tombs of the Roman period in the Punic tradition, or the Neo-Punic script).

Nereids: Sea-maidens, daughters of Nereus, the Old Man of the Sea.

Nilotic scene: A frequent theme of Hellenistic and Roman decorative art, both in mosaics and in wall-painting. Scenes are portrayed of life in the marshes of the Nile Delta, with fishermen in boats amongst the reeds, ducks and other water-birds, crocodiles and other forms of wildlife.

Nymphaeum: A monumental public fountain (originally dedicated to the Nymphs).

Opus africanum: A building technique, particularly characteristic of North Africa in the classical period. The main framework of a wall is composed of tall vertical blocks with spaces between them which are infilled with small rubble masonry.

Opus sectile: A decorative treatment, mostly of floors, in which a pattern is composed of shaped tiles of different coloured marbles.

Opus tessellatum: Coarse mosaic paving.

Opus vermiculatum: Extremely fine mosaic decoration, consisting of up to 60 stones per sq. cm., usually reserved for small *emblemata* (q.v.).

Orchestra: The semicircular space in a theatre between the spectator seating (*cavea*) and the stage. Originally used in Greek theatres as a performance space for dancers, in Roman times it was occupied by the (portable and comfortable) seats of the wealthier citizens.

Orthostat: An upright stone block (see *opus africanum*).

Ottoman: Culturally/chronologically related to the period 1551–1911, when Tripolitania and Cyrenaica were provinces of the (Turkish) Ottoman empire.

Palaestra: An exercise-ground.

Palmette: A decorative motif in painting or architecture, in the form of a stylized and symmetrical palm-frond.

Peristyle: A courtyard or garden surrounded by a colonnaded portico.

The Peutinger Table: A twelfth- or thirteenth-century copy of a map of the later second century AD, covering the world known to the Romans. It shows named locations (with a variety of conventional symbols), the roads joining them and the distances between them.

Phoenician: A cultural term for the inhabitants of Phoenicia in the Middle East (approximating to the Lebanon of today). Extended to the Phoenicians who settled at Carthage and elsewhere in the western Mediterranean and sometimes used interchangeably with 'Punic' (q.v.).

Pilaster: A flat-faced, barely projecting, representation of a column on the face or end of a wall. To be distinguished from an engaged column, which is fully rounded but against the wall and linked to it above and below; and an engaged semi-column, half of which projects from the face of the wall.

Podium: The platform upon which a temple or monument stands to raise it above its surroundings.

Praeses: 'President,' a widely-used title under the late Roman Empire, sometimes applied to the civil governor of a province.

Praetorium: The residence of the commanding officer in a Roman fort.

Principia: The headquarters building of a Roman fort.

Proconsul: The civil governor of a province in the early years of the Roman Empire, notionally appointed by the Senate of Rome.

Propraetorian legate (*legatus pro praetore*): An official appointed by the Roman emperor, particularly the commander of a legion.

Protome: A representation in art of the forepart only of an animal.

Punic: An adjective used to describe the culture of the Phoenicians who settled in the western Mediterranean, primarily at Carthage. Hence used in Tripolitania of the pre-Roman culture of the region.

Qasr (pl. qsur): Castle (Arabic); often applied to any ancient monument. In the present guide it is applied principally to the communal granaries of the Jabal Nafusah and to the fortified farms and military outposts of the pre-desert region.

Qibla: The wall in a mosque which faces in the direction of Mecca.

Quadrifrons: See **Tetrapylon**.

Quadriga: A four-horse chariot.

Regio: Conventionally used by modern scholars to denote a subdivision or district of a city.

Rostra: A platform from which speakers may address the people in the open air. The term literally means 'bows', and is derived from the platform in the Roman Forum, which was decorated with the bows of ships captured in a naval battle.

Sanam (pl. asnam): 'Idol' (Arabic); often used of standing stones such as the uprights of olive-presses or of tombs.

Satyr: A mythical attendant of the god Dionysus, of human form but with pointed ears and a horse's tail; lustful and always represented with an erect phallus.

Scaenafrons: The elaborately decorated façade of the stage-building of a Roman theatre.

Scriptorium: A writing-room or clerical office.

Sima: The crowning element of a cornice, or parapet.

Spandrel: The concave triangular space contained between the curve of an arch and its surrounding rectangular frame.

Stele (-ai): A vertical stone marker (similar to a tombstone).

Stoa (-ai): The Greek term for a portico.

Stylobate: The linear foundation for a colonnade.

Sudatorium: see **Laconicum**.

Taberna: A shop.

Tabula ansata: A frame for an inscription or the like which is rectangular with projecting dove-tails ('handles') at either side.

Tepidarium: Part of a Roman bath-building: the warm room which provided a transition between the hot and cold rooms.

Tessera: The small stone cube of which mosaics are composed.

Tetrapylon or **Quadrifrons:** An arch (over a cross-roads) which faces four ways.

Theatre: A place of entertainment with a raised rectangular stage and a tiered semi-circular auditorium (or *cavea*), for the presentation of plays.

Tholos: A circular pavilion or monument.

Tondo: A circular decorative feature, such as a roundel or medallion.

Tophet: An open-air Punic sanctuary and place of sacrifice, in which are found urns containing the remains of sacrifice – at an early date, human infants, but more usually remains of new-born animals.

Travertine: A hard, whitish building-stone, related to (but distinct from) both limestones and marbles. Particularly characterized by coarse voids in the stone. Most famously quarried at Tivoli, near Rome, and used in the construction of the Colosseum.

Tribunal: A raised dais from which judges presided over judicial proceedings (in a civil basilica), or from which a commanding officer might address his troops (in a military fort).

Triclinium: The dining-room of a Roman house. The word means a room with three couches, and typically a decorated (mosaic) floor will reflect this arrangement, with the principal decoration in the area immediately inside the door and simpler patterns around the three sides, which would largely have been covered by furniture.

Triglyph: An element of a frieze above a Doric colonnade, composed of three vertical ribs (thought to have originated as a representation in stone of the ends of the roof-beams).

Triton: A merman, fish-shaped from the waist down.

Tuscan: An order of architecture, not unlike Doric, but characterized by unfluted column-shafts with very simple, moulded but otherwise undecorated, capitals and bases.

Unguentarium: A small flask for perfumes or unguents. In the Hellenistic period these are of clay and are fusiform (like a bobbin, with a long neck and a tall foot); in the first century AD this shape is replaced by a piriform type (still with a long neck, but with a pear-shaped body and a flat base), and then in the later first century by a similar shape in glass.

Vomitorium: A vaulted, radial access passage in a theatre or amphitheatre, leading to the seating from outside.

Voussoir: A wedge-shaped block used to construct an arch or vault.

Zawiya: The Muslim equivalent of a monastery or college.

Chronological table

In the table below, ellipsis (...) is used to indicate that an event occurred at some time between the dates indicated.

BC

814	Traditional date for foundation of Carthage by Phoenician settlers from Tyre
c. 630	First evidence of occupation at Lepcis
Later 5th cent.	First evidence of occupation at Sabratha
c. 515	Attempt by Greeks under Dorieus to settle at the mouth of the Wadi Caam; driven off by the Carthaginians
264–241	First Punic War between Carthage and Rome: Carthaginians driven out of Sicily
218–202	Second Punic War between Carthage and Rome: defeat of Hannibal
162–161	Massinissa, king of Numidia, takes control of the Tripolitanian emporia from Carthage
149–146	Third Punic War: final defeat and destruction of Carthage. Territory becomes the province of *Africa (proconsularis)*
112–105	Rome at war with Jugurtha
111	Lepcis signs a treaty of alliance with Rome, becoming a *civitas foederata*
48	Roman Civil War between Pompey the Great and Julius Caesar; Lepcis hosts supporters of Pompey
46	Pompeians defeated at Thapsus; Caesar reduces Lepcis to the status of *civitas stipendiaria* and imposes an annual tribute of 3 million pounds of oil. The Numidian kingdom annexed as the province of *Africa Nova*
40/39	The two African provinces united, with their capital at Carthage
31	Roman Civil War ended when Octavian defeats Mark Antony and Cleopatra at Actium off the W coast of Greece. Egypt becomes a Roman province
27	Octavian takes the title *Augustus*
19	Saharan expedition of L. Cornelius Balbus

AD

17–24	Revolt of Tacfarinas
64...70	Earthquake in Tripolitania
69	War between Oea (which calls on the Garamantes for assistance) and Lepcis Magna (which calls on Rome). The provincial governor Valerius Festus routs the Garamantes and pursues them into Fazzan

74...77	Lepcis Magna becomes a *municipium*
86–87	Expedition of Suellius Flaccus against the Nasamones
92	Trans-Saharan expedition of Julius Maternus
c. 110	Lepcis becomes a *colonia*, Oea and Sabratha possibly become *municipia*
Mid-2nd cent.	Sabratha and Oea become *coloniae*
145	Birth of L. Septimius Severus
193	Septimius Severus becomes Roman emperor, undisputed from 196
c. 201	Construction of legionary forts at Ghadamis, Qaryah al-Gharbiyah and Abu Njaym
202–3	Septimius Severus visits Lepcis
211	Death of Severus at York
235	Fall of the Severan dynasty
244...246	*Centenarium* built at Qasr Duib
253	Army withdraws from Abu Njaym, and probably from the other desert forts
293...305	Revision of administrative system of the empire: Lepcis becomes capital of the new province of *Tripolitana*
306...310	Earthquake in Tripolitania
363–364	Raids by the Austuriani on coastal regions
365	Devastating earthquake and tsunami in the eastern Mediterranean, possibly one of a chain of such events
439	Vandals capture Carthage
455	Vandals take control of Tripolitania
476	Odovacar king of Rome: end of the Western Roman Empire
533	Reconquest of Africa by Belisarius, on behalf of the Byzantine emperor Justinian
543	Massacre of 79 Berber chieftains at Lepcis Magna by Count Sergius
642–645	Conquest of Cyrenaica and Tripolitania by the Arabs under Amr Ibn al-Aasi. Advent of Islam
670	Foundation of Arab capital at Qayrawan (Tunisia). Tripolitania henceforth loosely under the domination of governors (*emirs*) at Qayrawan or (after 915) Mahdia
698	Fall of Carthage to the Arabs
800	Aghlabid dynasty established at Qayrawan
909	Overthrow of the Aghlabid rulers by the Fatimids
969	Conquest of Egypt by the Fatimids and subsequent move to Cairo, leaving Zirid governors in Tunisia
1051	Invasion of the Bani Hilal; end of remaining urban settlements apart from Oea/Tripoli

CULTURALLY DEFINED PERIODS

This is a 'thumbnail guide' to terms used in this guide to place monuments or events within broad and approximately defined chronological limits. They apply specifically to the history of Tripolitania, and may have slightly different meanings elsewhere. (For further detail, see the **Glossary**.)

Punic	Seventh to first centuries BC.
Hellenistic	323 to 31 BC
Roman	31 BC to late third century AD
Late Roman	Late third century to 455 (or 533)
Vandal	455 to 533
Byzantine	533 to 645
Islamic	645 onwards
Medieval	Eighth to fourteenth centuries

SELECTIVE TABLE OF ROMAN EMPERORS

Julio-Claudians

31 BC–AD 14	Augustus
AD 14–37	Tiberius
37–41	Gaius (Caligula)
41–54	Claudius
54–68	Nero
68–69	Galba, Otho, Vitellius

Flavians

69–79	Vespasian
79–81	Titus
81–96	Domitian

96–98	Nerva
98–117	Trajan
117–138	Hadrian

Antonines

138–161	Antoninus Pius
161–180	Marcus Aurelius
161–166	Lucius Verus
180–192	Commodus
192–193	Pertinax
193	Didius Julianus

Severans

193–211	Septimius Severus
211–217	Caracalla
218–222	Elagabalus
222–235	Severus Alexander
235–238	Maximinus Thrax
238	Gordian I
238	Gordian II
238–244	Gordian III
244–249	Philip the Arab
249–251	Decius
251–253	Trebonianus Gallus
253–260	Valerian
253–268	Gallienus
268–270	Claudius II Gothicus
270–275	Aurelian
275–276	Tacitus
276–282	Probus

Chronological table

282–285	Carus, Numerianus, Carinus
284–305	Diocletian
285–305	Maximianus Herculius
293–306	Constantius I Chlorus
293–311	Galerius
305–313	Maximinus Daia
306–312	Maxentius
306–337	Constantine I
308–324	Licinius
337–340	Constantine II
337–350	Constans I
337–361	Constantius II
361–363	Julian (the Apostate)
363–364	Jovian
364–375	Valentinian I
364–378	Valens
367–383	Gratian
375–392	Valentinian II
378–395	Theodosius I the Great

Western Empire

393–423	Honorius
425–455	Valentinian III
455–465	Petronius Maximus, Avitus, Majorian, Libius Severus
467–472	Anthemius
472–476	Olybrius, Glycerius, Julius Nepos, Romulus Augustulus

Eastern Empire

395–408	Arcadius
408–450	Theodosius II
450–457	Marcian
457–474	Leo I
474	Leo II
474–491	Zeno
491–518	Anastasius
518–527	Justin
527–565	Justinian I
565–578	Justin II
578–582	Tiberius II (I) Constantine
582–602	Maurice
602–610	Phocas
610–641	Heraclius
641–668	Constans II

Further reading

Guidebooks/picture books

My debt to D. E. L. Haynes, *An Archaeological and Historical Guide to the pre-Islamic Antiquities of Tripolitania* (3rd edition, Tripoli 1965) will be readily apparent. This was an excellent guidebook in its time and still contains much of value.

R. Bianchi Bandinelli et al., *The Buried City: Excavations at Leptis Magna* (London 1966: Weidenfeld & Nicholson) was the first picture book in English devoted to this site, and contains many useful plans and drawings.

R. Polidori, A. Di Vita, G. Di Vita-Evrard, L. Bacchielli, *Libya: the Lost Cities of the Roman Empire* (Cologne 1999: Könemann) is a lavish picture book, three quarters of which are devoted to Tripolitania. It has an authoritative text by archaeologists with direct experience of the region.

Journals

There are three scholarly journals dedicated specifically to archaeological research in Libya. *Libya Antiqua* is the official organ of the Libyan Department of Antiquities (available from L'Erma di Bretschneider, below); *Libyan Studies* is the journal of the Society for Libyan Studies, 31–34 Gordon Square, London WC1H 0PY (http://www.britac.ac.uk/institutes/libya); the *Quaderni di Archeologia della Libia* are published by L'Erma di Bretschneider, Via Cassiodoro, 19 – P.O.Box 6192 – 00193 Rome (http://www.lerma.it).

Earlier work carried out by the Italians in the colonial period (1911–43) was initially reported in *Notiziario Archeologico* (Rome 1915–27: Ministero delle Colonie) and *Africa Italiana* (Bergamo 1927–1941: Istituto Italiano d'Arti Grafiche).

Monographs

There is an extensive series of *Monografie di Archeologia Libica*, published by L'Erma di Bretschneider, which represent the major reports of Italian research in Libya, published from 1948 onwards. Other works relevant to this volume are:

P. Romanelli, *Leptis Magna* (Rome 1925);

R. Bartoccini, *Le terme di Lepcis (Leptis Magna)* (Bergamo 1929);

R. Bartoccini, *Il porto romano di Leptis Magna* (Rome 1960).

The Society for Libyan Studies has published or distributes numerous monographs on British research in Libya. These are generally listed in *Libyan Studies* and on the Society's website. The following are of particular relevance to Tripolitania:

J. Reynolds (Ed.), *Libyan Studies. Select papers of the late R. G. Goodchild* (London 1976);

O. Brogan and D. Smith, *Ghirza: a Libyan Settlement in the Roman Period* (London and Tripoli 1984);

J.B. Ward-Perkins, *The Severan Buildings at Lepcis Magna: an Architectural Survey* (London 1993);

G. Barker, D. Gilbertson, B. Jones and D. Mattingly, *Farming the Desert: the UNESCO Libyan Valleys Archaeological Survey* (2 vols., London, Paris and Tripoli 1996).

See also:

J.B. Ward-Perkins and R.G. Goodchild, The Christian Antiquities of Tripolitania. *Archaeologia* 95 (1953) 1–83;

P. M. Kenrick, *Excavations at Sabratha 1948–1951: a report on the excavations conducted by Dame Kathleen Kenyon and John Ward-Perkins* (London 1986: Society for the Promotion of Roman Studies);

D. Mattingly, *Tripolitania* (London 1995: Batsford);

R. J. A. Talbert (Ed.), *Barrington Atlas of the Greek and Roman World* (Princeton and Oxford 2000), especially maps 35 and 37 (compiled by David Mattingly).

The wider background
P. MacKendrick, *The North African Stones Speak* (London 1980: Croom Helm);

S. Raven, *Rome in Africa* (3rd edition, London 1993: Routledge);

B. Rogerson, *A Traveller's History of North Africa* (Moreton-in-Marsh 1998: Windrush Press).

Index

Index